Praise for *Real Talk*
and Rafe

REAL TALK *for*
Real Teachers

Advice for Teachers
from Rookies to Veterans:
"No Retreat, No Surrender!"

Rafe Esquith

PENGUIN BOOKS

PENGUIN BOOKS
Published by the Penguin Group
Penguin Group (USA) LLC
375 Hudson Street
New York, New York 10014

USA | Canada | UK | Ireland | Australia
New Zealand | India | South Africa | China
penguin.com
A Penguin Random House Company

First published in the United States of America by Viking Penguin,
a member of Penguin Group (USA) Inc., 2013
Published in Penguin Books 2014

THE LIBRARY OF CONGRESS HAS CATALOGED THE HARDCOVER EDITION
AS FOLLOWS:
Esquith, Rafe.
Real talk for real teachers : advice for teachers from rookies to veterans :
"no retreat, no surrender!" / Rafe Esquith.
pages cm
ISBN 978-0-670-01464-4 (hc.)
ISBN 978-0-14-312561-7 (pbk.)
1. Teaching. I. Title.
LB1027.E758 2013
371.102—dc23   2013007096

Printed in the United States of America

Book design by Daniel Lagin
Set in Sabon LT Std with Archer

PENGUIN BOOKS

REAL TALK FOR REAL TEACHERS

Rafe Esquith has taught at Hobart Elementary School in Los Angeles for the past twenty-eight years. He is the only classroom teacher to have been awarded the president's National Medal of the Arts, and he has also been made a member of the British Empire by Queen Elizabeth. His many other honors and awards include the Compassion in Action Award from the Dalai Lama, the American Teacher Award, *Parents* magazine's As You Grow Award, Oprah Winfrey's Use Your Life Award, the Kennedy Center's Sondheim Inspirational Teacher Award, *People* magazine's Heroes Among Us Award, and the Bammy Award. Esquith presented at the prestigious TED conference in 2012. He lives in Los Angeles with his wife, Barbara Tong.

For the Hobart Shakespeareans,
who put something back in the tree

CONTENTS

PART II
Growing Up

PART III
Master Class

Real Talk for Real Teachers

Prologue:
The Sistine Chapel
and My Wife's Kitchen

I love my wife.

A couple of summers ago, Barbara and I were given an amazing gift. A concerned friend thought we were working too hard and used his travel connections to send us on a practically free trip to Italy. We had always wanted to go. Among the many highlights, perhaps the best of all, was an unforgettable evening when we were given a private viewing of the Sistine Chapel.

Any person who has ever seen it will tell you (forgive me) that it is a religious experience. It is impossible to convey its astonishing, overwhelming effect. No picture or film even comes close to seeing it in person. One can actually sit back in a special chair with a headrest and practically reach heaven absorbing the soaring images above on the ceiling.

But what was more interesting to me was the painting on the front wall of the sanctuary.

As our guide taught us, Michelangelo painted this section of the chapel twenty-three years after the ceiling was completed. And it's different. It's bleaker than the joyous images overhead. Michelangelo had become gloomier since his younger days, and his paintings reflect this growing cynicism. Age and experience can do that to a person. I am definitely more pessimistic than I was thirty years ago when I began teaching. It was nice thinking I had something in common with Michelangelo.

I realized we shared something else. Even though he was gloomier, he was still painting. He had grown, changed, and suffered, but he remained true to himself. He was still an artist. I am proud that I am still a classroom teacher.

Michelle Rhee, the former chancellor of schools in Washington, D.C., is often at the center of many emotional arguments regarding education. She once stated:

Nobody makes a thirty-year or ten-year commitment to a single profession. Name one profession where the assumption is that when you go in, right out of graduating college that the majority of people are going to stay in that profession. It's not the reality anymore, maybe with the exception of medicine. But short of that people don't go into jobs and stay there forever anymore.

This might be true but that does not mean it's a good thing. I think it's actually a sad reminder of something that is wrong with our society. Lack of commitment is seen in every facet of our daily lives, from personal relationships to the renegotiation of contracts.

I am still teaching after thirty years. I say this not to criticize the many terrific people who have left the classroom to become administrators or move on to entirely different professions, but there is something to be said about a teacher who stays on the front lines. With years of experience, and professional maturity, one can change lives and reach children who previously were beyond reach. In this fast-food society, veteran teachers are a reminder that no one is a fabulous teacher in the beginning. A person might be a wonderful second-year teacher, but no one is truly outstanding with only a year or two of classroom experience. It takes a lifetime to become a master instructor.

I am a fortunate teacher. I have been helped by colleagues, former students, celebrities, and the business world to create the magical classroom known around the world as Room 56. Every day is filled with happy moments as youngsters discover the best in themselves. On an almost daily basis I am visited by returning students who drop in to say thank you and share a laugh about a past adventure.

Even more rewarding, after an exciting day of teaching I get to go home to a woman I adore. We have been happily married for more than twenty years, have lovely children, and now grandchildren. I have done my best to give Barbara my love, good times, and a best friend.

But there is one thing she wants that I have never been able to deliver. My wife wants a new kitchen. We live in a beautiful home built in the 1930s. Barbara, the smart one in this marriage, bought the house when buying one was still possible. It is a beautiful place to live, but the kitchen is adequate at best. Barbara would love to remodel it with modern conveniences, but it hasn't happened yet.

I am a public school teacher. I do not make a lot of money, and, in fact, am at the bottom of the salary scale for teachers in Los Angeles. A teacher can climb the pay-scale ladder by taking additional classes after school, in the evenings, on weekends, and even online, but I have chosen to spend those hours teaching. I am not complaining, and neither is my wife. But I know she would love a new kitchen.

Having put four kids through college and graduate school, we don't have a lot of money left over for luxuries. We live a fairly simple life and rarely go out. Because we are careful, a little bit of money can be saved every year. By my calculation, if I can teach for about five hundred years we should have enough savings to get Barbara the new kitchen.

Therefore I have 470 years left to keep teaching in order to get Barbara the kitchen she wants. And that's fine with me. I have been fortunate to gain a great deal of worldly experience thanks to this job. Nothing is better than teaching the children in Room 56.

Simply staying in the classroom does not make an individual an outstanding teacher. Any honest observer accepts the fact that some teachers should not be teaching at all. Nevertheless, I hope this book inspires young teachers to keep teaching even against impossible odds. Readers take notice: honor those heroic veteran teachers who fight on and achieve true excellence, even when our society treats them shabbily. I yearn for there to be many potentially brilliant class leaders who get to the mountaintop by remaining in the classroom for thirty years.

If we all keep teaching and develop into extraordinary professionals, we can challenge and mold students who will change the world and make it better. And then perhaps we can all get a new kitchen.

PART I
Once Upon a Time

CHAPTER ONE

Badlands

Over the years, thousands of young teachers have visited my classroom, asking numerous questions about education and child care. Without a doubt, the most frequently asked one goes something like this: "Rafe, if you could tell a beginning teacher one thing, what would it be?" This is an excellent question, one that deserves a thoughtful answer. I usually offer the following sugarcoated advice:

Welcome to the profession. It is wonderful to have you working with us. We fellow teachers are fortunate to have you as a colleague, and the kids are very lucky to have you as their instructor. There is one thing you must know before you start.

During your training, you have most likely been given some excellent ideas of how to begin. You will learn about classroom management, lesson plans, and motivation. If you have been lucky, you have had the opportunity to observe master teachers who make the human race look good.

Your preparation and dedication is to be commended. But here is what I really want all young teachers to know:

You Are Going to Have Bad Days

I am sorry to be the bearer of bad news, but it's true. You are going to have bad days. Awful days. There are going to be classes where you do everything right and *still* have a bad day. You will have fabulous lesson plans and well-thought-out methods of instruction. Your subject matter will be relevant and interesting. You will remain positive. You will be flexible when things go wrong. You will have consulted other teachers and used their insights and wisdom to strengthen your program. And you will care deeply for each student, making sure that every one of them feels valued, respected, and important.

And you will still have a bad day. No amount of preparation and training can equip you for what can go wrong in a classroom. You will go home more depressed than you have ever been in your life. In many instances, you will cry yourself to sleep. There will be times when you might wonder if law school would have been a better choice.

As you mope, you will look for inspiration. Perhaps you will pop in the latest Hollywood movie about teachers. There will be some superstar class leader who amazes the world. And in the film, this savior rescues everyone. Every student loves the teacher, and they all pass the big test at the end of the film, win the big game, or give a triumphant performance.

And you feel even worse, because that's not you!

Will you please remember this: It's a Hollywood movie. It's not real.

If there is only one thing I hope a new teacher learns from me, it is this: when you have a bad day, you are not a bad teacher. I have been teaching for many years. And I have bad days all the time. Even after all these years, I still have terrible days. All teachers have them.

One year on the first day of class, I thought things were going well. Surprisingly, attendance was perfect—not a common occurrence at a large public school. I had been warned that one of my students, Joey, was incredibly difficult to handle. As the kids filed into the room I looked for a boy who might be trouble, but noticed no one. Some of the kids looked a bit tired or nervous, but no one looked like a ticking time bomb.

As we went over our class schedule, I told the students about lunch at school. Most of the kids get a free lunch because they are poor. I reminded them to eat lunch every day and explained its importance for good health and good work in school. I also, quite generously, I thought, told the kids that if they lost their lunch tickets I would be happy to give them the dollar they would need to buy lunch. I asked if there were any questions.

That's when a boy over on the side of the room raised his hand. Well, not his hand exactly, but rather his middle finger. I was so stunned to receive this universal suggestion from a ten-year-old that I was at a complete loss for words. But he had plenty to say for both of us.

"Well, you're gonna have to give me money every day. My sister's a slut and she spends all the money we got on drugs. And I ain't got no lunch tickets."

"Joey," I replied, "how nice to have you in class."

We had a good year together, but it was not easy. Joey was a true contrarian, and loved to push everyone's buttons. And he was quite good at it. No kid I have ever taught could ruin a science experiment, disrupt a history story, or disturb a literature lesson better than Joey. He was a considerable factor of many bad days, but it could have been much worse. Had I been in my second year of teaching, he would have practically single-handedly destroyed my classroom. But I was in my twenty-sixth year, and Joey did fine in class. Old age and treachery will always defeat youth and skill.

Still, even with more than a quarter of a century of experience there are difficult days. Currently it is true that there are fewer bad ones, but the job is never easy. Bad days come far too often, and from a variety of sources. Children, parents, colleagues, and administrators are all equally capable of crushing the heartiest of spirits.

I met a young teacher from Pennsylvania who was in his third year of teaching. He was off to a flying start. As a married man with two young children of his own, his personal experience with his own kids had shaped his considerable communication skills with his students. His classroom was a shining example of how a rigorous curriculum and high expectations mixed with the right amount of nurturing could produce a great environment for learning. His students were excited about education and couldn't wait to come to school every morning.

The parents loved him, too, and with good reason. Their children came home daily bubbling over with happiness. If any young teacher should be headed for sunny days and smooth sailing, it was this man. He was the poster boy for success stories about teaching.

As he loved teaching history, he decided that a trip to Washington, D.C., would be a marvelous way for his fifth graders to truly experience what they had been reading about in class. This trip was not an impossible dream; his school was only a couple of hours away by car, and many parents enthusiastically supported the idea of a trip to the nation's capital.

Our star teacher was no rebel. He did everything by the book. He filled out the proper forms and went through all the correct channels. He spent much of his third year of teaching planning the trip. Everyone was onboard. The excursion would take place just a few days after the children finished their year with him. The district gave him approval and the necessary funds were raised. Several parents and fellow teachers agreed to chaperone. Short of a natural disaster, nothing was going to prevent this teacher from achieving something wonderful and his students from having a life-changing experience.

Three days before the year ended and summer began, an official letter arrived. Someone at the district office had changed his mind. One official—one—did not think the teacher had enough experience, and that was that. The teacher was furious and the kids were devastated. It would be one thing, he argued, if he had never been granted permission, but to have it revoked so suddenly and illogically was more than he could fathom. This was a very bad day, one that would sap his strength to teach for many sleepless nights.

This sort of dramatic and unfair reversal of fortune is typical of teaching's darker moments. Such stories make good radio sound bites or plots for a Hollywood movie, but there is an endless supply of small disappointments that make it harder to walk into your classroom with enthusiasm and hope. Consider what happened to me just recently during this past school year.

I stay with students after school to teach Shakespeare and, after a year's work, put on an unabridged production. The show includes not only Shakespeare but a high-powered rock and roll band and intricate choreography. It is unique in the world, and even left the Royal Shakespeare Company speechless when they came to watch a show. Any student in our school from fourth and fifth grade is invited to participate.

Sometime after we began work on one show, a boy named Eddie came to my classroom and asked if he could join the Shakespeare group. Eddie was a fifth grader and very sweet. I mentioned to him that the class had been going on for almost four months, and I asked why he was asking to join at such a late date. He assured me that there was a misunderstanding of his eligibility because he was coming from another classroom. This seemed possible, as communication at Hobart could always stand some improvement, and I proceeded to go over a few of the basics. Eddie promised me that he understood the meaning of commitment, and that as a part of a team his classmates would be depending on his best effort each day of rehearsal. His teacher, one of the best in our school, told me that although this student was not brilliant, she had found

Eddie to be reasonably reliable. She thought his participation would be a good thing. I completely agreed with her assessment of the situation.

That night, after a hard day, I took the time to go to a bookstore to buy a copy of the Shakespeare play we were performing. With a new student off to a very late start, I hoped to use every possible opportunity to get this rookie up to speed.

I also burned a CD of various parts of the play, which Eddie could take home to help him understand the new book by not only reading but also listening. In addition, I recorded all the music the class had already learned (fourteen songs) and printed out the lyrics so the songs could be memorized. After all, it takes time to see the connection between Shakespeare, Led Zeppelin, Elvis Costello, and The Kinks.

When his first week of rehearsals was over, Eddie was happy to be invited to a huge party before winter break. The party included a very good dinner we provided for the kids, along with games and prizes for each child.

During the first day back after vacation, Eddie came to me with tears in his eyes. He told me he was quitting Shakespeare because his mother wanted to spend more time with him. As the class was after school, Mom had insisted her son come home immediately. It was terribly disappointing to hear this, but teachers are supposed to be supportive, and I let his long face know that it was enjoyable while it lasted, but it's totally understood that family must come first.

Soon after, I found out that the story of a possessive parent was a complete lie. The truth was that Eddie had discovered that Shakespeare meant a lot of work, and he preferred hanging out on the playground after school. I felt numb. There are so many days when you try to do your very best and have it amount to absolutely nothing. That, my friends, is a bad day.

There's not much you can do to feel better about it. I did find

Eddie near the playground eating hot Cheetos and felt it necessary to kindly but firmly express my feelings that he was very wrong to lie. I hoped he would consider the effects of his actions, which included hurting a person who had been nothing but kind to him and, more important, letting down classmates who had given him complete support and trust. Eddie shrugged his shoulders and ran over to the playground. Granted, this experience was not near the end of the world for me. It was not hearing from the police that a student had been arrested or hurt or killed in a gang-related incident. It was not a case of someone abusing a child. But such moments of apathy and, truth be told, betrayal can build up. It is easy to become demoralized by so many straws that even the strongest camel would wilt.

So remember when you have many bad days that you are in good company. You will in time learn how to cope, but meanwhile, please find the strength to move forward when you have them. I had to remind myself that while one child had lied to me and gave up, forty others were waiting for me to teach them more Shakespeare.

As you read this, I am probably in Room 56 at Hobart Elementary School in Los Angeles, trying my best to help ten-year-old children see that they can control their own destinies and make their lives extraordinary. If I am not there, or on the road with my students, I am probably at home with my wife discussing how we can help one of the kids or on the phone with a former student in need of a sounding board. And despite these constant efforts, I fail every day of my life.

Do not doubt yourself. There is a reason you are having a bad day: teaching is an incredibly difficult job. We are trying to teach kids to be honorable in a world where dishonor stares them in the face constantly. We are trying to convince kids to be decent in a world where indecency is not only the order of the day but shockingly celebrated in the media and, as a result, by much of our population.

But there is good news. Your bad days will become better ones. It takes a long time. No one is a good teacher right away. You might read an article or see a news special about some miraculous teacher, but it's usually hype. There are no great teachers who have been teaching for only three years. To become truly outstanding at anything takes more years than many people want to give. The finest gardeners, architects, musicians, baseball players, and, yes, teachers, do not reach instant nirvana.

If at all possible, do not go through your bad days alone. Teaching can be a tragically lonely experience, and as you sit in defeat, isolated within four walls, you might think no one understands your pain, self-doubt, and frustration. You are mistaken.

There are heroes in your school, old hands who have been where you now sit and lived to tell the tale. They are your most valuable resource and best friends. They will help you through your bad days. When you go to more experienced teachers and honestly trust them with your pain and despair, they will think more of you and not less. They will respect your honesty and sincere desire to do better.

I ask you to heed one warning. Most of the teachers you meet are the best sorts of people. They are caring and sensitive. Their value cannot be measured by a series of test scores. But there are some teachers you need to avoid. Sadly, they are in practically every school I have observed. They usually hang out in the lunchroom or parking lot nursing a bad attitude toward teaching, the principal, their students, and often one another. These negative folks do not thrive in solitary confinement, and they invite discouraged young teachers to join their circle of misery. I urge you to stay away from them. These teachers are of no good to you and certainly of no benefit to the students.

In the same way we caution students to hang out with the right kids, you need to hang out with the right teachers. The good ones will help you through your toughest times. They will give you valuable advice and help you craft your style. You will continue to have things go wrong, but disasters will happen less often. And when the road gets bumpy, with time and experience you will be better equipped to handle mishaps, eventually learning how best to prevent them.

You will have bad days. You will meet kids who are so incorrigible you will completely lose your cool. You might be in an unfortunate situation and feel absolutely no support from your administration or the parents. And you will pick up the newspaper and get no love from society either. But if you keep moving forward and not surrender to all the awful things that can happen in a school, one thing is certain. You will get better. Good days filled with joy and laughter, and lots of them, are coming.

Embrace your mistakes. Learn from them. One day you will be a master teacher. You have years to become outstanding. Through reflection and failure, and the understanding that there are no shortcuts, those dreams you have of changing lives will not simply be dreams. They will become a living, breathing reality. You will make a difference.

Day 1 is here.

CHAPTER TWO

First Things First

After spending a day in Room 56, both beginning and veteran teachers have thoroughly enjoyed observing and interacting with the kids. They love the fact that the children are engaged. There are no serious discipline issues. The students are learning at the highest levels of scholarship.

And invariably, this comment is made:

Rafe, I wish I could see you on Day 1.

Most people would be very disappointed.

Everyone is interested in the first day of school. It seems like so much has been written and talked about concerning this day that it has become overemphasized. Of course the first day is incredibly important. But the truth is, in my class, Day 1 looks a lot like Day 91. Nothing magical happens on the first day of school.

That is not to say it is not crucial to get off to a good start. I take the first day very seriously, but then, good teachers take every day seriously. On the first day of school I introduce several key themes that will be a part of every class for the entire year. I do not expect the kids to understand my goals, even after they have reviewed a paper with the class objectives clearly stated. It's just an introduction.

Legendary NCAA basketball coach John Wooden ran the same practice every day. The drills the players executed on the first day of practice were the same drills they worked on the night before their team played for the championship. There is a consistency in Room 56 that makes the children feel safe. Important principles are established in the beginning. The kids hear about them, though they rarely understand the complexity of our class structure. After all, they are ten years old. And I am not in a particular hurry. I simply want to set the table. The meal, one that takes an entire year or more to digest, will be served every minute of every day.

I speak far less on that opening morning than one might imagine. I do not even learn each child's name immediately, and I am not worried that the kids don't either. I spend only seven to ten minutes speaking on that first morning. I want the kids to be excited to be there. And I want them to take their work seriously and do their best in whatever task they are trying to accomplish. As a result, if class officially begins at 8:00 A.M., we are working by 8:10 A.M.

This is a working classroom. In many classrooms students often have to be told on Day 1 that essential materials have not yet arrived. Perhaps the math books are not there yet, or the science materials are being delivered next week. I never allow that to happen in Room 56. I want the kids to be prepared, and that means my classroom is running at full speed right from the start.

When the kids enter the room, they see strikingly beautiful rugs hanging from the bulletin boards. They cannot be missed, and as the students enter, many ooh and aah. I ask the children if they like the tapestries, and a chorus of voices expresses their delight. Then I wait about five seconds and ask, "Would you like to learn how to make one?"

After a unanimous shout of assent from the kids, I respond calmly, "Glad to hear it. You will start yours in about three hours." A deafening silence falls over the room, a moment of disbelief mixed with suppressed excitement. The students have just learned something about their new class. This is a working classroom, and we do not wait. Assignments and projects happen constantly, and the future is now. Supplies are here, and their teacher is ready. Once, a reporter talked to one of the students, amazed by the attention span and focus of the youngsters. The child was asked by the intrigued adult, "Don't you guys ever go to the bathroom?"

"I might miss something," whispered the kid, slightly annoyed that someone was interrupting his concentration.

Though the children cannot possibly comprehend on that first day the scope of the classroom objectives, several themes are being presented. They're something like the Ten Commandments of Room 56, but they have nothing to do with rules. In fact, there are no rules written anywhere on the walls of the classroom. Nevertheless, the students are extraordinarily well mannered and behaved. Your creed does not have to resemble mine, but here is a sheet the kids get before I even call roll the first day. It is simple and has very little explanation. The conversation it prompts will be at least a year long, but you have to start somewhere.

HOBART SHAKESPEAREANS

1. Our mission: Be nice. Work hard.
2. Our motto: There are no shortcuts.
3. Hobart Shakespeareans are honest.
4. Hobart Shakespeareans show initiative.
5. Hobart Shakespeareans take responsibility for their actions.
6. Hobart Shakespeareans are aware of time and space.
7. Hobart Shakespeareans are never afraid to ask questions.

8. Hobart Shakespeareans understand the importance of presentation.
9. Hobart Shakespeareans are organized.
10. Hobart Shakespeareans are humble.

As we move through the year, the children will be reminded constantly how the skills they learn are directly connected to these maxims.

In the days ahead, as we work on our math, or geography, or baseball, we will return to this code. It is not some sort of official lesson. It is simply part of the conversation woven into the activities. But in the weeks to come, each point will be repeated often and expanded upon.

Of course lists are subjective. Your objectives might have some things in common with these or be radically different. However, I suggest you keep things simple. And be patient. These are lessons designed to last a lifetime.

Be Nice. Work Hard.

I like nice people, and in conversation you will find that most kids do, too. Nice people help one another. They listen and show respect. This means we are quiet if another student has a question because she does not understand something. We do not mock someone for striking out in baseball. If we are finished with a project, we look for a fellow student who might require some help. In our class, we are never actually finished, because there is always more to be done to support or help one another. I constantly ask the kids, "When are we done?"

The chorus always answers, "Never."

We are an "all-the-time class." Being nice means being nice *always*. I have found the following example very useful in getting the point across to the kids. I call a student up to the front of the room and set up a situation in which I am inviting him to come to a baseball game and talking to his parents to get their permission. "Mr. Gomez, I'd like to take Ricardo to a baseball game this Saturday afternoon. I will take care of him *some of the time*. Will that be okay?" The kids hoot and make faces and begin to laugh at the absurdity of the question. I try again. "Okay, Mr. Gomez, I understand your concern. How about if I take care of your son *most of the time*?" You can guess the reaction. The kids realize that it is my job to take care of Ricardo *all of the time*.

The same thing goes for being nice. We are nice all of the time. It does not matter whether a teacher is present or not. It does not matter if there are unfair teachers, bossy playground coaches, or rude peers involved. Being nice is an all-the-time job. It's like the old saying, *You can't be a little bit pregnant.* In Room 56 you're nice or you're not.

Working hard is the second part of the mission. We try our best as we do our work. We strive to write well, calculate precisely, and think constantly. We try to get better at what we do. We take our work seriously, and we do it all the time. But it's not grim at all. We laugh a lot in Room 56. I have learned that it is absolutely possible (and a lot more fun) if we laugh while we work hard and strive to get better. When we make mistakes, we laugh at ourselves. We remind ourselves that when the harmony of one of our songs is off-key it can be ear splitting and simultaneously hilarious. But when the laughter dies down, we are back at work. And we keep working until the voices are in perfect harmony. We set the bar high for ourselves.

For the entire year, in every lesson, we are nice to one another and we take our work seriously. It is internalized in the hearts of the children. It is part of our classroom culture, and it fuels everything the students do.

There Are No Shortcuts

This classroom motto hangs at the front of our room. The kids will eye it for a year of their lives. They are consistently reminded of it in practically everything we do, beginning on Day 1. I like to get this lesson across with the art project we start on the first day of the year.

I mentioned earlier the latch-hook rugs that the students see hanging up on a bulletin board when they enter the room. They are beautiful. In the back of the room, I have about thirty-five new rug projects stacked up on display for the students to see along with pictures of the finished rugs, featuring animals, cartoon characters, beautiful landscapes, flowers, and colorful designs. By recess most of the kids have taken a good look at the samples and decided which one they'd like to make.

When they begin assembling their rugs they are told that it will take a long time—more than a month. The larger rugs might take up to four months.

And though they start their projects that very afternoon, they do not begin hooking the rugs on that first day. They will spend many days simply sorting through the yarn in their kits and separating the strands by color. This is not as easy as it sounds; many of the hues have very subtle differences The students read their instructions and discover they will be using not only red, blue, and yellow but also spice, coral, cream, and auburn. It typically takes them several days to read and understand various color charts I have given them. Plastic bags are carefully labeled for the separated colors of yarn to be place inside.

And as they do this, they are not only having fun making a rug but taking the first of many steps toward understanding a key lesson: there are no shortcuts. After an hour or so, almost none of the children will have finished sorting their yarn. But more often than not, the kids have had fun, and they are not complaining. Instead, they have begun to realize that the process is more important than the finished product. They will continue this lesson tomorrow, when we start with baseball. We will be learning about the sport, but we will not play an actual game for more than a month. For the first week, the students will simply learn how to throw and catch a ball. We are not in a hurry in our classroom. It takes a long time to do things well, and we take our time and enjoy the process. There are no shortcuts.

Hobart Shakespeareans Are Honest

On Day 1, I tell the students something that many of them have already figured out. They have had at least four or five teachers in their short lives, and each one has been different. Rules varied in each class. I take a few minutes during the first day to tell the kids that practically nothing upsets me. Missed homework assignments, spilled paint, lost books, and rude behavior in class are all mistakes, but not matters of life and death. But there is one thing that will change our relationship.

Hobart Shakespeareans are honest.

On the first day of school, this really has very little meaning. The kids have heard countless times about the importance of telling the truth, at home and in practically every classroom they have ever sat in. But they hear it from me anyway. If they lie, I tell them, I will still do my best for them as their teacher, but it does change our relationship. It is the one mistake I have seen in school that really cannot be fixed.

During our first math lesson of the year, I observe and learn if my fifth graders know how to add and subtract. Usually, there are several who cannot. Some may have forgotten things they had learned in the fourth grade, while others never grasped some basic concepts in the first place.

The most important moment comes with about ten minutes left in the math hour, as we correct the twenty or thirty problems that have been assigned. I ask the students who feel they have not gotten everything right to raise their hands and ask me to go over problems they have gotten wrong. Often they have not understood the work, despite my explanations and circulation around the class-room as problems were completed. And there are other kids who might have gotten answers correct but know, deep inside their hearts, that they were lucky, and did not fully grasp the concept.

So I ask for questions. At first on this first day, no hands go up.

I wait.

I wait some more.

And one brave soul usually raises her hand. It's a courageous act. By the age of ten, most children have already experienced the embarrassment of having an impatient teacher utter a remark such as "We've been over this." Even worse is the scar from having been laughed at by classmates for getting something wrong and asking a question.

But on Day 1, I simply look for one child to raise his hand and ask. And several things happen. The question gets answered, and I make sure the child is praised for asking a question. The kids may not learn much on that day, but at least they see that in our class-room all questions are answered. I have told the kids that I will be happy to help them, and they discover that I am a man of my word. Honesty begins with class leaders. It is the first step in removing the fear that prevents so many young people from becoming the best they can be. In being honest, their lives will be better.

However, modeling this behavior on Day 1 does not build a lasting and trusting relationship with students. Kids have seen plenty of teachers use their best manners on the first day of class, only to slowly watch their instructors get worn down and grouchy as the year ground on. You must not let that happen in your class. Day 1 is not special, but it is your chance to let the kids know that you are there to answer their questions every day without exception. As the trust level increases between the students and you, so will their learning and self-esteem.

Hobart Shakespeareans Show Initiative

On the first day, I spend a couple of minutes discussing the word *initiative*. It is one of the spelling and vocabulary words the children learn in class.

Most kids in school are trained to wait for their teacher to give an instruction and to ask permission to get a drink of water or go to the bathroom. It's understandable. Many teachers have to deal with children who take advantage of any freedom they are given. Good teachers are reasonably worried about losing control of a class, and when students are not focused on their lessons, nothing will be learned.

But I have discovered that if children are given the opportunity to show initiative, make decisions by themselves, and do so responsibly, a class will function on a much higher level than with a teacher being the puppeteer and the students mere marionettes.

On the first day, when someone asks to go to the bathroom, I show a look of puzzlement and ask, "Why would you ask me if you may go to the bathroom?"

The response is usually something like, "In my other class we had to ask."

So begins a yearlong conversation about initiative. This is mixed with the very real explanation to the children of the actual reason teachers do not grant permission to leave the classroom. The kids realize that their teachers do not trust them. Often the children have given their teachers good reasons not to trust them.

Before I allow the student to go to the bathroom, and after I ask the first question, I make sure he has told me the following things before he leaves the room:

Rafe: Why are you leaving the room?

Student: I have to use the bathroom.

Rafe: Tell me about your trip there.

Student: Huh?

Rafe: Describe how you will get to the bathroom.

Student: Huh?

Rafe: Will you run? Will you slide down the railing on the stairway, which is a dangerous thing to do?

Student: (starting to catch on) I will walk.

Rafe: Why? Is running a bad thing? I love to run!

Student: Huh?

Rafe: There are wonderful places to run and to make noise. Can anyone name some of them?

The class: The playground . . . the beach . . . the park . . .

Rafe: Exactly. So why are we walking quietly to the bathroom?

Student: You don't want me to get hurt or disturb other classes.

Rafe: That is absolutely right. Tell me what will happen in the bathroom?

Student: What?

Rafe: Will you be fooling around in there?

Student: I'm just going to go to the bathroom and come back.

Rafe: What will you do after you have gone to the bathroom and before you come back?

Student: (a pause, with some real thinking going on) I'll wash my hands.

Rafe: With what?

Student: With soap if there is any there (the class laughs bitterly at the recognition that our school bathrooms are often out of supplies).

Rafe: That's a good point. If there isn't soap, we have some right here in Room 56. What will you do with the paper towel that you use to dry your hands?

Student: I'll throw it in the garbage . . .

Rafe: . . . and not throw the wet towel up to the ceiling, yes?

Student: (impressed that I know what lots of kids do) I won't do that.

Rafe: One more thing. I think you are ready to go. But what would happen if you do not do these things? What would happen if you were found running, disturbing the school, or fooling around in the bathroom? In other words, what would happen if you broke my trust?

Student: I won't be able to use the bathroom anymore.

Rafe: Nope. Of course you can go to the bathroom. But you will have to be accompanied by people to watch you, as you would not be ready to do things by yourself yet. I think you are. Do you think you are?

Student: Yes.

Rafe: Then go to the bathroom! We have work to do!

In the year to come, the kids will learn many lessons that revolve around the concepts in this simple exchange. One is to use the bathroom during scheduled breaks so as not to miss part of a lesson. But the truth is, sometimes people have to go even during math or reading. The children begin to see the way things are done in our room. I give them my trust, and they will begin to take charge of their own lives. They do not need my permission to go to the bathroom or get up out of their seats to get a drink of water or a tissue for a runny nose.

They also clean the room when it is not their job. They polish their musical instruments. They begin working on math that has not even been assigned yet. Students who are not playing a particular character in the class production memorize that part for fun. Once students grasp the importance of showing initiative, the limits placed on a child's growth by waiting for a teacher's permission or approval are gone.

It's all about responsibility. When young people are given the freedom to show initiative, they begin to take charge of their own lives. By giving up some control and even allowing kids to make poor choices and stumble, teachers can help their students learn to value and embrace an essential piece of the character puzzle that leads to success and happiness.

Hobart Shakespeareans Take Responsibility for Their Actions

It's always interesting to note the language students use to describe their grades on a report card. When they have done well, children often remark "I got an A." If they have done poorly, the comment is "He gave me a D."

In an age when no one seems to want to take responsibility for anything, it's time to take a stand. In our class students are held accountable. They are expected to do their work while being considerate of others. If they have done something wrong, their explanation should begin with the word "I," not "He."

I often notice kids coming to school with parents who carry their backpacks for them. I have seen students call home a few minutes before school begins because they have forgotten to bring their homework, a book, or a form that the school needed signed by a parent. In our class, children are taught that it is better to simply tell me they forgot something. That can be fixed. But it is not the responsibility of a parent to make an extra trip to the school because their child forgot something.

My students are told that school is their job. They need to do it carefully. Their desk and materials need to be kept in order. If things are going well for you, I tell the students, take the credit. Accept the blame if things go badly. And please leave me, your teacher, out of it. I am only that—your teacher. I am here only to give you opportunities to become the best that you can be. Your growth and accomplishments are entirely about you.

If you are fooling around during science, I tell them, you will miss that day's science experiment. If you are misusing art supplies, you will not be participating in art that day. It's your loss, and your life. Actions have consequences. This conversation begins on Day 1, and it is begun in a friendly, comforting voice. It is meant to liberate children from waiting for someone to make their lives better.

It's a start, but let's be real about the road ahead. The students in my class believe they are entitled to a free breakfast and lunch because the school has given them one since their first day of kindergarten. They are given paper and pencils. I have even seen schools that give children alarm clocks if they are constantly late to school.

Such assumptions can be difficult to overcome, but I do my best to get kids to take charge of their own education. I can help them. I can open doors and show them how to do things that were previously a mystery to them. I mention to the children that very wise and good people continue to argue about how we as a school can help the students succeed. Many say the teachers are the most important factor in a child's education. Others say it's the parents. Still other voices point to poverty as the reason kids fail or succeed. All of these points of view need to be chewed, swallowed, and digested.

But in Room 56 the kids learn on that first day that the future is completely in their hands. By the end of the year, most of my students will learn how to go to the market and with very little money bring healthier food to school than the awful stuff that is placed in front of them daily. When they begin to do this, and feel stronger, and do better in school, they realize that they have control. In the year to come, the children will learn not to look at me but to look inside themselves. In the years to come, they will be the ones to make phone calls, fill out forms, and seek out people who have information that will be useful to their futures. They have more answers than they realize.

Hobart Shakespeareans
Are Aware of Time and Space

It's usually quiet in Room 56. It's not silent, but it's quiet, even when dozens of children are talking. On the first day of school, I explain to the kids that I have no problem with noise. But I initiate an exchange that gets the kids thinking about the importance of context. We do this through a discussion of time and place:

Rafe: Who likes screaming and yelling?

Kids: (usually very little response; the question is weird, and being that it's the first day of school, past experiences have the kids worried about giving the answer they think their teacher wants to hear)

Rafe: I love to make noise. Does anyone here like to make noise? (now many hands go up) Great! Now here's the harder part of the question. I love to scream my head off when I am surfing a huge wave at the beach. Is it okay to scream at the beach?

Kids: Yes, sure, it is, of course . . .

Rafe: Can anyone think of other places where making noise is appropriate?

Kids: The ball game . . . the park . . . a swimming pool . . .

Rafe: How about at the hospital?

Kids: (laughing with incredulity) Of course not!

Rafe: A funeral?

Kids: Nooooooo . . .

Rafe: Are there places you think it is more appropriate to be quiet?

Kids: A hospital . . . church . . .

Rafe: Exactly. Here's an important question. Are you quiet in a hospital because there is a rule written on the wall that says to be quiet?

Kids: No.

Rafe: Are you quiet in the hospital because you are afraid you will get in trouble because you are not supposed to be running around?

Kids: No.

Rafe: So what you're telling me is that you are quiet in the hospital because you actually understand why it is important to be quiet. It has nothing to do with some rule. Being quiet in a hospital makes sense. We wouldn't be mad at a three-year-old making noise in a hospital. Why not?

Kids: He doesn't understand.

Rafe: Absolutely right. But you do understand. As we grow up, we become aware of the world around us. We understand that our actions have an effect on other people. And those people matter. We are quiet in a hospital to allow doctors and nurses to do their best work. Patients need to rest. Visiting families are under all sorts of pressure and we do not want to disturb them.

Being considerate is the goal here, and simple lessons like this introduction are part of a much more complex and subtle journey. People need to be considerate of one another, and this means thinking at all times about context: in what time and place are certain types of behavior appropriate? Eventually, my students will be yelling while they play baseball and become immediately quiet as they leave the baseball field and walk back to the area of the school where classes are in session. No one tells them to modulate their voices. This value is preached often, especially at the beginning of the school year.

It helps that I speak quietly at all times. I do not raise my voice to the students even when I am upset with them. The word *modulation* is one of the first vocabulary words they learn.

It's quiet when I teach a class, and it's quiet when students ask questions or have discussions. It's noisy during a party, but quiet during our literature period. Considerate children do not have to be threatened with consequences when this sort of consideration is modeled and consistently discussed throughout the year.

You are creating a powerful model here, where children face the consequences of disappointing themselves by not living up to their own values. Once a student discovers the excitement of taking charge of his own education, learning becomes joyous. The kids treasure the time they spend in your classroom, and those sacred moments and lessons will be carried by them to other times and places for the rest of their lives.

Hobart Shakespeareans Are Never Afraid to Ask Questions

I've been teaching for almost thirty years, and have listened to several thousand children. Without exception, all of them have been afraid in school, and it happens far too often. They are afraid of bullies. They are afraid of being yelled at. They fear bad grades. They fear in general, and sometimes existentially.

But the number one fear on their hit parade is that of being laughed at by peers. This sort of cruelty happens all the time and leaves scars that last a lifetime. One of the many sad consequences of this fear is that children become afraid to ask questions. Any teacher with experience knows well that moment when we ask the kids "Are there any questions?" and the response is a deafening silence. Frustrated teachers—those who genuinely want to help— try to assure the class that they are more than willing to patiently clarify any mystifying question or point. Even with such assurances, many children would accept not understanding something before risking the agony of ridicule.

Creating a class culture where questions are encouraged and happily answered is no walk in the park, but there is one thing a teacher can do that might be the most underrated first step in helping the kids understand that they are safe in your class.

You can smile.

It seems insanely simple, but it's very effective. Yet too often, we encourage the exact opposite behavior in novice instructors. I have hosted thousands of young visiting teachers over the years, and many of them have told me that in various graduate school courses or in talking to other teachers, they have been advised

NOT to smile on the first day of school. Some have even told me they were advised not to smile until Christmas. One teacher told me she was taught to kick the trash can on the first day to let the kids know who is boss.

Just last year, an amazing little girl pointed out to me the importance of smiling. When Janice was a fourth grader, she joined the after-school Shakespeare program that I teach. She is a remarkable young lady. Brilliant, sensitive, kind, and an incredible worker, she is a teacher's dream. Janice is so amazing, the best thing a teacher can probably do for her is to stay out of her way. This kid is a winner, and all she really needs from a teacher is to have a few doors opened. She will do the rest on her own.

Her mother works in a tiny beauty shop, and Janice spends her evenings there reading quietly in a corner while Mom works as late as ten o'clock. On several occasions, I was happy to give Janice a ride there after our Shakespeare class was over. Her mom is a terrific and supportive parent, and I was happy to help her because Janice was staying late at school. On one of our trips to the shop, I asked Janice to tell me about her first five years of school. She went over each teacher she had in each grade. Janice is the type of kid who generally likes her teachers, and she had been a fortunate student, as she had been in the classrooms of several of Hobart's most deservedly recognized class leaders. I asked her if she had a favorite year at school. Janice immediately picked one grade because of a specific teacher. I knew this woman to be a very good teacher, and yet I was surprised. I had thought Janice was going to choose one of two teachers who were famously respected for their top classes and high-achieving students.

I asked Janice why she liked her experience in that particular class best of all.

Janice replied, "Mrs. C had the best smile."

Try to remember what it was like for you to have a waitress or salesperson who did not smile. Imagine having a nurse who did not smile. Now stand in the shoes of a kid and imagine that child looking at a teacher who does not smile.

It is no wonder kids do not ask questions!

If our goal is to set a high standard of learning for the kids, scaring them to death is not the answer. I am a tough teacher. I expect my elementary school children to master mathematics and literature far beyond most people's expectations. But being tough does not mean being intimidating. Many teachers try to scare the kids into working hard and doing well on tests, but I discovered a long time ago that if a teacher is willing to take the harder route and work diligently to create a friendly environment, two things will happen: One, they will become friendlier because you are modeling compassionate behavior. And two, more students will ask questions. Nice people do not laugh at others. Friendly people are considerate. They know from personal experience that it can be scary to ask questions.

Please remember to smile on the first day and every day after that. And remember Janice, who is now eleven years old and about to enter the sixth grade. She has been in school for close to six thousand hours of her life. After all the projects and assignments, one of her strongest memories is the lovely smile of one of her teachers.

Be firm and strict from the beginning? Absolutely. Demand excellence from the students? It's essential. But the kids will reach their potential if they know they can ask questions without any fear. Your smile, and one that you flash often, will be the safety net that inspires their trust when they take that first step toward asking honest and thoughtful questions.

Hobart Shakespeareans Understand the Importance of Presentation

I've never been in favor of school uniforms, though I completely respect outstanding educators who are smart people and have endorsed the idea that strict dress codes or uniforms will improve behavior, and consequently aid the learning environment. But I have always believed that in the end a uniform seems to be more concerned with the outside of a child. I am more interested in the inside.

That being said, I do believe that presentation matters. When the students prepare their first written assignment for me, neatness and an organized paper are not only expected but required. Any paper turned in that is not neatly presented will be handed back to the student with the comment "dreaded rewrite" written across the top. Presentation matters, I tell the kids. I explain that, unfair as it may be, you might have written something fantastic, but if it is a mess the reader will lose interest before she even begins reading.

And that's just their papers. Presentation matters all the time. That's why when the students enter the room on the first day the room sparkles. Even though there are stains on the ceiling and sagging tiles from a roof that has not been properly fixed for more than a quarter of a century, the room is shiny and bright. Bulletin boards have new backing and the trim is colorful and new. The college pennants that cover the walls have been thoroughly cleaned after collecting air-conditioning dust over the summer. Plaques featuring the names of hundreds of former students who attended those colleges have been sponged and cleaned. The picture frames holding colorful pictures of past students doing all kinds of wonderful things have been polished, as have the students' desks. The insides of the desks have also been washed, and the floor scrubbed. Room 56 looks good and smells good the first moment the new students arrive. Presentation matters.

I dress well when I teach. Although it is not required by the Los Angeles Unified School District, I wear a shirt and tie every day. My hair is combed, and, like the room, I come to school well scrubbed.

There are two lessons here. Presenting yourself and your work well develops self-worth and confidence. In addition, a good presentation encourages others to be interested in what you have to offer.

I want the children to do their work carefully and neatly. I want them to internalize the fact that though they might write the next *The Great Gatsby,* if it is sloppily presented, no one might take the time to discover their brilliant work. Although the kids do not know this at the beginning of the year, the room environment and my own appearance give me the right to ask them to present work that is fit to be hung on a museum wall. Our room does not have to be immaculate and neither do I. It's a choice I have made because I am a professional. I want the children to be professional in their approach to their own work, and this message is received far more openly if I set the example.

In the months to come, presentation will be an ongoing discussion. When former students return to show my class college application forms and essays they have written, they also show the young students that forms incorrectly filled out or essays with grammatical errors are rejected by universities overwhelmed by applications and looking for any reason to toss one from the pile.

Even walking across our own campus prompts many of the children to verbalize some astute thoughts. They see that some teachers are incredibly sloppy in their appearance. This does not make them bad teachers or people not worth knowing. Still, as I explain to the children, suppose we are having a parent meeting to invite the kids on a class trip or special activity. It could be something as simple as a parent conference. If I am sloppy in my presentation, it might very well provide an unnecessary barrier to encouraging the parents to trust my leadership and judgment. And it's an easy barrier to remove.

Eventually, the kids conclude that packaging does not simply include the wrapping. If we are late to events, that is also part of the way people will perceive us. As we walk down a hallway, our manners and noise level are part of the whole picture. Over the year, many students begin to internalize that, more than ever, in a world where we are watched constantly by cameras and recorded by microphones, our conduct is scrutinized practically twenty-four hours a day.

It takes almost a lifetime, and certainly many years growing up, to fully understand that perception becomes reality. On the first day, make sure your room sparkles and reflects the totality of how you expect your students to present themselves and their work. Take a good look in the mirror in the morning and at your room before the kids enter. Is your desk neat? Are the papers you are passing out printed legibly? Are your clothes pressed?

When they are, you are ready to ask the kids to turn in neat and carefully constructed work. The pursuit of excellence begins.

Hobart Shakespeareans Are Organized

It's important for a child to learn the value of being organized. This is a daily topic in Room 56. The children hear that to be successful in anything, being organized will help them achieve their goals.

Having things in order takes time and practice. Eventually, I hope each child has carefully organized his backpack, his desk, his bedroom, and, perhaps most important of all, his time. People often laugh lightheartedly when they see a student's desk filled with old candy wrappers and papers left over from the Eisenhower administration, but it really isn't funny. We want students who are clear thinking and methodical in their approach to solving a variety of problems both in the classroom and in real life. Students who understand that a carefully planned environment helps them focus can more easily make the leap to see that the process of thinking requires the same meticulous organization.

Which brings me back to our first-day rug-making project. Earlier in my career, I kicked things off with a fabulous string art project, but a few years ago I switched to the rugs because they require more organization. The assignment better reinforces my goal of helping children see the value of having a place for everything.

It is sad how so many children come to us without a clue of how to put things away or remember where things are. We can blame bad parenting, television, or video games, but I have found the blame game to be wasted energy. Of course it is wonderful when supportive parents work hard to prepare their children by teaching them important values, and that is often the case. But the fact that more than a handful of children are clueless as to how to take care of things should steel our resolve to try to teach students skills that are important—even if they are not on the test at the end of the year. I buy the rugs we make at Michael's art supplies store, but they are easy to find online. It takes many hours for the kids to divide up the thousands of strands of yarn by color, place them in bags, and label their merchandise. It is not easy to do this.

It begins a way of life that is the foundation of our classroom. The children are careful when they organize their folders. Parts of each weekend are spent going through old work and making sure essential materials are kept while obsolete ones are recycled. The kids spend a few minutes each night packing their things before they go to sleep, so that homework assignments or sheets of music are ready to be used the next day in school.

Many of the kids joke about becoming a bit obsessive about organization because they truly see its value. Eventually some of them begin keeping specially constructed diagrams of their baseball teams and lineups. Students show up very early at school or stay late to make sure our cabinet supplies are arranged carefully, and even to alphabetize our music books in order by composer.

Homework is not only finished on time but always ready when asked for. Next year's class will not be missing any hammers for art projects because the previous group carefully put their tools back in the same box in the same place and facing the same way as the kids from the year before.

Being organized is contagious and becomes a way of life. It starts on Day 1 with our rug project, and is present every day thereafter. Whether you are a kindergarten teacher or a high school physics instructor, teaching your kids to be organized is time well spent, and important enough to find its way into your class from the first day of school.

Hobart Shakespeareans Are Humble

Not everyone agrees about teaching humility. It seems these days that humility is out of fashion. With Andy Warhol's prophecy of short bursts of fame for all, modesty might be the last thing on young people's minds given the world in which they are growing up. Ryne Sandberg, the great second baseman for the Chicago Cubs, pointed out in his Hall of Fame acceptance speech that too many players know where the red light is in the dugout, but are not aware of how to advance a teammate to the next base. Reality television has created celebrities who are famous simply for being famous while accomplishing absolutely nothing.

This makes it very difficult to teach young people to be unpretentious, which is why I work so hard to expose kids to a different way of living their lives. The best teachers I have observed bring their own beliefs to a classroom and do not simply follow a district script of what to teach. That script should be the beginning of a lesson, but you, the class leader, are the period at the end of the sentence.

In the case of our class, that sentence includes being unpretentious. While we do not have humility lessons, I do raise the issue on the first day with one example. Our school gives out awards to students and classrooms for a variety of accomplishments, including math competitions. It's reasonable for a teacher or a school to take a moment to acknowledge excellence.

In fact, on the first day, as my class walks down the corridor of the main building, I point out a case that holds trophies that have been awarded to our school for having outstanding attendance. Attendance is a big deal at Hobart. Classrooms compete with one another to have more students who never miss a day at school. Sadly, I have noticed that there are times when such competition can cloud the mission. Perfect attendance is a worthy goal, of course, but hopefully kids are coming to school because they enjoy learning and discovering opportunities.

Soon after that walk down the hallway, we are back in the room. I point out to the kids that we do not hang certificates in the classroom. There are no awards anywhere. And I remind them that I hope in the year to come they buy into the premise that Hobart Shakespeareans are humble. We accomplish a lot quietly.

We do not do a touchdown dance or show up the opposing pitcher during a home run trot. We do not scream and whoop for joy when a perfect math test is returned. There will be a great day reading *To Kill a Mockingbird* when the children walk down a lonely street with Atticus Finch, rifle in hand, facing a rabid dog. Like his own children, my students will be amazed to discover that this quiet man was actually the best shot in town. And after they are surprised, just like his son, Jem, my students understand. After giving a great performance, we do not jump around and celebrate.

Instead, we save that energy so we can applaud and cheer another classroom's performance.

This is not the fashion these days. But over the year, I make every effort to convince the kids that humility is a good thing. It may be an uphill battle, but, like Henry V, we teachers are the makers of manners. When our class works hard to bring desperately needed supplies to homeless children, we deliver them to the shelter and do not wait for any sort of acknowledgment. After a year's work to put together an astonishing Shakespeare production, kids are scrubbing floors and packing up props thirty seconds after a performance. They're a quiet bunch.

Some observers have commented that my students are shy. Others have suggested to me that they need more confidence. Television sound bites have sold many on the images of excited children screaming out answers with hands thrust eagerly toward the ceiling in an effort to gain the teacher's attention. That's fine, but we do things differently in our class. We often do not raise our hands even when we know an answer. It does not matter if others know that we know. We know.

For the next year, through literature, film, and real life, these children will be exposed to the concept and attractiveness of humility. Some of the kids will eventually reject this value, and that's fine. That's their choice and should be. But the beauty of teaching is that good teachers make sure their favorite recipes are on the classroom menu, and humility is never the special of the day in Room 56. It's a featured dish every day.

Day 1 comes and goes. The lessons last all year.

The students are told what I expect of them. They understand some of what I hope they will. They discover that we work constantly in our class. I do not raise my voice. I smile and laugh. I talk all the time about what will be coming in the future, from as soon as the next hour to the next day to next week and the months to come. Words like *initiative, modulate, organization,* and *humility* are mentioned often.

By the end of the first day I take the first steps in establishing a firm but loving relationship with the students. I make sure I am the person I want the kids to be. They are watching even when it appears they are not paying attention.

I make every attempt to get the kids off to a good start. There are a lot of smiles when the first day ends, and some of the kids are excited about what will be happening tomorrow and the next day and the day after that.

Make no mistake about it. Nothing magical happens on Day 1. But on that day I set the table with a huge selection of choices that the kids will consider in the months to come. And slowly, patiently, and sometimes painfully, the Magic begins to happen.

For Your Consideration

- The kids will not grasp your program on Day 1. Introduce it and get to work.
- Be the person you want the kids to be.
- Work hard to begin removing the fear of school that most of your students will bring with them from previous classroom experiences.
- Introduce your personal mission to the students. Tell them why you are here. You are here to help them have better lives because you care about them. You are excited about having them in class.
- Begin a dialogue with the students to help them understand the *why* of your classroom structure instead of the *what*.
- Be incredibly patient on Day 1. Because of your excellent work the previous year, it will most likely seem that the new students are miles behind where they need to be. Your last year's class was not actually better, but achieved a lot because of

your excellent teaching! You're back to square one, so be patient, and remember that you've done it before and can do it again.

- Have a personal decalogue that will drive every lesson you teach. Simplicity and consistency will inspire the kids to great heights.
- Have fun. The kids will if you do.

CHAPTER THREE

Everything Put Together Sooner or Later Falls Apart

Many young teachers spend time asking questions about Day 1. Far fewer inquire about Day 2. In my experience, while many things can go wrong on Day 1, Day 2 is closer to what a classroom really looks like. It's like the second date. On the first date, people are usually on their best behavior. As people spend more time together, reality sets in and discoveries are made. Familiarity can breed contempt.

Even if Day 1 has been a triumph for both you and the students, don't take a bow yet. It is true that the best is probably yet to come, but certainly the worst is still in the wings as well. It might not happen on Day 2, but make no mistake about it. There is going to come a day or an hour when all that you have built may fall apart. It's during those trying and awful moments that your ability to remember your goals can help you avoid the frustrating meltdowns and tears that can overcome hardworking teachers.

The prompts for such terrible moments can come from almost anywhere. Sometimes it's a simple flaw in your lesson. As an inexperienced first-year teacher, I once thought I had a terrific science unit planned. It was the second day of school, and I thought beginning our science curriculum with astronomy was a good idea. Kids love science, and they are always interested in space. I had spent several of my college years working both at a science museum and at the Griffith Observatory in Los Angeles, so I already had experience doing some demonstrations for school groups. Day 1 had gone well; the kids seemed to accept the fact that I was their teacher and most seemed willing to give me a chance to engage them.

During our first science lesson, I thought it would be fun to go back in time and show the children that people have always been interested in the universe. The plan was to teach the students about astrology, and how it had occupied many a mind before great thinkers like Copernicus and Galileo challenged our thinking. I prepared sheets to help the kids look up their zodiac signs and consider their futures according to the astrological charts I had printed up for them. I was organized, enthusiastic, and attempted to be funny in my presentation. I hoped the kids would laugh, or, at the very least, groan, but I did not expect them to begin crying. I was aware that my jokes were bad, but not that bad. Still, once the sheets were passed out, one little girl began to cry, and within sixty seconds at least seven or eight of her peers had joined in.

Antoine de Saint-Exupéry once wrote that the land of tears is a secret place. It took a few minutes for me to understand what was going wrong. And then I realized why all the planning of what I had thought would be a slam-dunk science lesson fell flat on its face before even one step was taken. The chart's first question stopped most of the kids cold.

Question 1: When is your birthday? _____

More than half of my students did not know their birthdays. And as it was the second day of school, I had not been given an official computer printout with all the students' personal information.

To look up their birthdays would have taken my going to the office and going through thirty-plus files. That would have to wait.

I apologized to the children and told them it was entirely my fault. I did not share with them my shock that ten-year-old children did not know their birthdays. I was a young teacher, and had much to learn. In the days to come, I was even more surprised to discover how few of the children knew their addresses or phone numbers. Still, such small disasters can be used to avoid future ones. A teacher learns that an understanding of what knowledge kids bring to a lesson is crucial in making that lesson a successful one. I apologized to the children for my mistake (Hobart Shakespeareans are honest) and told them that I would do a better job in the future. Lessons improved as the year went on and I knew the children better. After the initial shock at discovering that many of the students did not know their own birthdays, I recovered my wits and kept on teaching. For that particular day random birthdays were simply assigned so that the children could experience the astrological activity. This was a small matter in the great scheme of things.

On the other side of the spectrum are days of catastrophic disaster. Even with experience they can happen. The worst Day 2 I have ever experienced happened after what I thought had been a terrific Day 1.

Until a few years ago, Day 1 had always ended with our annual string art project, since replaced by our latch-hook rug-making project. It was always exciting for the kids. I used a sensational book of patterns called *The Beautiful String Art Book* by Raymond Gautard. It took more than a month to complete the project, and the finished work of students from more than twenty years ago are still displayed. The first day of work included the kids choosing one of a hundred projects they would create. Precut wood that would be the background for the string designs had been stacked in the corner of the room, and the kids would pick out their piece and spend about thirty minutes sanding the sides until they were as smooth as marble. The wood was then placed on a newspaper-covered table. The day ended with the kids painting their wood, carefully choosing an appropriate background shade that would accent the colors they would be using in the weeks to come to create their art.

This project was always a huge success. I had made my share of mistakes and learned from them. After ten or fifteen years of teaching this activity, I had learned (I thought) just about everything there was to know about the best type of wood to use and where to get it. I knew which paint to use and which brushes were inexpensive and yet of sufficient quality to make the projects shine. I had found a hardware store that supported teachers, and the kind folks there were happy to order nails for me in bulk, which saved me money and time. They also showed me that certain brands of nails were better suited for string art. I began each year confidently knowing that an occasional banged thumb or spilled paint was the biggest problem I would face.

But I had never met Bobby.

On Day 1 Bobby had burst into the room about five minutes late. His mother and older sister were with him, and they did not seem to mind interrupting me, as I had already been going over some of the basics with the new class. Bobby's sister did the talking, informing me that her brother had problems and I should let them know every night how he was doing. I smiled and thanked them for stopping by and introducing themselves. They left, Bobby found a seat, and I returned to teaching.

Later that afternoon, we began the art project. The kids were excited. I demonstrated how to use sandpaper carefully and how to avoid splinters. As usual, everyone did an excellent job. They went outside to do the work so that the classroom would not end up resembling the Sahara Desert, and then it was time to paint. As I had done for years, I demonstrated to the children how to dip their brushes in the various cans, and separated the kids into groups by the colors they were going to use. There were eight or nine small groups of eager kids ready to dip their brushes into the bright colors that glowed from the newly opened cans. The kids listened carefully to my instructions. They gently spread newspapers on the tables and watched quietly, focusing on me as I modeled the correct way to dip the brush, allow excess paint to drip back into the can, wipe the brush meticulously on the inner edge of the container, and paint the wood in the direction of the grain. The room was very quiet as the kids happily began painting, and they were delighted that their carefully sanded boards allowed the fresh paint to go on easily. It was a particularly good Day 1. The kids were doing a great job and, without even knowing it, beginning to internalize many of the values that I hoped to teach them.

And then Bobby turned his paintbrush into a lollipop. Kids around him gasped as Bobby dipped his brush into a can of hunter green paint, held it up for all to see, and began licking it. He got in two or three good strokes with his tongue before I could tell him to stop. He grinned and proudly showed his peers his bright green tongue and teeth.

Never before (but always since) had I instructed my fifth graders not to lick their brushes.

I felt I handled the situation well. The paint was kid-friendly and nontoxic, but there was no room to have Shrek in the classroom. After I made sure his mouth was clean, Bobby had to return to his seat and begin work on his spelling homework. I did not raise my voice or humiliate him in any way. The rest of the class was too absorbed in their own painting to care too much about Bobby, and many of the kids had seen Bobby behave in this manner in previous years, so his antics were no surprise to them. I told him that he had not demonstrated yet that he was ready to paint in our classroom, but that he would have another chance tomorrow. I was fair and reasonable, and the rest of the art lesson went well. Tomorrow would be a day when I could start to establish a better relationship with this troubled youngster, firmly but fairly drawing the lines for him to function in our class.

And then tomorrow came. Day 2 was going to be a busy one. In addition to teaching, I was hosting a group of high school seniors. They were in a special program with a wonderful teacher who was trying to inspire students to consider teaching as a career.

My classroom opens very early in the morning. On Day 2 I begin an optional Math Team for kids who want to do extra work learning how to solve complex word problems. The first session had gone well, and math materials were being put away around 7:55 A.M., five minutes before the official beginning of the school day. The rest of the kids were coming into the classroom, some with raised eyebrows, surprised to see other children already working. I walked over to the door to say good morning to the kids, and also to greet the fifteen or so high school seniors who were coming up the stairs to spend the day observing.

I met them at the top of the stairs, and before I could even finish a brief welcome, a shrill scream jolted us from the bottom of the stairs.

"HEY, YOU MOTHER**####. WHAT THE *%$ DO YOU MEAN ABUSING MY CHILD? I AM GOING TO $#%& KILL YOU. YOU &%&$#!!!

Believe it or not, I actually have cleaned up the language used by Bobby's mother. She must have set some sort of record for both swearing and decibel level. Her obscenity-laced tirade could be heard all over the school. Basically, she was furious that I had taken a paintbrush away from her child the day before. And so, after what had been a very good Day 1, Day 2 began with my class and the visiting high school seniors watching a woman practically assault me. She was spitting in my face. I stayed as calm as possible and gave up trying to explain about the day before after three attempts. I did try to ask her to speak to me away from the children, but my attempts only made her swear louder and longer. The philippic ended with her promise to visit my principal before going downtown to complain about me to the board of education.

By 8:05 A.M. that morning, the high school seniors had left. They politely told me that teaching was not for them. Although this was the worst day of the year with Bobby, no day with him was easy. He was obnoxious, selfish, and mean. Considering his home situation made things understandable, but not easy. I did my best with him. He never did finish his string art project, despite my efforts for four months to help him. Eventually we moved on to other projects. He finished some of them.

However, most things that fall apart are not as dramatic as Bobby. Teaching is a job that requires constant planning, and when things go wrong, it usually involves some minor occurrence that is merely aggravating and, if looked at properly, even funny. Such was the case with Stanley.

One year on Day 2, the children were about to leave for lunch. They were excited because I was offering them their first guitar lesson. During the lunch period in Room 56, kids may learn to play the guitar after they've gobbled down their food.

Before we go to lunch, I talk to the kids about the specific way they are to return to the room. Because of the chaos at the school, we have teaching assistants, known to the students as "coaches," who patrol the hallways and playground to ensure that children are where they are supposed to be. No child is allowed to return to a classroom during lunch without a pass.

The kids do not like the coaches. The students complain constantly that these officers are mean and scary. I ask the kids to stand in their shoes for a moment and to consider that it is not an easy thing to watch over one thousand children running all over the place and keep things orderly. I then carefully explain to the children that there is a way for them to return to our classroom during the lunch period without having any difficulties with the coaches.

First, I make a little pass for each child. It looks like a business card and explains that this license gives the carrier my permission to return to class for music lessons. The coaches have seen these cards and always honor them. I also tell the kids that they should remember a couple of things when they have finished their lunch and are about to head back to class. First, it is important for them to keep their lunch tables clean. I make sure the kids agree with me that it is not fair to the coaches or hygienic for anyone to leave their lunch area messy. I instruct the children to bus their tables and make sure food trays are put in recycling bins and plates in the proper trash receptacles. The kids nod that this is a reasonable request on my part, and I am happy to say that my class almost always does a fine job all over our school in taking care of their areas.

A second thing I mention before lunch is that the coaches do not tolerate two things: running and noise. I explain to the kids that if they simply leave the lunch area quietly and walk calmly toward our classroom, they probably won't even be stopped or asked to show their music passes. This is a theme that will be reiterated when the kids take to the road later in the year. When in hotels, we walk and are quiet. There is nothing wrong with running and making noise, I tell them, but they need to be aware of time and place, and coming to the class is not the same thing as playing baseball on the playground. If they walk quietly, they should not have any problems.

One year, this little talk appeared to go well. The kids had completed a good morning and happily walked over to the lunch area to ingest some very bad food before returning to the room for their first guitar lesson. As was my daily routine, I left the lunch area to go to the office and collect my mail. There is a large window there with an unobstructed view of the playground.

That's when I saw Stanley, one of my new students, who had only fifteen minutes before nodded with complete understanding when taught how to return to class. To his credit, he was walking and not running. Also, he took the direct path to our room, as I had requested. He had not tried to take a shortcut through the school hallway, as I had explained to the kids that if twenty of them did this it might very well disturb the office people working or other classrooms in session. Stanley did not try to sneak around the back of the school through the parking lot, an area deemed off-limits by school personnel because there is no supervision back there, and hence often a place where many of the school's most notorious kids hang out. Stanley was walking back to class exactly the way he had promised. However, he had made two minor but critical adjustments to our plan.

First, he was carrying a tray of food. He had not eaten his lunch, not an altogether unusual occurrence for Hobart students. More unusual, however, was that he was carrying his tray of food with him. Perhaps Stanley had misunderstood his instructions and thought he would be able to eat in our classroom during his guitar lesson. Realizing I had probably not been clear enough in my instructions, I headed out to meet Stanley so that I could send him back to finish his lunch.

But Stanley had other plans. As I walked toward him, I saw something that I had not seen before and have not seen since. He stopped in the middle of the playground and, holding on to his tray, threw all the food perhaps twenty feet into the air. Seconds later, the ground around him was covered with school food, which is not very appetizing looking at its best, and certainly being splattered all over the blacktop did not improve its appearance. Not finished yet, Stanley then began jumping up and down, grinding his food into the blacktop. He then turned his tray into a Frisbee and flung it toward of group of third graders playing dodgeball. His work done, Stanley then walked calmly toward Room 56 to have his guitar lesson.

I spoke with Stanley about what I had seen. I also remembered that this was his second day in my class and that I did not know this boy very well. I knew that less than sixty minutes before, he had appeared to understand my instructions to walk quietly back to our room. I had learned that his nodding meant nothing. I was upset with him, but kept my focus on the fact that I wanted Stanley to understand why our class does things in the manner we do. In the months to come, I would find out many things about Stanley. His home situation was a very sad one. He was a very good boy to whom life had dealt a lousy hand. I did not know this on Day 2, but from Stanley's point of view, listening to his teacher ramble on about the necessity for proper school decorum was about the last thing on his mind.

I talked to him quietly and away from the other kids. I was firm but did not embarrass him. I made sure that he would have other chances to learn the guitar, but the price for lessons was to walk quietly back to class and avoid using the playground for any experiments in the physics of the flight of food. I made certain Stanley understood that he would have other chances, but that if he continued to demonstrate that he could not follow proper procedures he would deny himself the chance for guitar lessons and a whole lot of fun. I kept calm and constantly thought about being his role model rather than his dictator. That's how in the months ahead he would confide to me the frustrating pain he was feeling. Things had fallen apart on Day 2, it was true, but good teachers learn how to put things back together. By the end of the year Stanley was the lead guitarist in our band.

Everything put together sooner or later falls apart. Even when things go perfectly one day, they can fall apart in ways and for reasons no teacher could anticipate. In the case of a great art teacher I know, things fell apart because he created something quite wonderful, only to have it destroyed by people who should have been celebrating his project.

I was fortunate to observe John when our staff toured middle schools to meet outstanding teachers. John is one of those teachers who change lives and happen to teach art, but he would have been just as effective if he were a basketball coach or a physics instructor. He is that good. Art happens to be his field of expertise, but the truth is that John is one of those master teachers who remind us of what a beautiful thing teaching can be.

His students created astonishing works of art throughout the year, and John decided to have an art show as a sort of culmination to celebrate the students' creations and thank their parents for all their support. He took his students to art museums throughout the year, and he had convinced a gallery to allow his class to use a couple of rooms for their show. It was going to be a wonderful evening.

It turned out even better than John could have imagined. People in the community had heard about the show and came. The work was so beautiful that many people offered to buy the paintings and sculptures. The money could be used for John's school, ideally to buy art supplies for next year's class. Like many teachers, John had constantly reached into his own pocket to make things happen. By the end of the second evening of the two-day show, John's students had raised several thousand dollars. Everyone felt great.

Within two years, a sad and familiar tale had played itself out. With cash up for grabs, people at John's school got very involved. It was one of those schools where test scores are everything, and so art was never considered a "real" subject. But *ca-ching!* Once people saw that money could be made for the school, previously disinterested folks not only thought the art show was a great idea, they began to take credit for it.

Faster than you can say Picasso, school officials hijacked the art projects created by John's students and put on an end-of-the-year extravaganza. Visitors came and watched the students sing, perform, and generally put on a dog-and-pony show to raise money. There's certainly nothing wrong with a school having an activity like this, but John and his students were lost in the shuffle. People who had absolutely nothing to do with the project took credit for student achievement and, indeed, spoke as though the art created at their school was their idea. More money was raised. None of it was spent on John's art supplies.

Everything put together sooner or later falls apart. John was upset, but really, what can a person do? If he complained he might appear to be self-centered and not a team player. After all, the school was benefiting from something he had started, even though his efforts and, more important, the students' art were not appreciated. Instead, John has continued to lead a classroom where his children create astonishing works of art. Many of his Saturdays are spent reaching into his shrinking savings to take kids to museums, study the masters, and also make sure they have some lunch. It's not a perfect situation, but the lesson here is that John has never lost focus when others around him have. He didn't let cynicism or bitterness win the day, because even though the art show lost sight of the kids, he knew he couldn't. Several years have passed. John's extraordinary teaching is often not appreciated by many around him, including some of his students. That goes with the territory. But his initial goal was to have children discover the wonder of art and the extraordinary potential that each of them has inside to create it. That still goes on every day in his class.

And that, my friends, is the most important lesson for you to remember in your early days of teaching. The best class leaders begin to figure out what it is they want a child to learn from them. Once you figure it out, you can develop a means to your ends. But even when things begin to flow, something or someone will gum up the works.

Count to ten and do your best to stay on task. When you discover that your students do not know their birthdays, teach them their birthdays. When Bobby's mother screams at you, stay calm and do your best with Bobby each day. After you have made sure Stanley has picked his squashed food off the playground blacktop and learned to walk back to class correctly, continue the guitar lessons. When bureaucrats corrupt your brilliant project, remember what made it wonderful and keep on molding new artists.

Everything put together sooner or later falls apart. Do you

know why? It's because nothing remains constant. Remember, despite your best efforts, there are things beyond your control. Good teachers are adaptive. There will be lessons that fall apart because kids do not know their own birthdays and days when unreasonable parents scream and rant and create havoc in the shaky world that you are trying to solidify. Seemingly understandable instructions regarding walking across a playground and disposing of leftover food can turn into flying vegetables and mashed burritos on the blacktop. Children's masterpieces can be hijacked and used to make money rather than to focus attention on the artists themselves.

Everything put together sooner or later falls apart. But one thing does not have to change: you. You are the constant in the classroom. In your early years you have the opportunity to discover what your class will stand for and what lessons you want the kids to learn despite the constantly changing scene around them. Your consistent, patiently delivered teachings will be the foundation that steadies your students in what is often a very shaky world. Remember on Day 2 that there will be a Day 3, 33, and 133. You have time to teach the children, but not as much as you would like. That's why every day counts. In stormy weather, you are the one who can right the ship and get it back on course. Smile when the food goes flying, and adjust the lessons when kids have a shocking lack of knowledge. With your help, the food will wind up where it belongs and the kids will learn a lot.

Things fall apart. You are there to put them back together.

For Your Consideration

- Things are going to go wrong in your classroom. From vomit to fistfights, on practically a daily basis something will go down that is not in your lesson plan book. When things go wrong, stay calm.

- Things can be fixed in the long run. If a valuable activity is ruined, remember the objective of the activity and teach it another day.
- Learn from your mistakes. When things go wrong, it's not a problem. If the same thing happens over and over again, either try a different approach or seek the counsel of others for a fresh outlook.
- Laugh at yourself and at the crazy things that can go wrong. Humor and honest self-deprecation are not only healthy but effective in fixing anything that is problematic in your activities.
- Every disaster that happens is an opportunity for you to get better. Nothing feels better than teaching a great lesson that failed the year before because of what you have learned.
- You are never finished. Things will go wrong in your twenty-fifth year that never went wrong before. Take solace in the fact that the job is never boring!

CHAPTER FOUR

An Inside Job

Visitors to Room 56 are usually amazed by the culture of the classroom. They love seeing kids who are ten years old reading books far beyond their grade level, solving complicated math problems easily, and reciting Shakespeare as though they were members of a professional company. At the end of the day, however, it is the behavior of the children that people find the most impressive.

During an art project that requires hammering nails into boards, some of the kids go outside to hammer so the noise does not disturb the rest of the school. Back inside the room, visitors see me working with kids who have completed nailing and are applying string designs to their projects. No adult stays with the kids outside hammering. Yet when the classroom door is opened, and one walks out onto the balcony to look down at the playground, anywhere from six to twelve children are hammering away. No one is off task. No one argues. It's an impressive sight.

It seems that now, more than ever, managing a classroom is more difficult. At every grade level, there are issues of behavior that are shocking to anyone not involved in schools. And it goes beyond the horrific violence that finds its way into the news when schools suffer awful acts of brutality. On a much less shocking level, just getting kids to sit down and listen has become a struggle for many teachers. As a result, classroom management has become the focus of many discussions about teaching.

I am often asked a reasonable and understandable question, particularly by young teachers who have struggled getting their students to behave themselves, pay attention, and function. It's usually asked with a combination of wonder and frustration. Here is the question:

"Rafe, how do you control the kids?"

My answer isn't meant to be flippant. It is something I have come to believe after many years of teaching. When asked how to control children, I offer this advice:

There is no control!

(But you can teach children self-control.)

Any book about teaching is really a cookbook filled with recipes. No one has all the answers, and the system of classroom management used in Room 56 is submitted here as simply one way to lead a group of students. It is not the only way or the best way. It is my hope that the following pages might stimulate teachers to apply anything they think worthy into their own systems to make their days more fun and effective.

I've already mentioned that a lot of popular literature on the subject of teaching features suggestions about managing a classroom: *Don't smile until Christmas. Take charge. Show them who's boss. Kick a trash can. Put the fear of God into them.* Basically, make sure that whether the students are first graders or high school seniors, they fear the consequences of bad behavior so much that they can be frightened into being the compliant little humans that would make each day of teaching easy.

Here is part of an actual letter I received from a caring and concerned teacher who was attending a mandatory training session about classroom management:

> I'm two weeks into the training and am fairly trauma-tized by the experience. I find myself at odds with nearly everything that is said at the seminars, and to me it basically feels like teaching us to bully our students into submission. Every lesson must be tied to daily objectives and end with a quantifiable assessment. Meticulous tracking must be done on every student's performance. These workshops are deliv-ered by immaculately dressed, corporate personas who break up sessions with thirty-second periods of deep reflec-tion but never encourage any degree of critical thinking or discussion. I feel like all of my favorite teachers—from high school, college, and people I admire like you—would be screaming at the ideology being espoused here. Should I just endure this brainwashing boot camp and then put as much love as I can into my kids when I start in the fall?

I have no doubt that the instructors running such seminars mean well, but I am also certain I would never want to be in their classrooms. My goal is to teach the children a set of values that they internalize. I want them to work hard in the class not because they fear a consequence but because they enjoy the work and also because they believe that good behavior is the right thing to do. This is a constant topic of conversation. Getting kids to buy into a value system that accepts the fact that there are no shortcuts and that being respectful matters is never easy. These days, when it often appears that incorrigible behavior is the norm in many schools, it is understandable that young teachers have been willing to try anything to get students to simply sit down and, forgive me, shut up. I am suggesting that while some of the latest trends may work in the short run, they are a quick fix. As you grow as an instructor, it's better if your lessons have a longer-lasting effect.

It is therefore predictable for novice teachers to use simple techniques to get their classrooms running smoothly. If you are an elementary school teacher getting your students' attention by clapping hands, ringing bells, or turning off lights, it does not make you a bad teacher. If your high school history students behave because they fear detention or your constant threats that parents will be called, it might be the best way you have learned during your early years of teaching to keep some semblance of order in the room. I hope, however, to present a vision of what is possible for you with experience. Some techniques teachers use that I do not care for would be called effective by many observers; particularly as a beginner, anything short of holding a gun to the students' heads that works and can get you through the day might very well be called good classroom management. I would suggest that some classroom management techniques are better than others. Let's take a look at one trend that is popular in some schools that has merits, but one that ultimately I would not use in working with children.

SLANT is an acronym that describes a method being used by some teachers who are working very hard to do well and care deeply about their students. Its proponents point out that no lesson can be taught if the kids are unruly and not paying attention, and SLANTing creates a foundation of attentive silence that allows a teacher to proceed. For the unfamiliar, kids who are taught to SLANT memorize the following rules:

S: Sit up
L: Listen
A: Ask and answer questions

N: Nod (I'm not kidding)
T: Track the speaker

I have observed many classrooms that use this technique of management, and frankly it's a little disturbing. To be fair, all the classrooms I observed were taught by passionate teachers with an unshakable commitment to ensuring that students master the lesson of the day. And the students *were* usually quiet and attentive. Yet it troubled me because the behavior was superficial. If the teacher was interrupted by a visitor or had to use the bathroom, the class deteriorated rapidly. I noticed that the students SLANTed only when the teacher was present, which inspired me to consider an important question I would ask any teacher who used this sort of management:

In your own life, do you SLANT?

I know I don't, but I am able to quietly listen and show respect to others.

Of course the goals of such techniques to control children are reasonable. We want kids to be attentive. We desire them to show respect to the teacher and their peers, and we certainly want them to ask questions when they do not understand the material. One of the problems with such techniques is the element of fear they create. Behind most strategies used to control a group of students, the underlying theme is that there will be a punishment to those who do not comply with the rules.

Some teachers count backward from a certain number, have the kids join in, and then become silent at zero. Other teachers raise their hand in the air, and wait for all the students to raise their hands as well, then proceed with the lesson when the room gets quiet. There are an infinite number of ways teachers ask for the attention of their students.

There is another way I have seen teachers control their classes.

It works like this. The teacher quietly says, "Listen up, everyone." And they do. This is what happens in my class and it can in yours.

It is not easy, and as a beginning teacher, this might seem like an impossible goal. It isn't. But there will be days early in the year when the kids won't listen or show you and their classmates respect. By modeling the behavior you expect of them, and teaching interesting and relevant lessons, the bumps in the road will become smoother with each passing day. Slowly, patiently, and calmly, your class will follow your example. You must give up some control. You must ignore some of the kids who are not paying attention. I do not demand that the students track me. Over time, I hope to show them that I am worth being tracked, and so is everyone in the class. I have found this to be a far more reasonable and effective way to maintain order to create the best possible learning environment.

A friend of mine who has his students SLANT told me that he does, in fact, SLANT at staff meetings. He told me that it helps him behave when meetings are boring. It helps him avoid a scolding by his principal because it appears that he is interested in the meeting when in fact he is not.

That is the hardest point, and one that is not discussed often enough. It is true that there are severe behavior issues in schools, and they often manifest themselves because of poor parenting, poverty, the deterioration of societal values—it is a never-ending list of causes. But often—more often that most teachers care to debate—students misbehave in school because they are bored. There will always be students who cause problems in school. Whether you are as mild as milk or as tough as steel, some of the kids will cause trouble.

It has been my experience, however, that the most effective way to keep a class in order is with an interesting lesson. When activities are fascinating and exciting, you have a more reasonable punishment for bad behavior. The punishment is the missing of the lesson, and very few students want to be left out when they actually believe they are going to miss something fun and stimulating.

Once a reporter was interested in a student in Room 56. This kid had stayed in during recess to work on some guitar pieces and had remained in class for almost four consecutive hours. The writer said to the student, "Don't you ever go to the bathroom?"

"I might miss something," replied the youngster, eager to get back to the challenging math puzzle that had been assigned as a supplement to the basic numbers work for the day.

It takes years to build interesting lessons. At first, it is reasonable and even necessary that you will do everything your department or grade level asks you to do. The district assigns a regimen of books, questions, and tests that each class must finish. But as you continue to teach, you will no doubt discover that some of these lessons are not particularly interesting or important to your students despite your most enthusiastic efforts. You will find ways to use your own experiences to supplement the basic curriculum you have been assigned to teach. Best of all, you will collaborate with first-rate teachers who are doing things that make their lessons more interesting and relevant. In most cases, the teachers who have the most captivating lessons have classes with the fewest behavior problems. It may be easier to threaten, bully, and scare the students into obedience when you first begin to teach, but it is not better in the long run.

And that maxim about the long run goes back to the concept in class that there are no shortcuts. This motto applies to us as well as to the students. During your lessons, things are going to go wrong. Some kids will misbehave no matter what classroom management strategy you employ. Please consider the following suggestions when the train goes off the tracks, when someone is not listening or making faces or being just plain rude.

The best instructors come to learn that teaching is an inside job. The ultimate goal is for students to behave well and listen because they want to instead of being forced to comply with a set of rules. Teachers all have similar goals. We hope our students pay attention, practice their lessons diligently, and play well with others. Young teachers discover quickly that this is not often the case. The unfortunate reality is that many students, and sometimes it feels like the majority of them, tune us out. Such students are totally apathetic to doing work and are downright cruel to others. As a result, many class leaders and professional development sessions are increasingly using extreme tactics to get Johnny to sit up, shut up, and work.

Try to set up your lessons as part of a grand scheme. While the focus that day might be on a fifty-minute lesson in math or a science project or a class discussion in history, try to work toward a bigger picture in your own head and in the minds of your students. During your lessons, you may find it effective to constantly refer to future lessons and projects that will connect with that day's material. When I finish a lesson, I often talk about what will be happening tomorrow that will connect with what is currently happening. I often stop reading literature with the kids at a point of extreme interest. They groan when they learn they will have to tune in tomorrow to see what happens. This strategy builds excitement in students. When I work with high school students on weekends, we read or study things that are directly connected to something they will be doing later in the year. They know this, and it motivates them to focus. By connecting your lessons to the future, the present will be far more peaceful.

Most young teachers jump on students when behavior is not perfect. It's as though we have the red pen in hand, circling every spelling error and editing ill-used phrases as an essay is graded. We teachers are trained to correct mistakes. It's in our job description. This becomes a problem if we attempt to control every bit of student behavior like a drill sergeant. If we do, we'll never get any teaching done. We should remember that the journey we are taking with the students is a long one. Some things can be overlooked and left for another day. This comes under the heading of "Don't sweat the small stuff." When I teach a lesson, I see dozens of little misdemeanors that might have received my immediate attention as a young teacher. Over the years I have discovered that the energy I once spent correcting behavior is better spent perfecting the lesson. In doing so, fewer have misbehaved, and more have learned.

Consider three students of mine who were difficult to teach. These kids were not in the same class, but all exhibited behavior within the first two days of the year that let me know they were going to try my patience.

RUDE AND MEAN

Anna was a pretty little girl and very bright. She talked constantly in class. Occasionally it was even about the subject being taught. Often, though, she interrupted others, tuned out her teacher, and figured that her considerable speaking ability would get her through school. She passed tests easily and had superior language skills, coming from one of the few homes of the children in class that year where a parent spoke English. However, Anna was also quite insensitive to others. At times she was downright mean, insulting peers and hurting their feelings with accurate but cruel observations. Some of the kids were simply afraid of her, as being caught in her crosshairs could result in the type of verbal abuse that could cause some long-lasting scars.

I was nice to her, something that surprised both Anna and her classmates. When she did not pay attention in class, I continued teaching. After a few days, I spoke with her privately about showing courtesy in class, which resulted in some tears and the explanation that she was misunderstood and had been treated unfairly by every teacher she had ever had. I called her mother, who was a very nice woman and gladly came in for a conference. We all spoke about my concern that Anna needed to work on being a bit more considerate of others. I described to her mother that she often did not pay attention to the other children in class when they had something to say. I also showed Mom how Anna had turned in some very sloppy assignments. Mom was only too pleased to explain to me that Anna often did not pay attention to others because of her extraordinary intelligence, and that sloppy work was fine because content was the only thing that mattered, and that my point that presentation was important was a stupid and childish thing to say. I smiled and thanked her for coming in to have the chat.

What should a teacher do? We all face situations where a student does not listen and there is no support at home. Still, we want the student to learn and we aspire for our class to run efficiently. This is why many class leaders use a rigid system of fear to get a student like Anna to close her mouth. By staying calm and not paying attention when Anna tuned me out, she learned that lessons continue in my class. Over time, Anna began to behave better. She learned that if she wanted attention from anyone, blurting out rude comments was not going to get it. Let's be clear. I did not change this young lady. There was no epiphany in which she mended her ways and morphed into Mother Teresa. But she did calm down over time, did well in class, and, best of all, the other students did not suffer any tyranny from their teacher because of the actions of one student. Anna was one of thirty-four kids in the class. She came to understand this, and the discovery that she was really a very small part of the room helped her and thrilled her classmates.

LAZY

Alex was a different sort of student. He did not hurt or bother anyone. He was highly intelligent and never rude. He had one small problem: he did practically no work. Rather than practice his math or work on an essay, Alex wanted to dream about video games. Each day he wore a T-shirt with a video game character. He constantly doodled figures from his favorite adventures. Not a day went by when I did not talk to Alex or sit with him to get him through his assignments. Homework was rarely completed. He had to make it up by finishing it in class. I deprived him of the opportunity to participate in certain art projects the class worked on each afternoon in order to help him finish his assignments. There was no hope of his finishing anything at home. His mother was rarely there, and when I spoke to his grandmother, who raised him, she explained that Alex was only ten and there was nothing wrong with a boy playing eight to ten hours of video games a day. He would rise at 5:00 A.M. to play them before school and had the joystick in his hand ten minutes after the bell rang to signal the end of the school day.

I once visited a school where the teachers told the students, and without tongues in cheeks, that they were going to drag them kicking and screaming to college. It is understandable to feel this way when we know what is best for a student. Most people would agree that a student sitting around doing nothing all day but playing games is missing many opportunities.

At this school I visited, when students did not finish work or were caught not paying attention in class, kids were given an unusual punishment. They had to stay after school and stare at the clock for two hours. A teacher sat in the room with the offender to make sure the task was completed. Given that this was a standard sight at this school, I would question whether it was effective. With several students a day in detention staring at clocks, it is possible that some of them would eventually pay attention to avoid such a dreary punishment. However, the most reasonable consequences help correct improper behavior without turning off the kid to the actual reason he should pay attention. Learning should be a joyous experience, and it's hard to find joy if paying attention in class is forced on a student instead of encouraged.

Of course Alex needed to face consequences for his unfinished work. On days when he did not complete basic assignments, he had to miss working on art projects he enjoyed to get his math or language work done. But the door was always left open. If he finished his work properly, he earned the right to participate in the rest of the class activities.

The mission of our class is to be nice and work hard. If I screamed at Alex when our mission was to be nice, that would be a mixed message! I spent time with him every day, speaking to him and listening to his thoughts. I coaxed him to finish his work because I wanted him to see me as an adult who constantly worked hard to help him. It was important for him to spend time with someone who believed in his potential, even if he gave very few reasons for that belief. Still, in the end, it had to be Alex who ultimately made the decision to work. In the current environment, in which schools proudly hang banners declaring *All of us will learn* and *All of us will go to college,* allow me to make two predictions. Despite the admirable sentiments expressed in such goals, it won't happen. When their students don't achieve these goals, young teachers become discouraged and give up. High expectations are important, but unrealistic expectations do not help anyone. I do not think Alex has a bright future. I know he does not if he continues on his current path. That is why I encouraged him every day. That is why I hope that someday, years from now, my explanations as to the value of working in school might begin to become a part of Alex's thinking. Of course I could have browbeaten Alex into doing his work, but in truth it would not have helped him. Eventually Alex is going to have to work by himself; I have learned that screaming and handholding really is not in the student's best interest. Students also must come to understand that even the neediest cannot expect a teacher to be with him all the time when other children deserve attention and support as well.

THE CRIMINAL

That may sound a bit harsh, but when kids steal, let's not sugarcoat their behavior. There are students in school who steal. It might be interesting to dissect why students believe they have the right to take something that does not belong to them, but when it happens, there is often not enough time to play Freud and delve into the psyche of a thief. Family values (or lack of them), greed, peers, and a host of other factors can be a part of the problem.

In our classroom we have an economic system in which kids have jobs and receive monthly paychecks. We also have "cash" lying around the room. It resembles Monopoly money, with some humorous pictures and class mottoes printed on the paper. The denominations come in $25, $50, and $100 bills. The kids do not touch the money, which is often sitting on the ledge of a whiteboard or a back table. Hobart Shakespeareans are honest, and it is a value the students take quite seriously.

But one year, a "banker" was stunned when a girl came to him with a huge amount of money to deposit. Even the best students in class had not earned close to the amount of cash this young lady was holding in her hand. The banker came to me immediately and I took Deborah aside to ask her where she got the money. After a few unconvincing denials she admitted that she took the money during recess when I was teaching some of the children classical guitar.

Stealing is serious. It's not chewing gum in class or missing a homework assignment. Deborah and I had a long talk, and I pointed out the awful reality that this young lady had not considered. When I called her parents in to discuss the situation, they were appalled by what had happened and completely supportive of my efforts. They told me they had two other children who had never done anything like this, and, having taught one of the siblings, I knew they were sincere and correct.

Deborah had broken the trust that is held sacred in Room 56. As a result, there would be serious consequences. She was removed from all optional class activities until the class and I felt she was worthy to have the privilege of before- and after-school fun. Deborah was not allowed to go to the bathroom without being accompanied by another student. As a result of her dishonesty, Deborah had to know that even a simple request to use the bathroom in the middle of a lesson might reasonably be doubted. However, everyone in the class, following my example, was kind and polite to Deborah. She remained a member of our class, and eventually called a meeting to ask her peers for another chance. It took two of these meetings, but eventually Deborah was again participating in all class activities. She made a big mistake, but if a door is not left open for possible redemption, there is no motivation for a student to try to do better.

Dishonesty is often a serious problem not only in school but in society. Many teachers are understandably concerned about cheating on tests, and one way of preventing this is to place cardboard screens between students to make it impossible for one kid to copy off the paper of another.

I do not use dividers when the students take examinations. It is true that this gives kids a far better chance to cheat. It is also true that a teacher has the power to practically eliminate any dishonesty during a test. When a teacher uses dividers and circulates around the room like a vulture in search of carrion, most students would find it impossible to copy from the kid next to them or have some sort of notes under the table.

I have made a conscious decision not to do this. My classroom management goal is to teach students to manage themselves. Eventually, I hope to teach Deborah not to steal because she is not a thief. I am hoping, through example and a consistent message, to inspire students to internalize a code of honesty in which classroom money lying around is left alone and a child would prefer getting an answer wrong honestly over a correct one dishonestly.

Given the fact that some recent polls show that 95 percent of high school students admit to having cheated in school within the previous year, the quest to build real moral character in anyone might be rightfully categorized as quixotic. So be it. I am happy to mount Rocinante and tilt at windmills. I might prevent an entire classroom from cheating by using fear and force, but with this method these same students will eventually cheat in the future. My goal is to create opportunities for the students to do well on exams and, more important, develop a code of integrity from the seeds planted in my class.

AN ALL-THE-TIME CLASS

The language teachers use in explaining consequences is crucial if our message is to be heard. There is a phrase I have found effective that you might like to use with your students. A common occurrence in school is when a young teacher who has established a good classroom learns that the students misbehave when she is not present. If the students do well only when a particular teacher is around, it is actually a sign that they are not doing well at all. Whether kids work hard and behave because a teacher is charismatic or Draconian, the ultimate goal is for students to do a great job in school because the values are within them and not forced from without.

I've mentioned this already, but it's worth showing you again. Early in the school year, I call up a student and sit him down next to me as the class watches. We have a conversation that sounds something like this:

Rafe: David, I just got tickets to the Dodgers game, and I'd love to take you. If I asked your mother if you could join me for the game, and I promised her that I would take care of you *some* of the time, would she let you go?

David: No!

(Lots of laughter accompanies the ridiculous nature of the question.)

Rafe: All right. How about if I promised her that I would take care of you *most* of the time?

All: No! No way! Never! Of course not! (You get the idea.)

Rafe: I don't understand you guys. These are great seats!

David: You have to take care of me *all* of the time.

Rafe: Yes, I do.

The conversation begins. We are an *all-the-time class*. We listen all the time. We admire people who do the right thing all the time. We want our dentist to be focused all the time when he drills. Drivers on the road need to pay attention all the time. If we go to the theater, we expect the actors to speak their lines clearly all the time. The kids come up with dozens of interesting examples.

Finally the attention is placed on them. If they are nice only when a teacher is around, then they really aren't nice. When a guest comes to class and has something to say, we pay attention. We do so because we believe that paying attention is polite and the right thing to do. We listen not because a two-hour clock-staring session awaits if we don't but because we have come to understand that paying attention is a win-win-win situation. The speaker wins because his words are being acknowledged. The listener gives himself an opportunity to learn something that might be of value. And the other students in the room win because no rude person is denying them the right to learn something as well.

There are concerned teachers who force students to behave properly. Some might scold a student with the words "If you want to mess up your life, that's fine with me. But as long as you are in my class, you will do things properly. You are not going to screw up on my watch."

The passion is admirable. In the early years of teaching, you might very well find yourself going down this path. But consider this food for thought. The ultimate goal is for the student to internalize good behavior that will benefit him for the rest of his life. When we are unreasonable with students and humiliate them into submission, the benefit is really for the teacher and not the students.

It's an inside job. Use reason and logic and fairness. Be firm, of course, but keep cool when it's hardest to stay calm. Remember that in the end, it's not your watch that really matters; it's their watch. Keep this in mind, and one day you will have many students who conduct themselves with honor and dignity at all times. They don't care about your watch. They watch themselves.

For Your Consideration

- Language is crucial when dealing with classroom management. Be careful that you are not bullying the students into being docile prisoners. "Because I said so" might work in the short term, but a firm and reasonable approach to the rules of your class will be far more effective in the long term.
- Teaching children self-control takes a lot of time. At the beginning of the year, be prepared for the kids to make many mistakes after being given the opportunity to take charge of their own behavior. Use these mistakes as opportunities to teach students a better way of conducting themselves.
- Have class discussions outside the traditional hours to hear what the kids have to say about previous school experiences

with discipline. The lunch period is a great time to get the kids expressing themselves about both good and bad experiences they have had. When you show a genuine interest in their feelings, they will be more receptive to your suggestions on how to carry themselves both inside and outside your classroom.

• Try not to talk too much. The goal is for the students to take charge of their own behavior. The more you remove yourself from the conversation, the more invested the students will be in their actions.

CHAPTER FIVE
The Quiet Man

A terrific teacher I know once suggested to me that I write a book called *Everything's a *&$@#%$ Fight*. He was bemoaning his situation in a school where it seemed that there was an impediment to accomplishing even the most modest of goals. Some rule or regulation stopped every one of his ideas dead in its tracks. He bitterly remarked that if his class found the cure for cancer, a representative from a procancer organization would file an injunction against his students to prevent them from releasing the information to the world.

Okay, he was joking, but there is some truth to his frustration. In fact, a very successful businessman once visited my class to check things out as he was considering becoming a patron. He was so interested in the comings and goings of a teacher's life that his plan to spend a few hours in Room 56 morphed into spending an entire week with the students and me. He went to every meeting, observed the planning of lessons, and shadowed every encounter I had with current students, former students, parents, administrators, and visitors. At the end of his week, he became a lifelong patron and, better still, a wonderful friend. He also offered up this observation:

"Rafe, the most amazing thing about you is that in the last quarter of a century you haven't killed somebody yet!"

I laughed heartily but he interrupted me.

"No, seriously, how do you survive in this place and not lose your cool? How do you stay so calm? There were people I met this week that I would have at the very least yelled at and at the worst punched in the nose! What's your secret?"

There are two answers to this question. The grand-scheme answer is to always remember that the children are watching. If we want our students to treat others with respect and courtesy, it begins with us. When people are disagreeable might be the most important time of all to be civilized. The students are watching, and we teachers can show them that they have choices in the ways they will conduct their own relationships with others, both in school and in the world beyond.

I have also found that it is best to be the Quiet Man for a practical reason. We teachers usually become upset because we care deeply about a student or a project we are doing that will help many young people have better lives. And this anger and the desire to fight for a cause is well intentioned. Give me a feisty teacher over an apathetic one eight days a week. But better than feisty or apathetic is the *effective* teacher.

Consider this letter I received from a caring young teacher who had so many bad days he left teaching, but he is considering giving it another try:

> I came into the job with my hair on fire, so to speak. As a musician, I found it imperative to teach my students music. The school I was teaching at had no music curriculum. The closest thing these children had was a "multi-arts" teacher who yelled at them every day they had her class. Needless to say, this took all the joy out of art. So I started the year by promising an early morning music club. I was teaching the

students to play guitar, glockenspiel, bass, and melodica. They loved it and so did I. Of course, I was teaching on my own time and not receiving payment. Despite this, my principal found it necessary to ask me for my lesson plans for the morning music club. When I told her that I was doing the same thing I had done for my master's thesis and therefore didn't have a lesson plan, she immediately pulled the plug on the program. This hurt me, but it devastated the children. I had promised something, and my promise had been broken. In a classroom that was supposed to be built on trust, this was the first in a long string of promises that I cold not keep due to the school policies and administrative limitations.

All fun was thrown out the window. I lived in fear of my principal coming in during our monthly auctions and other "extracurricular" activities (i.e., talking about life, feelings, and being good people). I eventually tried to continue these important lessons on days when the principal was out of the building, but by the time I had figured out how to do this, the students no longer took me seriously. I don't blame them. They were receiving mixed messages. I would act like a hard-nosed drill sergeant when the principal was around, and when she was gone I would try to remind the children that it's good to be smart, but it is ultimately more important to be a decent, considerate, and caring human being.

The fear that my principal instilled in me eventually found its way into my classroom and everything devolved from there. By the end of the year, I was breaking up verbal and physical fights on a weekly basis. I received severe reprimands regarding my classroom management skills and was told, "Perhaps you should consider a different profession."

Maybe she was right. I used to be proud of my accomplishments. But after last year, all of my hard work evaporated into a cloud of indecision, uncertainty, and utter despair.

After being bullied all year long, I was given a "satisfactory" performance rating by my principal. If my performance had been satisfactory, shouldn't I have been told? When she broke this news to me she explained that the district's standards were much lower than her own, assuring me that I didn't deserve a "satisfactory" performance rating. Of course.

And so I find myself selling European comfort shoes. The job comes along with very little stress, and with commission I can make decent money. It has been difficult to write to you. It has been difficult to even think about last year. There is so much pain wrapped up with my first teaching experience. I hope to conquer my fears and successfully reenter a classroom. If I give up, what kind of example am I setting for my own children?

Here is a good person with much to offer students. But even the best of people have a breaking point. It is sad that he had to leave the classroom, but the greatest tragedy is that the students were the big losers. If he returns to the classroom, the same frustrations await him. Staying calm is the best way to help yourself and your students.

Here is a suggestion to new teachers. Have a grand strategy each day you walk into your classroom. This is different than your lesson plan. Understand that despite your best preparation things will often not go according to the script. From something as simple as an emergency assembly to a sudden appearance by a district official with "concerns" about your lessons, days are often interrupted by someone or something that knocks the wheels off the wagon.

Each morning before school begins I choose two or three things that I feel must happen to call the day a success. There might be fifteen goals in my lesson plan book, but experience has shown that it is rare to accomplish all I had hoped to do. So I prioritize. To steal a phrase, I keep my eyes on the prize. When a hurdle is placed in front of me that is justifiably upsetting, I instantly remember the mission that must be accomplished. It is rarely the case that fighting with anyone gets a teacher where he wants to go. This is not to say that there are not causes worth fighting for. But I have witnessed many examples of outstanding teachers getting punched and, rather than losing focus or punching back, using righteous anger to help their students learn and succeed. The Quiet Man superficially loses the battle but modestly wins the war.

"TOO MANY BOOKS"

Miss F is a brilliant and creative fourth grade teacher I was fortunate to visit and observe. I must apologize if I carry on about her, but I knew her family when she was a little girl, and she hasn't changed a bit since then. She was a sensational kid and a fabulous student. Even when she went on white-water rafting trips with her family as a child, she always had a book with her to read by the river during a lunch break.

Her first couple of years of teaching were frustrating. As with all beginners, she suffered the growing pains of managing her classroom and finding her voice. Yet, as so often happens, the students were not her greatest problem. Her school used a scripted basal reader to teach reading, and Miss F wanted to teach reading using great works of literature. She felt that *The Chronicles of Narnia* would serve the students better than boring them to death with an insipid state textbook. By the middle of her second year of teaching, her fourth graders had caught the reading bug, and read constantly even when not in school. To feed their addiction, as so many teachers do, Miss F dipped into her own pocket generously to build a classroom library filled with exciting novels for her students to devour.

Unfortunately, a couple of well-meaning administrators visited her room several times a week and expressed concern. The young teacher was not using the proscribed reading program. One of the supervisors was particularly harsh in criticizing Miss F's work, and she spent many evenings worried about what to do. She believed strongly that her students were growing rapidly as readers, and the fifth-grade teachers at her school were thrilled with the students they received who had been in Miss F's class the previous year. The students she sent off were the best and most enthusiastic readers in the school.

But the criticism continued. The final straw came when her evaluation arrived at the end of the year. The official document mentioned that one fault of Miss F's classroom was that it contained "too many books."

Is it any wonder young teachers get discouraged?

Although she may have felt like ranting and raving, Miss F signed the evaluation, and in doing so agreed with the assessment. She superficially followed the suggestions of her supervisors and used the basal readers to replace the literature she preferred. As the months wore on, there were fewer visits to her classroom. Other teachers had apparently warranted the attention of these concerned coaches, and Miss F fell off their radar screen. Slowly, Miss F used the basal readers less often and used her beloved classic novels for part of her reading lessons. By her fourth year of teaching, this quiet teacher was using only literature with her students. The people who once were on her case had moved on and were not even at the school anymore.

Miss F just finished her tenth year of teaching. Ironically, the *Los Angeles Times* rated her as one of the top teachers in the city in their infamous Value-Added system of evaluating teachers.

FRIDAYS WITH MS. J

The struggles Miss F found trying to find her voice when others wanted to silence it happen frequently. In fact, when her classroom next-door neighbor began a tradition that was fun for her students, hurt no one, and did not deviate from the district curriculum, she also faced resistance.

Ms. J taught fourth grade, too. Her students were lucky to have her. She had high standards and a delightful personality. Students voluntarily spent many extra hours in the room with her, engaging in exciting projects. Ms. J, a mother of three, understood that a rigorous course of study works best with some good, old-fashioned fun mixed into the recipe. She wanted to build a relationship with her students that went beyond asking Pedro what circle he bubbled in for question 8. And so Ms. J decided to have lunch with her kids every Friday.

The plan was simple enough. On Fridays she would go with her students through the lunch line and then walk the kids, with their food trays, back to their classroom. They would eat together, talk about subjects ranging from the serious to the ridiculous, and get to know one another. In doing so, the kids would look back over the week they had just completed, reflect on what had happened, and consider the road ahead. No class time was wasted. No subject was missed. A dedicated teacher, like so many thousands of others, was more than happy to give up her lunchtime and sacrifice her break to help her students. She believed that her lunch with the kids could help them grow socially and emotionally. By the time the lunch period was over, the trays had been taken out to the appropriate bins for recycling, the room was immaculate, and Ms. J's students were back at work finishing their day and following the school curriculum to the letter.

Soon she was called into the office. These sessions had to stop, one supervisor explained, because food was not allowed in classrooms. The teacher was stunned and, quite frankly, upset. It was a very common sight to see pizzas being delivered to classrooms or parents bringing cupcakes for birthdays and special occasions. Why in the world was she being singled out? When she vented her frustration to colleagues, many were ready to go in to speak to the administration on her behalf. She wisely stopped them.

Despite the setback to her plan, Ms. J stayed quiet. Instead, she changed the plan but not the goal. Her school has a tiny patch of grass near one of its buildings. As this area is outside, no one could complain about food in the classroom. Now every Friday Ms. J has lunch with her students on the grass. It's a lovely sight. The kids are happy, their teacher is teaching important lessons, and no one bothers her; in fact, the supervisor who gave her a hard time left. It turned out that the grassy area was actually better for the Friday lunchtime sessions than the classroom. When she ran into an unreasonable administrator Ms. J could have fought back, but instead she kept her focus and got what she wanted in the first place. And of course the real winners were the kids.

THE SUPERINTENDENT IS CALLING

These might seem like minor issues, but at times situations arise when it is extremely hard to hold one's tongue. Even in these cases, though, it still might be the best thing to do. One time, a first-rate teacher who was distraught about his situation contacted me. He had been in the classroom for more than a decade and had been recognized often for his outstanding work. Like many good teachers these days, he managed his classroom in part by using a classroom economy. This teacher, happily married and a father of two, was creative and enthusiastic. Hordes of students wanted to be in his class, and parents sang his praises because their children loved the lessons offered and were learning how to save money and balance a checkbook, certainly important skills.

But one student in the class was very lazy, and despite the encouragement and multiple chances given by his teacher, he had no money in his bank account. When the class had auctions where children could buy school supplies, this student had to watch harder-working kids go home with goodies they had earned. As is too often the case these days, an angry parent blamed the teacher for her child's lack of production. It should be noted that the child had never done well in any class in school, indicating that the fault, dear Brutus, did not lie with the teacher but with the student.

The parent did not ask the teacher for a conference. She didn't even go to the principal. She contacted the district superintendent directly to complain about the horrible teacher who was unfair to her son.

Many veteran teachers can guess what happened next. The superintendent called the instructor and chastised him for running such a reckless and damaging program. The teacher tried to point out his exemplary record and the many citations he had received. The superintendent told him to stop the economic program immediately and the discussion was over.

One kid. One parent. And twelve years of work erased with a phone call.

It took some time for the teacher to calm down, but he did. He shut down his economic system for the remainder of the year. The result was one happy student and thirty-odd others who were sad and frustrated. Despite being angry, the teacher knew that he loved teaching the students about saving money and planning for their future. Because he hoped to teach for many years to come, he kept quiet. He did not protest or write to the district or the local press.

The following year his students were once again keeping ledgers, earning money, and acquiring skills that would be useful for the rest of their lives. The teacher may have lost part of a year, but by swallowing his justifiable anger he would be able to continue helping students for years to come. The good thing is that the teacher kept calm and saw the long-term benefit of biding his time. Despite the setback, his checkbook was clearly in the black.

THE RAIN AND THE KEY

Two months before I wrote this chapter was one of the best Junes I can ever remember. During this time every year about forty students aged eight to ten put on an unabridged production of a Shakespearean play. A lot of amazing professionals help with the show, and it's a lot of fun. This year's production had been *A Midsummer Night's Dream,* a play I normally shy away from because it has been done to death. However, a hilarious group of students brought fresh life to the show, and even some of the most jaded theatergoers told me they had never seen a better *Dream.* One woman told me she hurt her jaw laughing so hard. These were good times.

Yet just six months earlier, for the first time in almost thirty years, I had been ready to throw in the towel.

Our school had a new principal, a very bright and capable leader who had the added bonus of being a genuinely nice man. I was very glad when he was chosen to lead. The decision was announced the previous summer. The office manager informed all the teachers that when there is a changing of the guard, all keys must be turned in and accounted for to ensure security. This posed a problem for me. My previous principal, another terrific leader, had given me the keys to the school. This allowed my class to meet on Saturdays and during vacation periods. When the class was on campus during off hours, I always called the school police and the alarms were shut off. This had gone on for almost twenty years and there had never been a problem. The extra hours were a major factor in countless great times and life-changing activities for many deserving children.

I told my office manager that I needed the keys during the summer, and she told me not to worry. I would get them back in two weeks and we could go back to business as usual.

Two weeks later, I stopped by to pick up the keys, but was told I would have to wait until school resumed in September. There was a memo circulating from the district office that prohibited the keys from being given out, and as our new principal had not yet taken the reins, I had no one to go to for help. Two months of potential rehearsals for Shakespeare went down the drain.

September came and the Shakespeare program rebooted, but we were two months behind schedule. The students desperately needed Saturday mornings to get the production back on track. I went to the principal to discuss the situation. He told me he knew of the problem and sympathized, but he had called the district and been told there were no exceptions to the memo.

I walked out of the office in shock. It seemed that it should not be this hard to get a key. Surely someone could simply make a call, explain the situation, and the kids would be given the extra time they'd need to put together a spectacular show and learn lessons that would last the rest of their lives. But the rules had changed. In the end, we figured out that we would lose more than one thousand hours of time that had been used during the previous years. I kept quiet. The kids that year were an especially motivated and talented group, and the loss of rehearsal time seemed to motivate them to work harder than ever.

As winter break was approaching, I was told that the plant manager and cleaning crew would be on campus from 7:00 A.M. until 6:00 P.M. during the week before Christmas. The students all agreed that this would be a fantastic time to work. With the school open and alarms shut off, I was told it was fine to be back in Room 56.

On the first Monday, it was pouring. Our leaky room made use of six buckets to catch the excess water flowing in, but nothing was going to stop the rehearsal. It was going well, and all of us felt that in the first three hours that morning we had made more progress than in the previous three weeks. Spirits were high, and the best was yet to come. My former student Joann, studying for her doctorate in music, was coming to help our keyboardists with the more demanding parts of the production's score.

A little after 11:00 A.M. the door opened, and the kids cheered what they thought was Joann's arrival. Instead, one of the cleaning crew came in and informed us that the staff had decided to take the day off and go home. We would all have to leave campus, as the doors were being locked and the alarms set. I explained patiently that this was impossible. We were told we could be there, and there were forty kids who could not get home. Their parents were at work, and they could not leave to get their children in the middle of the day. The man shrugged and said he was sorry.

I took the kids outside to a small sheltered area near the filthy benches where students were corralled each day for lunch. It was still pouring. There were no bathrooms for the children to use as everything had been locked up. As I sat down trying to figure out how to get the kids home I realized that even if I could do that, many of them did not have keys to get into their apartment buildings. Head down and thinking, I glanced up to see Joann coming through the parking lot being blown around by the storm. When she asked why we weren't in our room, I explained the situation.

"Joann," I said, sighing, "I have to tell you something. I think that for the first time, I am getting close to the point where I don't think our class can do this anymore."

"Rafe," she said wisely, "it got to that point ten years ago. You just don't know it."

I smiled grimly and turned around. There, around the lunch benches, forty children were rehearsing a scene from *A Midsummer Night's Dream*. They were terrible, but they were rehearsing. They reminded me that the play's the thing. There was nothing to worry about. Neither a storm, the absence of a key, nor even the necessity of walking a couple of blocks to a gas station bathroom mattered.

When school resumed in January, many teachers came to my

room. They had heard about the key situation, and offered me help. They thought they should collectively speak to our principal, or call the district, or even summon the press. I declined their thoughtful and considerate offers. My energy was needed elsewhere.

And six months later, after the final show, I asked the beaming boy who played Oberon if this might have been the best month of his life. He agreed that it was "awesome," but told me that his favorite day of the year was the rehearsal outside on a stormy day. That was the day, he told me, when he knew we were going to have a fabulous show.

I still do not have keys to the school. Rubbing salt into the wound, each night men who work on wiring and pipes enter the school with access to everything. They have told me they love going into Room 56 and fooling around with all the instruments and equipment it has taken a lifetime of work to acquire. There have been mornings when guitars are missing or the soundboard for our music has been tampered with. Am I happy about it? No, it would be much better for the students and me if we had access to the room and strangers did not. Will I say anything about it? No, I will not. The class is already working on next year's production of *Measure for Measure*. And we'll get it done. Quietly.

For Your Consideration

- The greatest frustrations in teaching often have little to do with the students and more to do with school politics.
- Choose your battles carefully. When someone tries to prevent you from doing something innovative, the fight can usually be won without firing a shot.
- Stand in the shoes of your administrators. They, too, are under pressure to conform. Keep any disagreements you have with them as a professional discussion. Never make it personal.

- Remember that any pain or anger you feel probably pales in comparison to the awful situations your students face on a daily basis. By keeping the students first in your mind, it is easier to stay calm and do what is best for them. Having an explosive argument with an administrator or colleague is rarely in the best interests of your students.

- When an unfair decision is made about your program, you can use it as a lesson for the students. What do you do when things go wrong? Your calm and rational reaction to illogical school policy can help your students when they come up against bureaucracy and cant in their own lives.

CHAPTER SIX
19th Nervous Breakdown

We need to address an uncomfortable subject. I do not mean to sound overly dramatic, but there is a truth about teaching that should be examined.

This job can kill you.

There are students who are not golden drops of sunshine. There are children who bring so many issues to the classroom that no mortal, even an extraordinary one, can make a connection. And yet, despite this reality, there are many well-meaning policy makers and bloggers demanding that teachers reach every child. But some children cannot be helped, even when a teacher is willing to sacrifice her life to do so.

Teachers face mounting accusations that they are to blame for the turmoil in public education. To be fair, they share in the blame. There are bad teachers. Any good teacher will admit to that. There are class leaders who are lazy, disorganized, and incompetent. We've all had such a teacher. But the rest of the problem lies beyond the ability of any teacher to fix. Are incompetent doctors blamed for cancer? Reasonable people know that poverty and other societal ills are creating students who are not going to learn even if Plato, Socrates, and Aristotle were in charge of their education.

Young teachers, please remember this. All students deserve to be given our best. Good teachers never give up on an individual. But please balance your efforts to help a child with the knowledge that you cannot, and should not, be responsible for solving all his problems. If you listen to politicians or well-intentioned philanthropists demanding that we teachers save everyone, you are going to become incredibly discouraged when you don't.

Mrs. C is a lovely elementary school teacher. She cares very much about her students. At staff meetings she is constantly searching for ways to help them. She comes to school early, stays late, and does everything she can to provide her class with a rigorous curriculum combined with a warm learning environment. She's a good teacher.

One year she had a class that was very difficult. At least ten of her boys were savage to other children in the school yard and menacing in the classroom. A couple of them would run out of the classroom and the building, scale the sixteen-foot fence, and run away. As is too often the case in schools, Mrs. C received very little support from her administration. The incorrigible youngsters were simply rounded up and brought back to her class within a few days. They would constantly curse, spit, fight, and insult anyone in their path.

Mrs. C demanded of herself that she would save them. Society told her she must. If she did not help each one of these boys do well on their tests and become fine citizens, it meant that she was not doing her job. Of course this is ridiculous to anyone looking at the situation objectively, but there are many extraordinary class leaders like Mrs. C who deep down have started believing the unreasonable demands that are placed on teachers.

One day she collapsed in class. The strain was too much. Mrs. C was not an old woman, but she did have an irregular heartbeat that her doctor had warned should be monitored carefully. As this woman was being wheeled away on a stretcher to the waiting ambulance, several of the boys she had tried so hard to help yelled after her, *"We hope you die."*

Mrs. C recovered and is back teaching. Mrs. D was not so lucky.

I taught with Mrs. D for many years. She was a good woman, and she was strict, an old-school disciplinarian. She never missed school. She was always prepared, and her class worked hard. Many of her students made excellent progress after a year with her. Mrs. D took good care of herself. She was slim, she was a nonsmoker, and she dressed immaculately. She was a professional. I often sat near her at staff meetings and found her to be pleasant, caring, and sometimes frustrated with the behavior of her more difficult students and with a system that did not seem to hold such kids accountable for their actions. I particularly remember one day when she was upset because some of her students had been tagging on the bathroom walls and their only punishment was to clean off the graffiti. She felt strongly that the consequences should have been more severe. But that was Mrs. D. She cared a lot. She tried. She worried.

And then one day she just died. It was a Tuesday. I saw her at the staff meeting and she was the same as always. We had a brief conversation about a school event coming up, and walked out to the parking lot. She went home and died from a stroke that night. She was not an old woman. But she had taught for twenty-five years, and the frustrations and difficult days can wear down a classroom teacher. You pay a price for constantly dealing with mean children, apathetic parents, and the pressure that you must do better. I am not a doctor, but I shudder to imagine an autopsy that concluded "Death by teaching."

Young teachers, please take heed. It can happen to you. This is a stressful job. You will read critical articles and hear unsympathetic speakers proclaim that teachers complain too much. After all, lazy teachers get out at 3:00 P.M. every day and have summers off. They get tons of vacation days during the year. Considering the number of days teachers do not have to go to work, some people say the salary is actually high.

In some cases there is truth to these complaints. but for most teachers this is not accurate. Many of us come to school very early in the morning and stay far past the traditional end of the day. Vacations are often spent planning for the future, and, sadly, brooding about the past. The mistakes and missed opportunities haunt teachers during what many believe are sunny days at the beach but in reality are lonely hours at home wondering if it will ever get any better.

I have seen good teachers crying in their classroom during a lunch break because their outstanding efforts fell short of the impossible goals they allowed others to set. I have personally witnessed friends who had to attend the funeral of a child they had helped make enormous progress only to be killed in a drive-by shooting.

And now, in pursuit of the reasonable goal of holding teachers accountable for their work, even newspapers have joined in on the unfair attack. Some are printing the results of year-end state tests that are so scientifically inaccurate they should be laughable. But it's hard to laugh when people read such misinformed articles and pass judgment. These articles label individual teachers as good or bad, basing the rating on two or three days of students bubbling in answers on a standardized test sheet. Real teachers know that such test scores are a mere snapshot of some aspect of a student, and rarely show the whole picture. The great majority of teachers I have met have no problem being held accountable. They simply want to be judged fairly. Too often that is not the case, and it works both ways. There are teachers who are probably not as good as such ratings indicate, and marvelous teachers whose excellence does not show up on a standardized test.

These inaccuracies and unrealistic expectations put pressure on all teachers, especially those who are just starting out. You want to do well. You care. It would not be human if you did not try to measure your success. If Johnny scored 70 percent on last year's exams and after a year with you has improved to 77 percent, it is cause to feel good about the job you are doing.

But early in your career you will almost certainly discover some cold, hard facts that very few people seem to want to consider. Despite your best efforts, there are factors that might defeat you before you even begin your journey with a certain student. We like to think the teacher is the most important factor in a child's success in school, but I have not found that to be the case. You, too, will probably discover that the student's family will have more to do with his progress in your class than even you. Poverty can also play an enormous role in the student's attitude, potential, and eventual progress.

Thus, you are faced with a dilemma. Some teachers run into the frightening truth about poverty and dysfunctional families and give up. They throw up their hands and bitterly cry, "What can I do? I've lost the game before the first pitch has even been thrown."

Good teachers do not give up. There is always hope, and that is why they teach. But may I suggest that your heroic and even superhuman efforts must be tempered with the realistic knowledge that you cannot solve every child's problems. Should every child be given your best effort? Of course. Should you ever give up on a kid and decide he is not worth the trouble? Never. But at the risk of raising the ire of those who feel that every child must be saved, may I offer a little piece of advice:

There are times you need to go home and shut it off.

This is the fourth book I have written about teaching kids, and about the tremendous expenditures of time and energy I make on their behalf. Many thoughtful and caring readers have asked me: *Do you have a personal life?*

Of course I do. I do not write about my family because it would not be of interest to anyone. As a consequence, it appears that all I do is teach. While it is true that I spend many hours in the classroom, I do not live there. My wife and kids provide the necessary sanity a teacher needs after a day of lunacy. In other words, consider the following advice: *Don't do this job alone.*

When the stress mounts, walk away. After almost three decades of teaching I have learned that there are very few situations that are life or death. On those extraordinary occasions when I have had students considering suicide, or gone missing, immediate action had to be taken. But it has been my experience that most stress, no matter how painful and sleep depriving it might be, is actually not as awful after a night's sleep. Whether it is an angry parent threatening to go to your principal, a colleague treating you in an unprofessional manner, or the latest article you have read calling you overpaid and lazy, shut it down.

Play Frisbee. Go dancing, bowling, or hit a bucket of golf balls. Pet a puppy. Cook or spend time in a garden. Take a walk or pursue whatever it is that makes you truly happy. After spending time with my family, I personally relieve stress either by picking up my guitar, watching a baseball game, or cranking up some rock and roll to outrageous decibel levels. For anyone who wants to try this, I have found The Who's "Baba O'Riley" an especially effective stress reliever. Teenage wasteland indeed.

The bottom line is that if you have a nervous breakdown it helps no one. It might make for a good story on the news, but you are needed in your classroom, feeling strong and enthusiastic. By occasionally turning off your desire to save the world, you will live longer and healthier, and by doing so you will do a lot more saving.

There are hundreds of thousands of incredibly hardworking teachers, and I am proud to be one of them. But I have learned the value of rest and balance. I put in extra hours working weekends, vacations, and before and after school, but I also have romantic dinners with my wife several times a week, go to the theater, and work out at night. Remember, I need to teach for another 470 years to get Barbara her new kitchen. If I allow stress to kill me she'll never get it.

You are not being selfish to let it go. Most problems can wait until tomorrow. If you ever feel you are being a bad teacher by taking a breath and clearing your mind, never forget the words from act 2, scene 4, of Shakespeare's *Henry V:*

Self love, my liege, is not so vile a sin, as self neglect.

For Your Consideration

- Take care of yourself. You are no good for your students if you are overworked and allowing the stress of the job to turn you into a combination of Benito Mussolini and a constipated rhinoceros.
- Spend a little time at the end of your day debriefing with a sympathetic friend or loved one. Talk about the day, and then shut it down. A pleasant evening increases the chances that your next day of teaching will be better.
- Consider the source of criticism. It seems that practically everyone has an opinion on what is wrong with our schools. Most critics of teachers do not have the faintest idea of what they are talking about. They are entitled to their opinions, but try not to take ignorant criticism too seriously.
- Laugh with your students and laugh at yourself. This job should be fun. Don't let anyone cause you to forget that.

CHAPTER SEVEN

A Question of Balance

If your students are a bit reticent about participating in a class discussion at the beginning of the year, I've found that one icebreaker is certain to get them passionately involved This question never fails to stimulate even the shyest of kids to speak up.

I ask them for their opinions about homework.

Early in my career, I didn't give the homework issue as much attention as I should have. In generating homework assignments, I followed fundamental principles as to what most would consider a series of reasonable tasks. I hoped the work would help teach students to be responsible in completing projects and mastering important skills.

Then, many years ago, a student broke down and started bawling at the end of our first day together. The day had been a good one, and I was taken completely by surprise by Jane's crying. She explained to me that she was afraid to go outside, but not because of a bullying student. With a little help from her friends, she explained that her fourth grade teacher from the previous year would be lying in wait for her.

Three months earlier, at the end of the school year in June, Jane's teacher had given her a homework packet. This assignment consisted of at least seventy-five worksheets stapled together. There were hundreds of repetitive math problems and vocabulary exercises that would have ruined the appetite of the hungriest learner.

I walked Jane outside. The well-intentioned teacher accosted us and lit into this little girl with more fire than I would have directed at a convicted felon.

I stood by Jane as this teacher screamed at her and warned her that being in the fifth grade was no excuse for not turning in summer homework. When I met Jane's mother, I told her not to worry about this and that Jane did not have to finish the packet. She would be busy enough with her current workload. With the help of my principal, we straightened things out.

How did it ever get this crazy?

Teachers assign various amounts of homework. I give far less than most. In too many classrooms meaningless homework is piled on. In most cases, the culprits are class leaders who care about their kids, but whose best intentions are misguided and ineffective.

Many kids are far behind in school, which is how the homework crunch begins. Panic sets in when fourth grade teachers discover that children who have attended school for four years cannot read a basic sentence. High school teachers contend with students who cannot write a grammatically correct sentence or a coherent paragraph. It is shocking how far behind many of the students have fallen. Just this month, I welcomed a new group of students during the summer who wanted to sign up for the Hobart Shakespeare project. These were nine- and ten-year-old kids who liked school and wanted to devote their summer to the study of Shakespeare. The group included some of the most motivated and successful kids at our school. Yet when I asked them to fill out a form with their personal information, only six out of the thirty could write down their address and phone number. In a few months, the Los Angeles Times will rate my performance as a teacher based on the standardized test scores of children who do not even know where they live. The pressure is on.

Many teachers and parents have lost focus as to why children should have homework. Ideally, students complete homework to reinforce important skills that will be useful to them in the years to come. Homework can teach children about the importance of being organized and responsible. In addition, homework reminds a student that while school may end at three o'clock, learning should not. A reasonable, relevant assignment can help a student develop as a scholar and a person. Doing quality homework can potentially help a student's confidence and lead to success in the classroom.

Sadly, reasonable and effective homework is in short supply these days. The sabotage of potentially important lessons at home has been a twofold operation. First, more than ever teachers are finding students coming into their classrooms shockingly behind in even the most fundamental skills. This tragedy coupled with a system demanding immediate excellence on a never-ending battery of standardized tests has resulted in kids being sent home with an endless pile of mind-numbing worksheets and tasks.

Parents have unfortunately bought into this madness, asking teachers to send home hours of drill-and-kill undertakings. There are schools that boast of assigning three and four hours of homework each night to children as young as eight. High school students become nocturnal creatures finishing assigned readings and projects at three and four in the morning.

Most students, when comfortable speaking off the record, will admit that the only reason their homework is completed is to avoid some sort of awful punishment or poor grade for substandard work. Learning anything is far from their minds.

As if killing the joy of learning were not serious enough, too much homework is actually injurious to a child's health. Sleep deprivation is becoming an increasingly serious problem for our students. Although there is no magic number for how many hours of sleep someone should get, most experts believe that children between the ages of five and twelve should be getting between ten and eleven hours of sleep a night. Parents of teenagers who laugh when their adolescents become night owls don't laugh as much when their sweethearts are incredibly moody and grumpy when they get up in the morning. Studies illustrate that sleep-deprived children are more likely to be obese and have heart problems and diabetes. It is not surprising that students who do not sleep enough also have more problems paying attention. Ironically, even with the best intentions, teachers who assign too much homework often wind up with kids in their classrooms who are dull and moody, the exact opposite result of what one would hope extra work would produce.

The same forces that are driving the excessive homework assignments are at work even when on the surface the activity appears to be healthy and educational. The mad rush to help kids close the achievement gap or reach grade level often does more harm than good as schools ratchet up the intensity without considering the long-term, or even the short-term, effect on kids.

One time a school contacted me in the hope that some of their hardworking students could come and watch a Shakespeare production in Room 56. Nothing is more fun for my students than to perform for their peers, so I happily agreed. This was a middle school on the East Coast. They sent me their itinerary. Their plan was to catch a 7:00 A.M. flight. That meant the kids had to be up at 4:00 to be at the airport at 5:00. After the flight to Los Angeles, a bus was going to pick them up and take them straight to Venice Beach. After the beach, the students would be bused directly to our school to watch an almost three-hour production. I called a teacher at the school and pointed out that the students would have practically no sleep the night before their flight due to excitement. Our 7:00 P.M. show would actually be starting at 10:00 P.M. in the bodies of the visiting students, who would still be on East Coast time. The plan was to go to their motel after the show and head for Yosemite National Park the following morning.

"When will the kids sleep?" I asked.

"They'll sleep on the plane," I was told.

This is a school run by hardworking and involved teachers. They care and have lovely students who, due to poverty and other societal ills, have gotten off to a bad start. It's not the kids' fault, and they are lucky to have teachers who want to close the gap. Yet in their quest to help the kids "catch up," they are driving them to exhaustion. It really shouldn't be a race to the top. The journey is everything, and every voyage should balance adventure with rest.

As a young teacher, you are being placed in an impossible position. You might be teaching high school English to students who cannot distinguish a noun from a verb, or you might be a middle school teacher of thirteen-year-olds who do not know their times tables. Despite your best efforts each day, the kids are behind. You go home and watch the news and someone in the government or private sector is chiding you for not doing your job. It is often forgotten or brushed aside that these students are far behind because of factors beyond your control.

Let's be brutally honest. There are reasons students come to you without skills. These kids were not born four years behind their classmates in literacy. Their foul language or cruel manners did not happen just the year before they sat down in your class. Home situations, poverty, and a host of complex forces have all conspired to present you with students who might have turned you off before you even tried to make a connection. When a nine-year-old child comes into my class on the first day of school with a hood over his head and a scowl on his face, the road I had planned to help this kid become a fine student has been almost completely blocked. When he tells me on his first day that his father and he watched the film *Saw* the previous evening, it is a daunting task to consider that I have less than a year to sell this boy a different way of life. His test scores from last year are abysmal, and at our first staff meeting I hear that it is all on me to get this kid up to speed.

You can't give up and you shouldn't. Each child deserves your best each day. Believe in him. Listen to him. Encourage him. When work is substandard, it is necessary and often effective to give him extra work to help him catch up. But the most important thing to keep in mind is that his journey to grade level is going to be a long one, and that you don't have to be in too much of a hurry.

It may be easier said than done. Many young teachers are currently afraid that their jobs are on the line if their students do not do well enough on tests. Of course you should spend enormous effort and time getting kids ready for assessments. Exams are a reality, for better or for worse, and preparing students well is a necessity. The wiser teachers, however, balance test preparation and homework with a consistent message. Students need to hear about not seeing the forest for the trees. Tell them that, unfortunately, in our push to get kids to pass tests and make it to college, we lose sight of why school is supposed to exist in the first place. The best teachers help to guide young people to a place where learning is joyous. It can take years to find the right language and style, but it is essential for teachers to make sure kids know that the most important things learned in school cannot be measured on a standardized test. Given the unhappy reality that policy makers have overemphasized the importance of test scores, we teachers must be a buffer between preparing the kids to bubble in the circles and actually turning them on to the joys of mathematics, writing, sports, music, science, history, art, and even sleep.

It's a question of balance. In my early years of teaching, I assigned too much homework that did not result in the mastery of skills the projects were designed to produce. By observing some outstanding teachers, I learned to be patient, and to move students forward without destroying their pleasure of learning and/or their good health. Hamlet told his mother he had to be cruel to be kind. It is a logical attitude for teachers to have, but hopefully one of our goals is to inspire our students to be nice people. As we attempt to close the so-called achievement gap, let's not become ogres. I am more interested in closing the *opportunity gap*. By making sure the kids are enjoying school and getting enough rest, students will begin to do extra work at home because they are interested in something they are learning instead of being force-fed a worksheet.

There is no correct homework policy, but here are a few thoughts that I reflect on when I assign projects outside the classroom.

For Your Consideration

- Students need a good night's sleep. Stand in their shoes. Consider that they have a life and family obligations. Calculate the amount of time needed to complete homework, and be reasonable.
- Homework is usually assigned to practice and reinforce skills you have taught.
- Students should be told often that homework is giving them an opportunity to be responsible and independent.
- Teach kids to pack their homework before they go to sleep. It's an opportunity to practice their organizational skills. When students do not have work ready and say, "But I did it," you can remind them that part of the assignment was to have the work ready. You might remind them that we wouldn't trust a surgeon who shows up without his tools.
- Particularly early in the year, have a class discussion about what to do when things go wrong. A friend can be called. Many teachers allow their students to contact them via e-mail

or even cell phone to get some help. If you are a teacher who comes early to school, make sure students with problems know they can come to you.

- Homework should not be a punishment. Assignments are given to help kids learn essential skills.

- Discuss time management with the kids. Ask them what time they normally walk through the front door of their homes. Teach them to calculate the time they spend doing family chores, other activities, and dinner. Then figure out how much time the assignment will take and demonstrate how they can get it all in and still go to bed at a healthy hour.

- When students are unable to complete homework because of a difficult home situation, allow them to use your room. Most teachers stay after school to either grade papers or prepare future lessons. This is a good time to allow students with home problems to finish their assignments and simultaneously build a trusting relationship with you.

- Not all students are the same. If Eugene never misses a math problem in class or on tests, there is no reason to give him math drills that other students might need. Give Eugene either a different challenge or no homework at all.

- Kids who play music always have homework. Practicing an instrument is a fine way to spend an afternoon or early evening. Encourage your kids to play music.

- When students do not finish homework, consequences should be firm but reasonable. Putting kids on a bench or humiliating them defeats the purpose of the assignments. If in your class students must complete the assignment or receive a lower grade, that is fair. But leave the door open and show belief that a student who doesn't complete an assignment will become more responsible in the future.

- Discuss the very real problem of plagiarism. These days it is very easy for students to use the Internet or one another to cheat on homework. While many will not heed your warning, the students need to hear that your assignment is an opportunity to develop their honesty and character. Let's have a goal of taking the lantern away from Diogenes.

CHAPTER EIGHT

Even the Devil Can Quote Scripture for His Purpose

We need to assess our students. Good teachers need to take a student's scholastic temperature to see how the patient is doing. I have never met a teacher who thought that the concept of giving a test was a bad thing.

But we've gone too far. The reasonable desire to hold students and teachers accountable for what is being learned in school has snowballed into an avalanche of examinations that are hurting children and depriving them of a meaningful education. Assessments are putting young teachers in a very difficult situation.

You cannot run and hide. High-stakes testing is here to stay for a long time, given the fact that it has no political agenda. Most Republicans and Democrats have bought into a system so outrageously flawed that any scientist would throw out its data immediately as unreliable.

Tragically, the teachers are right in the crosshairs of powerful people who do not understand the damage they are doing. And, like it or not, all teachers have to make some truly difficult decisions as to how to work in a system in which they are judged by a series of numbers that have very little to do with educating a student.

Your first concern must be for your students. If we as mature adults are feeling undue pressure to get Johnny to regurgitate a series of facts on a standardized test (facts that will be forgotten before the results even come back), imagine how a student feels. Many are often miserable and scared, turning off to the potentially good things a school can offer them.

Some teachers and schools have bought the party line and spend every second of their year preparing their students to take tests. Sadly, many of these educators have actually convinced themselves that these scores indicate that their students have become scholars. The best teachers know this is not true and refuse to buy into the madness. Strong educators will not waste a student's or their own time preparing for tests that have little to do with real learning.

I have chosen a middle path. I consistently assess my students' work and have no need for the exams being thrown at the kids by the school district and state. I fantasize about starting a bonfire with those infamous testing booklets that stimulate a groan from my students faster than the bell made Pavlov's dog drool.

I follow a few principles that have allowed most of the kids to not only do very well on their exams but also to internalize a love of real learning. My students prepare for exams but also participate in a discussion about the shallowness of the belief that test scores are the most important data in assessing a child's worth. My students learn that men like Bernie Madoff and the Enron boys most likely had very good test scores. Can any decent human being label these criminals as successful? Can we even categorize them as successful?

Good students help other people. They are aware of the world around them. Real scholars know that the recitation of facts is a beginning, and not an end, of knowledge. There is a difference between identifying a speech as Hamlet's and being able to analyze the meaning of that speech. There is a difference between solving a math problem and applying that mathematical principle to a situation never before seen.

Because of this, the test preparation sessions in my class are taught separately from the subjects these tests are supposed to cover. My students read literature every morning. Reading comprehension practice exercises are never given during this sacred time. This is the period when students read, discuss, and reflect on the important themes of the material they study. Later in the day, the students might spend fifteen minutes practicing for reading comprehension exams by reading insipid stories and bubbling in answer sheets. They know such practice is a necessary evil. Students should be encouraged to understand that doing well on a test is wonderful, but not as wonderful as actually mastering a subject and joyously learning more about it at the library after school. Doing well on tests and learning are two entirely different things, and they are treated as such in my classroom.

Our test prep sessions are very basic. Any source that reviews test-taking skills will stress time management when taking an exam. Good test takers practice eliminating obviously wrong answers, increasing the chance of selecting the correct choice. Experienced students know that it is best to go with one's first choice and not to erase an answer unless absolutely sure a mistake has been discovered.

In class several times a week we create the conditions of the test. I never give students test prep materials as homework. They will not be taking the tests at home, and I have found many such worksheets to be a waste of time. It is more effective to set up one's classroom as though the students were taking a real exam. The room is silent. However, we run these sessions for short periods of time. We begin test prep on the first day of school, and practice for approximately twenty minutes a day several times a week. Less is more. I have found that the kids improve their scores by doing fewer problems that are then corrected in class and analyzed thoroughly. This has given my students better results than being force-fed hundreds of problems that are corrected but never analyzed with meaningful discussion.

High school teachers might consider having some periods delegated only for test-taking skills. The important curriculum should never be shortchanged to practice for tests. This is just one way of doing things. Many good teachers I know might teach a math concept for thirty minutes and then finish the session with twenty minutes of practice questions. I have found that making sure the kids truly understand the concepts will lead to higher scores faster than trying to use smoke and mirrors and techniques to "beat" the test.

Of course, good teachers give their kids exams all the time, but that is entirely different from the state tests now being used to hold schools and teachers accountable. A teacher-designed test created to see if the kids understand a concept is a good thing. If the kids do well it is time to move on, but these important assessments can help a teacher discover holes in a child's understanding, and that data can be used to reteach important lessons.

State tests do no such thing. And, sadly, they don't even help teachers with accurate data either.

STANDARDIZED TESTS ARE NOT STANDARDIZED

One day I saw two outstanding young teachers standing in our main hallway looking desolate and defeated. One had been crying. They had just been chastised for doing a poor job in school, as many of their students' test scores were lower than the year before. The conclusion was that these two teachers had not done a good job teaching the standards.

Incompetent teachers should be chastised. The problem here is that these two teachers were competent. The real issue was the fact that data means something only when it is accurate.

Standardized tests are not standardized. State tests are not given the same way in the same environment, and yet these scores are compared with one another to draw supposedly accurate conclusions. In the case of many schools, the crucial state exams are given in individual classrooms, proctored by the very teachers whose reputations are based on how well the students perform. You don't have to be Nostradamus to predict that there will be individuals, and sometimes even entire districts, that will dishonestly alter test results. Recently there have been scandals at schools that turned in tests with unusually high numbers of incorrect answers that were erased and changed to correct ones. It might be that some teachers are coaching kids or erasing answers themselves before the exams are turned in. And sometimes honest teachers turn in tests only to have supervisors "improve" test scores.

In the case of the two frustrated teachers, they knew what was going on. A year earlier, they had been given students whose test scores showed them to be "advanced" in math. A beginning-of-the-year assessment told the teachers that these children were anything but advanced. In fact, many of the kids were years behind. And the teachers' dilemma began.

They were honest professionals. There is no doubt that even their most struggling students improved in math during the year. But because of the inaccuracy of the scores from the previous examination period, it appeared that the two teachers had done a poor job because their young charges did not repeat their "advanced" rating.

The tears began. They had done their jobs and done them well. Despite this, their job approval rating will take a hit. These two young women were being punished for having integrity, and a colleague rewarded for lacking it.

Should they have said something? There was no way of

proving anything. Should they, in the future, bow to the pressure and boost their test scores by coaching students during exams that are not proctored? They chose neither.

Instead, they cried for a few minutes. Then they went back to their rooms and continued to do their jobs. The scores showed that they had not done as good a job as others. They knew that some people would believe the scores and pass judgment on them without the facts. It's a painful and high price to pay for integrity. For these two young teachers, as well as for hundreds of thousands of others who have come to the same conclusion, they will not gain the world and lose their souls over a test score. The best teachers choose character over reputation. It does not matter what misinformed people think about our performance. It matters who we really are.

THANKS A LOT

For young teachers, overemphasized test scores can lead to painful and frustrating moments, and sometimes a loss of income. For a veteran, they can make you question your entire life's work.

Faye Ireland was a special teacher. It was my honor to meet her during my first year of teaching. I was assigned to teach at an upper-middle-class school I have jokingly called Camelot in one of my books. The kids were well off and had supportive and educated parents. After-school hours were spent participating on swim teams and taking private violin lessons. It was a wonderful school filled with special teachers who had taught for decades with professionalism and wisdom.

I was the new kid on the block, filled with wild ideas of saving the world with a rock-and-roll soundtrack blasting in the background. Faye noticed me and took me under her wing. No one could be more different from her than I was in both temperament and style. Faye was old school. She was so square and demanding, she did not allow her kids to erase anything on their essays. If they made a mistake, they simply had to start over. Her students lined up with military precision and her classroom had the organizational look of a Swiss bank. Everything about Faye, from her classroom to her appearance, was order incarnate.

One more fact should be mentioned. Her students adored and respected her. She was no walk in the park, but everyone in that room mattered. She cared deeply for every student and her kids knew it. Each child left her room a better student and person when the year was over. She was a pro. And even though I admired her craft and precision, our classes were polar opposites in every way.

My class ran out to the field for baseball practice. Her class walked silently to the yard, and every one of her students knew exactly where to go and what to do. For a Christmas show her class performed "The Little Drummer Boy." My students shocked the school by performing "Father Christmas" by The Kinks, a choice that caused my principal to reprimand me. Even though the audience went wild, the scolding I received had me down in the dumps. Faye stepped in to pick me up.

We had many dinners together, and she would often stop by my class. She never asked me to change my style. In fact, she encouraged me and gave me countless wise suggestions on effective teaching. But as a consummate professional, she was never arrogant enough to believe her way was the only way. She saw something in me when others did not. She helped me survive my first two years, before I left Camelot for Hobart School. I heard from her only occasionally over the next thirty years, as she would drop me a line to congratulate me for an award I had been given. We were both busy teaching.

Enter the news media.

Two reporters had recently caught the fever that has spread through policy makers and school officials all over the world. Using a seriously flawed method known as Value-Added (about which you've already heard my opinion), these writers had taken a look at the test scores from elementary school teachers over the past five years and labeled each teacher as either highly effective, effective, less effective, or least effective. Schools were also rated. The ratings of every teacher and school were posted online for parents to gain "knowledge" about who was teaching their children.

Parents have a right to know about teacher quality. After all, they are the ones paying our salaries. However, as is so often the case when complex problems are oversimplified, this "data" was not nearly as accurate as it claimed to be. Across the board, my colleagues and I shook our heads in disbelief at the results. Many teachers rated as highly effective most certainly were not, and others with low ratings were doing an outstanding job. The Value-Added evaluation system did not take into account most of the truly important lessons students should be learning in school. It looked only at math and reading scores. And even if you thought the system was wonderful, some teachers being evaluated in math were not even *teaching* math—their students went to other instructors for that subject.

Supporters of this so-called evaluation pointed out that preceding the posted scores is a qualification stating that these labels refer only to the test results in two subjects and are not a complete picture of teacher effectiveness.

Well, thanks a lot. Let's get real. Once the scarlet letter is tattooed across a teacher's face, no one is going to read the fine print. When you call a person not effective, that is the only thing anyone is going to remember.

And now back to Faye Ireland. After the newspaper evaluations had been printed, a smaller follow-up article appeared that caught my attention. It told of Faye Ireland, one of the best teachers I had ever had the pleasure to know, sitting despondently in her apartment. Beside her lay a stack of hundreds of letters from grateful former students. On her other side was a copy of the *Los Angeles Times*. She had been branded as a "least effective teacher."

One might as well go ahead and label Thomas Edison "lazy" or Pablo Picasso "ordinary."

This is a woman who taught for forty-five years. Students who finished college and were leading successful lives kept in touch with her, grateful for her inspiration and her unshakable belief in their potential.

But in her last few years of teaching, her classes were filled with students who could not speak English. Faye knew that if they were not fluent by the end of elementary school, these children would often be put in middle school classes that placed them on a track to nowhere. Instead of preparing the kids for tests that would not help them, Faye spent most of her days making sure the kids were fluent in English. And in doing so, her test scores took a hit.

She retired after giving her students everything for almost half a century. By any reasonable measure this was a terrific teacher. Students, parents, administrators, and colleagues would all agree. And the *Los Angeles Times* classified her as a least-effective teacher.

Always the pro, Faye Ireland simply wished the paper had been a little clearer in stating that she was least effective in raising test scores. Deep down, despite the stiff upper lip, this teacher will always feel a sting of sadness unfairly applied by a test-obsessed society that has completely lost its focus on what really matters.

Teachers, stay strong. Go in every day, like Faye, and be a positive role model for your students. Always remember that test scores matter, but your students matter more. Students and their test scores are two very different things. Test scores eventually fade into oblivion and are forgotten, but your students will always remember you.

For Your Consideration

- Make sure your students know that the most important things they will learn both in and outside of school cannot be measured on a standardized test.

- Teach your students to understand the sad reality that good scores on standardized tests will help them gain access to more opportunities in school in the future.

- From the beginning of the year, set aside time for students to practice taking standardized tests. These sessions should be short and consistent. If students have practiced on a regular basis, the actual exams at the end of the year will cause far less stress. The readiness is all.

- During your early test prep sessions, spend some time listening to your students who have been through the testing process before. How did they feel about it? How did they prepare? You will often hear tales of apathy and misery and fear. Make it clear to the kids that your class is going to do well on the tests but prepare with purpose and reasonable expectations.

- When correcting practice tests, call on students to justify their answers. Rather than announcing that the answer to number 5 is B, call on students individually. Have them explain not only why they chose B but why they did not choose A, C, or D.

- Remind your students and yourself that a more accurate evaluation of your effectiveness is where your students are ten years after they have left your class, and if they are using skills you taught them. When students contact you when they are adults, having fun in college, entering the business world, or starting their families, those are results that will fuel you far beyond being labeled by a number on someone's ledger sheet.

CHAPTER NINE

There's No Place Like Home

I like being the Quiet Man.

At professional development meetings I say nothing when an expert gives a PowerPoint presentation overemphasizing the importance of test scores. I am silent when the newest reading textbook is presented and announced as the miraculous breakthrough that will make all the children literate. I'm even silent when a district official explains that all students will read from the same materials on the same day at the same pace. I disagree with these speakers, but there is no point in raising my hand. No one is listening.

But there is one statement made constantly that inspires me to say something. Presidents, authors, reformers, and talk show hosts say it all the time and someone has to point out that the emperor has no clothes.

Here is a direct quote from the Web site of the *Los Angeles Times,* but it is said in one form or another by well-meaning people who are far off target:

Research has repeatedly found that teachers are the single most important school-related factor in a child's education.

I have never found this to be true. And I've seen a lot in three decades.

Let's be clear. A good teacher can change a life. It happens every day around the world. But to conclude that teachers are the most important factor in a student's success is not true. Some qualify the assertion by taking a step back and claiming that the teacher is at the very least the most important factor in a child's progress *in school*.

Still, I disagree. A child's family has more influence on what happens in school than teachers, systems, materials, and any other influence.

Don't get me wrong. You can alter, improve, and even save lives. Optimism is the foundation of all good teaching. But to diminish the importance of family is naïve. Parents who are apathetic and, even worse, downright destructive will lower your batting average faster than Sandy Koufax.

Even more tragic are wonderful families in dire financial situations. Poverty can have an impact on the kids in your class in a lot of different ways. Even a cursory glance at the effects of poverty reveals that poor children are not participating on an equal playing field. Poor nutrition coupled with a lack of access to books is not a recipe for success. In addition, there are parents working several jobs, which prevent them from spending time with their kids and helping them define and reach their personal goals. With almost fifteen million children growing up in poverty, no real teacher can ignore the fact that the odds for these children are against success.

The family situation of every student, both emotionally and financially, is the primary influence on a child's success or failure in school.

A TALE OF TWO FAMILIES

Let's examine two students who were in the same class. Roy and Daniel were both bright young men. Roy made an impression immediately, constantly making acute observations and expressing himself brilliantly. Daniel was equally impressive, and was an intrinsic learner. I had rarely seen a student smile so often just because he was learning something. I had high hopes for both of them.

However, it's a long and winding road, and both of these boys hit major bumps along the journey. In Roy's case, early in the year it became clear that although he was highly intelligent he had no friends. He was sarcastic and downright mean to many of his peers. He thought his comments were amusing, but the targets of his jokes were not laughing. Unfortunately, it turned out that he knew full well of the pain he was causing others. He simply didn't care.

About the third week of class, I wrote his father a note and requested a parent conference. I explained that I had high hopes for Roy, and that I thought if we worked together we could all help him with his peer relationships. Roy's father called me the same night and scheduled a conference after school the following Monday. It was hard to read his tone on the telephone. He seemed to be annoyed with my request, but he could have been having a stressful day, and I made sure my tone was professional, concerned, and positive.

The following Monday, several of my students came into the room around 6:30 A.M. to ask me if I had heard the news about Roy. I did not know what they were referring to, and they told me that he had been arrested for shoplifting at a mall about three blocks from the school. Roy had been trying to sneak some electronic games out of a store and set off alarms.

After school that day, Roy's dad arrived and the three of us sat down. I did not mention the shoplifting incident; the purpose of this meeting was to let the father know that his son was being very rude and often mean to his peers. I did my best to explain that the behavior was unacceptable; it was hurting not only the other children but Roy as well. I got the father to admit that no one ever called the house and that Roy was never invited to play with anyone.

I told Roy that this was a solvable problem, and that with a change of attitude he could become a respected class leader with his dance card full.

When I was through, the father began cursing me and told me I needed to mind my own business. My job was to teach his child math and not to stick my nose into his son's peer relationships. I immediately backed down and thanked Roy's father for coming in. It was only the beginning of the year, and I was going to do my best to help Roy with or without his father's support.

I stood up, but the man said, "Not so fast. I need you to do something for me."

He asked me to write his son a letter of recommendation for a private school he hoped Roy would be attending the following year. I replied that I certainly could not write such a letter about a child I had known for only three weeks. When Roy's father pushed for the recommendation, I explained that I could not recommend someone who had been stopped by the police for shoplifting. The father stormed out of the room and screamed that he would go to the head of the district to complain about me.

The following evening I received an apologetic and concerned phone call from Roy's mother, who had divorced her husband and moved out of the state several years ago. She had heard about the shoplifting incident and decided she needed to raise her son. Her ex-husband, she felt, was not fit for the job. Roy had been babied and spoiled, she explained to me, and she was coming home to take over the job of raising him. She said she would be in Los Angeles within the week.

She never came that year. Roy's father never showed up in my classroom again despite many phone calls and requests from me. Roy tolerated my class, passed all his exams, and moved on. His friends told me that he was often getting into trouble in middle school, where he was then in the sixth grade.

The following year I was at a market near the school when I

saw a surprising sight. A woman, who at the time I did not realize was Roy's mother, was with him. She had followed through on her promise to come back to Los Angeles to raise her son. I noticed her only because several people in the market were staring. Roy, now a seventh grader and twelve years old, was sitting in a shopping cart being pushed around by his mother.

Roy had an equally bright classmate in Daniel. Daniel was disorganized, and because he was very bright, he had been able to slide by for practically all of elementary school. He did well in my class, but there were signs that eventually just being bright was not going to be enough. Sure enough, Daniel had many problems in middle school and eventually was asked to repeat the seventh grade.

His parents were consistently supportive. They met with Daniel's teachers and also came to me. They loved their son and knew what he was worth. As a result, they administered several new reasonable guidelines for Daniel to follow. They had the highest expectations for their son. He needed to improve his scholastic achievement immediately and they made it clear that they would not accept anything less than his best effort. By high school Daniel was the captain of several academic teams and a participant in school athletics as well. Eventually, he received scholarship offers to several of the finest universities in the country. He accepted one in California because he wanted to be close to his parents, and his choice of schools allowed him to come home on weekends.

Here are two students from the same class with the same teacher. I did my best to help them both. I treated them as individuals and made myself available to these young men above and beyond the call of duty. One had an incredibly supportive and understanding family that worked hard with their kid and collaborated with several teachers and schools. One had a father who spent much of his time howling at the moon and a mother who pushed her adolescent son around the market in a shopping cart. Is it any wonder that one of these boys went to a top university while the other fell off the edge of the world? There are so many factors that play key roles in the development of a child. Teachers can and should work hard to be one of the most important pieces of the puzzle. But never forget that your most superhuman efforts will rarely supersede the student's family's influence. More often than not, family dynamics are the foundation that can either support a child or contribute to his collapse.

WARNING: DON'T GO THERE

This leads to the next question. When you have families that do not support your efforts and even work against your best intentions, what do you do?

Sadly, some teachers will give up. People who once cared deeply throw up their hands in frustration and ask, "What am I supposed to do? This kid doesn't stand a chance." There is often truth in such tragic predictions.

Please don't give up. It's not over. While it may be the case that the odds are a million to one against you, if the teacher quits, it's a million to *none*. It doesn't happen very often, but there are students I have been able to help despite a family situation that made teaching very difficult.

When things are impossible, return to your personal code. I constantly model the importance of organization even to children whose backpacks are a mess and whose desks resemble Pigpen from the *Peanuts* comic strip. I have witnessed a student who did poorly in my class for an entire year, leaving me discouraged and defeated, yet returned years later in a better place than I could have imagined citing our days together as a turning point.

It's so hard to celebrate the turning point because we teachers rarely see it. In fact, the students themselves rarely see it. But once in a while, though not as often as we like, the fact that we didn't give up pays off.

Joey is a young man who wrote me a letter from college. He was not born with a silver spoon in his mouth. His parents were separated from him for much of his childhood because of immigration problems. He was passed around several relatives who did the best they could, but this was not a young man born with the sort of advantages fortunate children inherit. But in his junior year he wrote to me from one of the top universities in the country. I had not heard from him in about eight years:

Hey Rafe!

I am Joey from your Saturday class.

I hope you are well. =)

In four days I will be a junior in Chemical and Biomolecular Engineering.

Your Saturday Classes added to my discipline regarding academics and I am faring well in classes with a 4.03 GPA (A+ = 4.3)

I am involved in an undergrad research in my department.

In my free time, I play ukulele, work out, play soccer and hang out with my friends. I continuously aspire to learn from them.

I am grateful to be where I am at and, thus, happy.

I understand that your help and support as my teacher and mentor greatly shaped my American adventure. I wouldn't be where I am without you.

Thank you, Rafe

Occasionally the stars line up correctly and a child growing up in poverty can beat the odds. There are kids who are able to overcome the most dysfunctional family situations and accomplish the extraordinary. These children remind us that we must never give up. But if extraordinary efforts are not tempered with the knowledge of the reality of factors beyond a teacher's control, the constant defeats and failures will crush the heartiest of spirits. Once a teacher feels defeated, the chances of receiving a letter like Joey's are reduced from slim to none. It's painful, but coach John Wooden defined success as peace of mind knowing you did your best. Young teachers often beat themselves up over students who were lost because of family situations. If you have been told that you are the one who will make or break a student, it simply is not the case. Coming to this realization will not only get you through many awful situations but will steel your resolve when the next case comes along.

Alejandro was a delightful young man who had enormous dramatic talent. He was a natural comedian, and a class leader. He was a good-looking and athletic young man with no father and an involved mother. His mother hated my class, dousing her son's enthusiasm for our activities each night with a diatribe against the false promises and lies I was pouring into her son's brain. Mom finally went to my principal to demand her son be put in another class. My boss, who was terrific about having her teachers' backs in such situations, called in Alejandro to ask what he wanted. He begged his mom to let him stay put, but his mother was adamant and he was moved in the middle of the year. He called me that night in tears, and I told him not to worry. He didn't need my class; because he was so talented and bright, nothing would stop him.

A couple of months after school ended I ran into them walking through the neighborhood to a bus stop. As I greeted Alejandro he scowled at me and turned his back. I was shocked. I understood that he was his mother's son, but we had always had a wonderful relationship and I never thought I would be treated by him as someone with a highly contagious disease.

Eight years later one early evening I was grading papers in class when a stranger walked into the room. Fans of Pink Floyd know the shocking story of the band members not recognizing their troubled founder Syd Barrett when he returned to the studio during one of their sessions. This young man identified himself as the fine boy I had known all those years ago, but life had taken a terrible toll. He looked awful, with bad skin fueled by bad nutrition written all over his face. Dark circles under his eyes indicated a lack of healthy sleep. This was a young man who had suffered many years of neglect.

Alejandro had come back to tell me he was enrolled in a junior college. He had spent the last eight years in hell, he explained, jumping from place to place all over the country because of all sorts of family problems. He came by to say hi and to tell me he had made it to college. He was the first in his family to ever do so. He spent five minutes with me, walked out, and I have not seen him since.

Young teachers, that is what winning looks like.

It's not pretty, but, battle scars and all, Alejandro had beaten the odds. There was still realistic hope for a better life than the one he was leaving behind. But it was a hope tempered by reality. George Bailey's friends were not there with a basket of money. When young people grow up with serious family and economic problems, it's not a wonderful life. Please remember this when you read that a child's failure to produce in school is predominantly your fault. It's not. Do all that you can. Some days, do even more. But never forget the very real hurdles you face.

For Your Consideration

- Accept the fact that you do not have more influence over a student than the child's family or economic situation. Continue to be the best teacher you can be every day for every student despite the reality that the odds are stacked against you.
- Listen to the students talk about their problems. If possible, spend time with students during lunch, or before or after

school. Once you know a child's mind-set, you will have a better idea of where he might want to go.

- Empathize with your students, but encourage them by letting them know that everyone goes through some awful times; challenge and inspire them through your own and other people's stories that courage and hard work can overcome the most difficult situations. Stay positive.

- Use former students to mentor your current ones. Students who do not see the light at the end of the tunnel will be motivated if they see actual students from their situation who have made good decisions and profited from them.

- Try not to be discouraged when policy makers blame you for all of society's ills. Most of the people who are preaching that teachers are to blame for all of our problems do not teach. If they did teach years ago, their stories of reaching every child are not accurate. Remember the words of Mark Twain: "I remember everything from my youth, whether they happened or not!"

CHAPTER TEN

Haters

When I was seventeen years old I saw an enormous pile
of excrement. To this day I do not know what it came
from. Although the evidence is that the dinosaurs are
extinct, my only guess was that it came from a brontosaurus. It
was sitting in the middle of an auditorium stage and was placed
there to prevent a group of six-year-old children from rehearsing
a play.

I had taken a summer job working at a camp to earn a few
bucks to take out a girl I had a crush on, and our camp leader ran
a program in which groups of children gave a performance at the
end of the season. There would be songs, dances, and a variety of
skits. My little group of kids thought it was cool that I could play
the riff from Pete Townshend's "Pinball Wizard" on a guitar, so
we put together a skit based on The Who's rock opera *Tommy*.
Several of my friends helped with a little staging, and as the summer wore on, the kids became astonishingly good and had a ball,
too. I did not know it then, but the groundwork was being laid for
the Shakespeare plays my classes would perform years later.

We practiced all the skits and songs in a park, and the day
before Parents' Night was set aside for dress rehearsals. Each group

leader was given thirty minutes to take the kids to the park auditorium so that the children could acclimate themselves to the stage. Each group was randomly assigned a time slot. There were about twelve groups performing, and my children were slated to rehearse last at the end of the day. We walked in from a baseball field, entered the empty auditorium, and discovered the enormous pile of dung awaiting us in the middle of the stage.

I was so naïve I did not even consider how or why such a thing could happen. I simply found a park attendant, borrowed a shovel, and cleaned up the stage while the kids waited. It took so long, they were not able to rehearse. It was no problem; they were ready to rock, and their performance the following night brought down the house. Without even trying I had begun to discover the importance of art in a child's development.

Many years later it dawned on me that a coworker tried to sabotage our little rock-and-roll show. It is almost impossible to conceive of a mind so small as to want to prevent a group of six-year-olds from singing and dancing a couple of songs.

Haters.

I am sorry to raise the issue, but it's an important one, and something all good young teachers will likely encounter. We live, as Don Henley sang in "The Heart of the Matter," in a "graceless age." Time and time again, when I meet outstanding teachers, they relate a tale about a coworker who was mean to them simply because they were doing a good job. Jealousy is an ugly emotion that often leads to unprofessional and cruel behavior.

Over the past few decades it has gotten worse. With the social network now dominating many lives, it seems people are at liberty to say practically anything. A cursory glance at comments on the Internet reveals surprising nastiness. If a well-known person has died tragically it is a sure thing that someone will spew hateful comments that are better left unsaid. It is a necessary but ultimately sad price we pay for our freedom of speech.

This mean-spiritedness is a constant and annoying presence in too many schools. In my rookie year of teaching, I first saw its effects when people gathered around a bulletin board next to our main office one Friday. A new display had brought the hallway traffic to a dead stop. The artwork was so beautiful it was as if a curator from MoMA had loaned a few masterpieces to an elementary school. Astonishing oil paintings created by fourth graders decorated the panel. Jaws dropped. The paintings were spectacular in their form and content. I was inspired. I would come to learn that these children had been working with a brilliant art teacher. I know very little about painting, but even a brief glance at the work told the viewer that these children were learning things that extended far beyond brushstrokes. These works displayed persistence, creativity, risk taking, and joy. They were marvelous. I stared at them and knew two things immediately: I wanted my students to be artists, and I wanted to get to know the teacher of these young Rembrandts. I was dying to know his strategies, as my students would never be able to accomplish such outstanding work as long as they had me teaching them. I needed to get better, and I was excited to meet someone who could help me improve.

A trio of teachers stood near me commenting on the work. Their snarky reviews made it clear that they thought the display was a fraud. Their poisonous comments flowed easily and quickly, one observation after another. "No way students created these paintings." "The teacher *actually painted the pictures and claimed it was students' work to show off.*" "If the kids did any of the work, it was because they were gifted children and it was easy to get such *kids to paint masterpieces.*" "If we had those students they could do the same project."

I felt so sad listening to them. I thought this would be a profession where everyone cared deeply about children and about one another. I was too inexperienced to appreciate the sad reality about some people. The art teacher eventually left for another district.

I lost the chance to consult with a possible mentor, and the students at our school lost much more than that.

Hate can arise over the simplest of issues. One of our school's teachers was on maternity leave, so a substitute was brought in to finish the last several months of the year. She was outstanding. One could not ask more of a replacement. Rather than simply going through the motions, this woman wanted the class to finish strong. She began a book club during their lunch hour to help the students discover the joy of reading. She was bothering no one. She simply stayed in her room during the lunch hour reading with children who voluntarily joined the activity.

A few teachers who taught the same grade approached her and asked why she did not come to the teachers' lounge and join them for lunch. She said she would love to, but she had started a lunchtime book club that had picked up steam and significantly helped some of her students. This information was greeted with an infamous question:

"What are you trying to do—make us look bad?"

Any good teacher has winced upon hearing this. Of course the substitute was doing nothing of the kind. But it depressed her to have fellow teachers frown upon her effort. The majority of the staff admired her work, and some teachers began similar clubs. Still, she told me that she felt uneasy every time she passed this small group of colleagues infected with the green-eyed monster.

It can and probably will happen to you. When it does, it hurts. No amount of advice can take away your pain if you are a sensitive person. Ironically, that sensitivity can be a blessing and a curse. It drives you to do more for the students because you care deeply about them, but it provides very little armor against tactless comments.

Try not to take it personally. It has nothing to do with you and everything to do with the person slinging the arrows. Your school is not unique. I have had the privilege to speak with teachers from all over the world and the story never changes. From Bangkok to Taipei to Rio to Main Street, U.S.A., every school has mediocre individuals who tear down rather than build up.

Two veteran teachers hoped to become nationally board certified. For the uninitiated, this is a series of classes and examinations geared to teachers who want to broaden their knowledge of the field of education. A lot of hard work and time spent can earn a teacher the prestige of certification, and those who achieve it are considered top professionals.

The two teachers had taught at the same school for more than a decade and both were known as consummate professionals. Their classes were well organized and the children learned their skills. Parents praised them, and their administrators were not surprised that these two chose to take the certification classes. They were the type of teacher who constantly wants to grow.

After a couple of years of work, the results came in. One of the teachers passed and was nationally board certified. The other did not.

The one who did not pass has not spoken since to the one who did.

The teacher who passed did not flaunt her success or condescend to anyone. Yet what should have been a fulfilling time for her grew bittersweet because a colleague refused to acknowledge her with so much as a "Good morning" when they passed each other in the hall.

It's ironic that a teacher trying to reach the pinnacle of her profession would act so unprofessionally. But that's the whole problem with haters. The worst thing about this phenomenon is that haters forget that we teachers model behavior for the students. Pettiness, hostility, and jealousy are the last things we should be showing our students. Never forget that even the youngest children pick up on far more than we think they do. The teacher who did not get her board certification missed an opportunity far more important than passing her exam. Had she told her students that she failed to achieve her goal and was trying again, she would have motivated them to get up off the mat when they are knocked down. She could have praised her colleague for an outstanding accomplishment, and in doing so teach her students the importance of graciousness and true respect for other people. Unprofessional behavior hurts the target, diminishes the instigator, and damages the children who are supposed to be the reason we are teaching in the first place.

Spitefulness is not limited to one type of teacher. It can even infect class leaders with outstanding records of achievement. Early in my career I reached a crossroads. I was having some success at my elementary school despite making more mistakes than I'd like to remember. Passion and hard work had gotten some results, and a very nice principal called me. She was the leader of a gifted magnet school in a wealthy area of Los Angeles that had a sudden and rare opening the following year. She wanted to know if I would be interested in interviewing for the job.

It felt good to be courted. I didn't yet feel married to Hobart despite loving the kids and having wonderful colleagues. In those early years the importance of staying put and making a stand had not occurred to me. I still thought other pastures had greener grass.

The idea of teaching brilliant kids with supportive families in a school where your shoes didn't stick to the bathroom floor intrigued me. There were days when I was frustrated by working with children who were far behind. I did not yet fully understand that such children were waiting for me to level the playing field. And so, eager to test new waters, I agreed to meet with the principal.

She invited me to her office, but when I arrived she wasn't alone. The interview included twenty-nine other people waiting to evaluate my worth. Administrators, teachers, and parents came to grill me. As my home school did not even have a PTA, I was a bit shocked to see such a large group waiting to fire away.

It took more than an hour. The questions were tough but fair. The basic tone of the conversation was that their school had remarkable children who needed teachers who could go far beyond normal expectations. What could I bring to the table that would excite and motivate these bright children to excel? I described some of my classroom activities at Hobart, with particular emphasis on presenting challenging math problems and teaching Shakespeare after school. I promised to produce and direct an entire production of a play each year and not expect to be compensated for the work, which can total more than a thousand hours.

I thought the interview went very well. The parents seemed thrilled, and when the session was over several teachers approached me with a desire to collaborate on the Shakespeare production. I went home feeling that a new door had opened for me.

The following week I received a very nice note from the principal telling me that she could not offer me a position. Looking back, it was not the lost position that discouraged me but the rejection. As there was no explanation of why this decision had been made, and I had thought the interview had gone well, I called the principal and asked if she could tell me where I had gone wrong in case I was ever in a similar position.

She was embarrassed to tell me what had happened. The school had a policy concerning its interviews. A candidate had to receive a yes vote from all thirty members of the committee. One no meant rejection. The vote after my interview had been twenty-nine to one in favor of offering me a position.

I asked whom I had offended and she hesitated. She told me I was very young and was about to learn a very tough lesson. It is the lesson I hope to share with you about this sad but all too true problem that happens in schools.

"Who voted against me?" I asked a second time.

"Our school's most popular teacher," she replied sadly.

It was a hard pill to swallow. But such moments can still be viewed as an opportunity. The best way to deal with haters is to take the high road. I returned to Hobart and did my best to grow as a professional.

Success is the best revenge. The year after the gifted magnet school rejected me I was fortunate to be awarded the Walt Disney National Outstanding Teacher of the Year Award. The school called me and invited me for another interview, but it was my turn to politely send a rejection letter.

For Your Consideration

- Never forget the words of an extraordinary teacher named Jeanne Delp. She once observed: "When what you are reminds others what they are not, hostility results."
- If you come up with a new idea or do something different in a school, someone will be unhappy with you. Your class could be discovering the cure for cancer and a hater will criticize you for it.
- Good teachers do not hate extraordinary educators. They emulate and collaborate with them.
- When feeling down about a colleague's unprofessional behavior, take solace in the fact that many of the teachers in your school are fabulous human beings. A couple of bad apples can make a person forget the fact that the majority of educators make the human race look good.
- Always remember that you do not have the power to make anyone look bad. Bad teachers look bad all by themselves. They don't need your help.

- As difficult as it can be at times, take the high road when dealing with a hater. If necessary, reread chapter 3 of *To Kill a Mockingbird* and watch Atticus Finch handle the wheelchairbound Mrs. Dubose. She is hell on wheels (literally), but Atticus treats her with respect and dignity. Being polite to disagreeable people is a strong message to model for your students.

CHAPTER ELEVEN

Keeping It Real

You don't have to be Plato to know that if your class is not listening or focused on their lessons the students won't be learning. The kids have to be under control, and teachers use a variety of strategies to keep them that way. Some scare the kids; others are talented performers who can dance and rap and joke their way through lessons. I'd like to suggest to you a bit of language that can be a powerful tool.

Visitors to Room 56 are impressed with the children's ability to stay focused for long periods of time. During a ninety-minute Shakespeare rehearsal no one squirms. The kids, all of them, sit still while reading Mark Twain for more than an hour. The room is calm and quiet. Here's the secret. Approach a student working in school and ask him one simple question: Why are you doing this activity?

No matter how many times you ask a student this question, you are likely to hear some of the following answers:

"Why are you working on your multiplication?"

"The teacher told me to."

"Why are you writing this essay?"

"I have to."

"Why are you outlining this history chapter?"

"There's a test on Friday."

"Why are you studying these vocabulary words?"

"They're going to be on the test at the end of the year."

Saving the best for last, my favorite answer to the following question, which you will hear a lot:

"Why are you doing this?"

"I don't know!"

If you approach one of the students in my class and ask, "Why are you doing this?" he will answer with the following sentence:

"If I learn this skill, my life will get better."

I tell the students constantly that in my class they will be learning things they will use in their lives. I am not teaching them to get ready for a test. The test is only to see if they understand the material, but it has no connection whatsoever with why they are learning to calculate or write an essay.

Relevance is the key to truly motivating students for the long run. Superficial dangling carrots such as grades, prizes, and parties may work temporarily, but creating activities that are truly germane ensures that your entire classroom will run more calmly and efficiently.

Try as much as possible to introduce this concept in every lesson you teach. It must be repeated consistently throughout the year.

When I teach students decimals, I ask them, "Why are we doing this?"

I wait until the students are able to answer, "If we understand decimals, our lives will be better."

"When will we use them?"

I then read them an article from a newspaper about a patient in a hospital who died because someone put a decimal in the wrong place and he was given ten times too much of a prescribed medication. The students gasp.

"So let's be clear," I tell the kids. "Understanding decimals can actually be a matter of life and death." Then we go to work.

MISSING THE POINT

Here is a sad high school tale. Jason is a former student of mine who recently stopped by and told me something about his tenth grade English class. Their teacher had assigned Harper Lee's *To Kill a Mockingbird*.

Forty students were told to read the book at home and prepare for a multiple-choice exam to be given two weeks later. Jason took an anonymous survey of his class. Two students had actually read the book. The other thirty-eight had turned on their computers and read outlines and various summaries of the novel. All forty students in class passed the exam.

The tragic point here is that the students missed an opportunity to make reading a relevant activity. Teach your students that all great books are about *them*. At all levels of school, we teachers must constantly read with the kids and help them connect the dots between the printed page and their own lives.

RIGHT ON TARGET

Rudy was a young man in my class who came from a very difficult home situation that practically blocked all roads to success. Fortunately Rudy spent a year in fifth grade discovering the joy of reading and internalizing the important lessons of great literature.

Many years later, Rudy attended New York University. Financial aid was never enough to cover expenses. I dipped into my pocket to try to help. I had a few hundred left in my checking account and wrote my former student a check. He rejected the money and sent me the following letter:

Dear Rafe:

As far as the money goes, I cannot ask you to give of yourself like that. As I said, I CAN do it on my own. I just need to work a little harder and cut down on my expenses. I would feel terrible knowing that energy that could be devoted to a kid started on the path YOU got me on would be wasted on me, when I can manage just fine. I appreciate your willingness to help me. But I'd much rather the money you are offering me go to the class so that one day maybe some other kid will be in a position like mine.

Rafe, I honestly believe I would be dead right now if it wasn't for you. I was headed down a dark path, where drug dealing didn't seem so bad and the acceptance of a gang was looking like the only way to be accepted. You SAVED me from that and now I am at a top University, studying an art that I would never have tried had you not cast me in a play. You showed me a better life, a better way to live. When I tell people about the class and you, I have found myself comparing what you did for me to Plato's Allegory of the Cave. I knew only pain and disappointment and thought that was the way of the world until I met you. I thank God that I did and had you in my life.

THIS is what reading is supposed to look like. I had to look up Plato's *The Allegory of the Cave* to make sure I understood what this boy was expressing. But after laughing at my own ignorance, I realized that this young man was a reader not to complete an assignment or take an exam but to take the wisdom off the page and apply it to his own life. This can be the result when every hour of every day we teachers make sure the kids see the relevance in what they are doing.

Today Rudy is a graduate of NYU, and he remains an avid reader.

For Your Consideration

- Constantly ask the kids: Why are we doing this? The answer must be: If I learn this skill my life will get better.
- Make sure the children make the connection between the lessons they are learning and how they will apply them in real life. Have the kids explain the connections rather than listen to you.
- When the curriculum is drudgery, such as preparing for the SAT, connect its relevance by explaining that it is part of a flawed system. By playing the game and beating the system at its own game, a student can open doors to create a more relevant existence for himself. Learning when to fight and when to play the game might be the most relevant lesson of all.

Congratulations if you have made it through five years as a classroom teacher. Your class is in good order. You have survived those first terrifying days of watching the clock and waiting for the day to end. You have had bad days and been strong enough to come back for more, hopefully a bit wiser. You've even laughed at yourself when things have gone wrong. You are making a difference, and your students are lucky to have you.

You are calmer than when you began. You have found your voice, and are more confident. It's a good life.

But now you have reached a crossroads. You are competent enough to begin to take it a little easier. You're a bit older, you are raising your own family, and the kids in your class seem to be slower, meaner, and more apathetic than your classes of only a few years ago. And it's time to make a decision.

You can phone it in. Many teachers do this. They establish a routine, teach the curriculum, collect their disappointing paycheck, and go home.

But you can also take the road less traveled. You are ready to connect with students previously beyond your reach. You have tools and experience now that were not with you before. You are about to enter what might be the most exciting ten years of your career.

It is time to grow up.

PART II
Growing Up

You've been teaching at least five years. You dread professional development meetings. They are often geared toward new teachers; worse, the meetings are spent repeating things you've heard a dozen times before. You're tired, and you are upset that the passion you once felt for the classroom is waning.

Part II is for you. Consider it fodder for dedicated teachers who need answers to questions that time did not permit to be asked during the early years of struggle. Now that your classroom runs efficiently and the students tune in more than out, it's time to reach higher.

CHAPTER TWELVE

Bitter Fingers

One Friday as I was walking down the hallway I passed a teacher heading for her classroom. "Happy Friday," I said, figuring the thought of a weekend would make most people smile after a long and tiring week.

"I hate Fridays," she growled back. Before I could ask the obvious follow-up she clarified her response. "I hate Fridays because it just means that Monday is that much sooner."

Now, *that's* a glass-half-empty attitude. This woman is a good and caring teacher. But she was tired and worn out. Teaching can do that to a person, and it is difficult not to become bitter after years in the classroom.

Through how many hoops can a thinking adult jump? When "new" approaches to teaching are preached at staff development sessions, often completely contradicting what experts were preaching just a few years before, it's hard not to become jaded. Throw in some truly difficult students and an administrator who offers no support. Finish it off with grading the essays of illiterate tenth graders, and the recipe for bitterness is almost complete. For dessert add a monthly magazine article citing teachers as the reason schools are failing. These ingredients can cause the most idealistic class leader to deteriorate into an angry, pessimistic, and sarcastic instructor.

After teaching for five years or so, you reach a crossroads. You've made it, more or less. You have survived some frustrating days. Your class is normally under control and functioning. You have taught long enough that even with a switch in grade level or school, your previous experience has provided you with enough tools to establish order in the classroom. You have begun to find your voice and have made real connections with some of the kids. And now you have to make a decision.

Are you going to basically keep doing what you are doing and phone it in for the next two decades? Or will you challenge yourself to keep growing?

Many good people phone it in. The job is tiring, and if you have started a family you cannot be expected to come back to school at night for a function. Even if you want to continue to go the extra mile, there are dozens of small defeats that make good teachers slump down and wonder, *What's the point?*

THE ROAD TO NOWHERE

Denise entered the profession for all the right reasons. She had discovered a love for children while working at a series of child-care centers when she was in college and graduated with a degree in early childhood education. She struggled during her first few years of teaching, but she battled through her tears and sweat to become a fine young instructor. By her third year she was taking an active role in school leadership, and she gained a reputation as a rising star among the parents and staff.

Enter Valerie, a nine-year-old student with a mother who made school personnel miserable. This woman would burst into a class-room in the middle of the day and scream at her daughter's teacher about whatever was making her unhappy. Valerie was a capable student, but in her mother's eyes she was Einstein, Mother Teresa, and the Virgin Mary rolled into one. If Valerie brought home a paper that was not covered with glowing comments, Mom would go to the principal or district office to register vicious complaints about the teacher. One day she pounded on Denise's door when school was in session. She said she was picking up her daughter because she had a doctor's appointment and wanted company. When Denise told the woman that Valerie was missing too much school and it was hurting her education, the mother cursed the teacher in front of the class and took her child anyway.

Denise was very upset and went to the principal demanding that something be done to prevent the mother from interrupting the class and removing her daughter for all sorts of ridiculous reasons. The principal explained that he had met with the mother several times, but in the end, the mother's weekly invasions needed to be tolerated; there was not much that could be done. Denise was furious. She felt that her administrator needed to stand up to the parent, even to the point of throwing her off the campus. When this didn't happen Denise grew frustrated. She began treating Valerie rudely, growing short with her when she asked for help and often ignoring her raised hand.

Feeling unappreciated and let down by the principal, Denise quit all her leadership roles at the school. She refused to help an administration she believed did not support her. This is a very common tale. Denise made a deliberate turn at the fork in the road and went nowhere. She still teaches today and is adequate. Her classroom is in order and most of her students spend a year in a sterile environment, numbly doing their work and for the most part passing their tests. The class is a far cry from the happy and hopeful environment Denise had begun to create in her early years.

It is said that a Shakespearean tragedy is tragic not merely because it is a sad story but because it's a story that could have been joyful and instead had its potential bliss cut short. We weep for Hamlet not simply because of his death but for the king he might have been. Teachers who allow the frustrations of the profession to turn their potential into bitter fingers are indeed tragic figures. They lose their potential excellence.

And of course their students are the biggest losers of all.

TWO OUT OF THREE AIN'T BAD

It's astonishing to reflect on all the factors that embitter teachers. Anger at the administration is common. Working with students who come from families who show absolutely zero interest in their education is another factor. High-stakes testing, schools in disrepair, mean colleagues, and an unappreciative society all pile on a teacher's psyche to produce a bunker mentality. The dismissal bell on Friday signals the end of another week of torturous and pointless work. But nothing can quench an educator's fire faster than a student who foolishly chooses not to pass through doors that his teacher has worked so hard to open. When you've put in extra time only to fail, it makes it that much harder to go the extra mile the next time a situation arises where you might do some good. King Lear's "How sharper than a serpent's tooth it is to have a thankless child" has in one way or another resounded to many a teacher trying to help a child in need.

I have often been asked why I do not burn out. Had I continued, as I did in my youth, to try to fix every problem and help every child in need, I would have certainly flamed out years ago. Some see teaching as a thankless job, but it might be better for the psyche to think of it as a service job. The reward for teaching is the teaching itself. Of course it is gratifying to receive heartfelt letters and thanks from a grateful student and his family, but to expect and hope for such recognition is a slippery slope that can erode the joy of teaching.

All students must be given an opportunity to learn and have

fun. Some will and some won't, but most teachers love to teach. The bitterness comes when our efforts are pointless. If you are going to do something extra, such as stay after school to tutor a child in trouble or spend a Saturday afternoon with the kids at an art museum, know that you are likely to have one of three outcomes.

First, the student might grow from your extra effort and show appreciation, thus steeling your resolve to do more. Cards and letters from former students now in college or happily married are some of the most wonderful rewards a teacher can receive. There is not a teacher I know who does not read such letters after they've had a bad day. Such appreciation rejuvenates our tired souls and reminds us why we stick with a job whose rewards are few and far between. A Saturday afternoon spent at the wedding of a beautiful young woman who was once a little girl in your class is an incredible experience. Having that woman acknowledge that your efforts were an important part of her growth and development is a feeling better than standing in Stockholm and receiving a Nobel Prize in education.

Second, students might grow from your extra efforts, show no appreciation, and have better lives without even realizing they owe some of their good times and success to you. This happens a lot, and can make one sad. Don't let it. If you do extra work with the mind-set that most kids (hey, most people) often do not appreciate their blessings, you can keep your spirits high by feeling good about a job well done. I once had a student with Tourette's syndrome raised by a single parent who did not have the knowledge or connections to get his child help. My wife drove the parent and child to see a series of doctors, including a top pediatric neurologist who told them there was medication that might be able to help if the boy was able to take it safely. Three weeks and several thousand dollars later, we had radically changed this child's life for the better. Most of his tics were under control, and he developed friendships and began to do well in school. In one year, he went from being viewed as a freak by ignorant classmates to being a valued member of their community. We never received a thank-you from this child or his parent. The boy went on to college and today is married and successful. Do I wish he would make a contribution to our class foundation to help others the way he was once helped? Of course I do. Do I feel bad because I failed to instill in this young man a generosity of spirit? Absolutely. And yet I never get to the point of bitterness, because the goal was to help a young man and I did. Helping and a job well done are the rewards.

Number three is the downer: complete failure. This is just an awful feeling, and it happens a lot. You wouldn't be human if you didn't just throw up your hands and cry out, "Oh, what's the use?" After three decades I have personally gone the extra mile for many kids when there was no point in doing so. The work was not only unappreciated but completely ineffective.

I once had a student in need who I believed could benefit from my extra assistance. I didn't just go the extra mile, I practically ran the marathon for him. In the end, I did not help this young man at all. I worked with him over summers. Believing in this young man's potential to beat the odds, I helped him get a scholarship. He went to a top university, and I bought him plane tickets during his breaks so he could return to spend time with his family.

Years later, my wife and I ran into him at a Christmas party. We had not seen or heard from him in almost ten years. He had become a bitter and angry young man. He was very drunk and his behavior was awful. He spent the evening insulting everyone within earshot, with particular barbs directed at the family who had invited him. I hoped he was having a bad night because of some personal crisis. I learned from his peers that he was like this all the time. He was completely unrecognizable from the young man I had placed my faith in all those years ago.

These are the situations that can bring you way down. Too many experiences like this one can result in your entering the classroom without a bounce in your step and a twinkle in your eye. Your students (and you) need both. So go the extra mile when you can, but go with care.

START ME UP

Here's a little thing I do each day in the parking lot at Hobart Elementary School before I get out of my car. It may seem silly, but it works for me, and it doesn't hurt to share it. I usually pull into the lot between 6:00 and 6:05 A.M. It's dark and there are one or two other cars there as well. It's quiet, especially after I turn off the Beatles or Kinks blasting from my car stereo.

For about a minute, I focus on things that have me worried or sad. You might call it a prayer, or a moment of meditation. But whatever you call it, I take a few moments to pause and just think in the darkness. Perhaps I think of my daughter, who has been struggling with a difficult pregnancy. My wife had not been feeling well, and fortunately tests at the hospital last week indicated that her problem was not a serious one. I know that later today part of the lessons will be interrupted by a ridiculous assessment being given by the school district that will not help the kids. I think of everything possible that could get me down. And I remind myself to leave those problems in the car. They have no place in Room 56. There are kids there with problems far greater than mine, and without the adult sensibilities to handle them. They need a positive, supportive, and happy human being in front of them all the time. There is no room for fatigue, sarcasm, or pessimism in any classroom. It's hard to write a song with bitter fingers, so do your best to recognize the enemy and leave it in the car. Joy must carry the day.

For Your Consideration

- Do not pretend teaching is always a happy experience. Recognize the bitterness that can come from the lack of appreciation and learn to deal with it rather than whine about it.

- Develop the ability to have amnesia and forget bad moments. When a difficult parent or colleague does something insensitive or awful to you, feel bad about it for a few minutes and then move on. Stewing about the craziness of the job won't help you or your kids.

- It's not an exact science, but be careful about doing too much for your students. It might feel noble to try to save that one child no one else could reach, but often there is a reason no one succeeded before. Tilt at a few windmills, but if it becomes a habit you might lose the desire to fix some kids with solvable problems.

- There is a tiny group of teachers whose achievements are recognized by the community and the school district. Unfortunately, most teachers, even outstanding ones, are rarely given their due. Coming to that understanding can help you remain positive and effective. It is nice to be recognized. We all need a thumbs-up from others. Realistically, the greatest satisfaction in teaching is good teaching itself, noticed or not. Remember coach John Wooden's definition of success: peace of mind knowing that you've done your best.

CHAPTER THIRTEEN

Middle Man

There's an old bit of wisdom passed along among teachers and it bears repeating. When asked "What do you teach?" many class leaders will answer with something like "I teach first grade" or "I teach high school physics." With some experience under your belt, you come to learn that there is a wiser answer: "I teach students."

For many beginning teachers that is not always the case. Most of us thrown in front of the children spend a lot of time thinking about the subject being taught and additional time thinking about ourselves. When you've worked extremely hard to be interesting and pour your last ounce of energy into each day, there's nothing to be ashamed of if you collapse at home thinking about your many failures and your badly bruised ego. When one looks at a teacher's lesson plan book, practically all the notes are about the material being covered.

After a few years of finding one's style and rhythm, good teachers begin to spend more time locked in on the audience rather than on the assignments.

In an age of a standards-based curriculum and a never-ending battery of assessments, anyone who has actually taught school discovers an inconvenient truth: standards may be the same for all ninth graders, but not all ninth graders are the same. Even in a classroom assembled based on previous test scores, grades, or teacher reports, a supposedly homogeneous group of twenty-five students will showcase a remarkable differentiation. It's hard to teach to a huge range of abilities in both scholarship and behavior. Many classrooms contain some students ready to make the jump to college and others whose plans involve jumping out the window.

This past year, for example, I worked with thirty-four fifth graders. Some of them were brilliant students, even classified as gifted. And this classification described not just their ability but their performance. They were bright and happy students who looked forward to school every day.

Wouldn't it be nice to have an entire class like that? No question, but those shining stars constituted only about eight of the thirty-four students. Other students followed the path of least resistance. There were two ten-year-old girls who openly spoke of having their first babies at fifteen, just like their mothers. There was also Michael, a young man who just a few months before joining my class entered the girls' bathroom, assaulted a fourth grader, pinned her to the ground, and spit in her face. Nice.

There are endless ways to work with students. I'd like to share with you *one* way—not *the* way—to approach classroom management that I have found effective. It does not reach everyone. I have never met an honest teacher who believes every student bought what he was selling. But the idea is to reach as many as you can.

As I get to know my class, I mentally place each child into one of three categories. This is a gross oversimplification of establishing a relationship with the kids, but it's a start.

KID ONE

Kid One is the gift from God. He comes to school on time because he loves to learn. He also is highly intelligent and adored by his peers. He is funny, compassionate, and sensitive. Not only is his artwork ready to be hung in a museum but his spare time is spent assisting others. He comes to school early to help set up, and verbally expresses sincere gratitude for the valuable lessons you are teaching him.

His parents contact you the first week of school. They run a dry-cleaning business and want to let you know that if you ever need your shirts done they would be happy to help. When Kid One's parents come to conferences, they are on time. They know all about the class because they have dinner with their kid every evening and have meaningful conversations about the importance of education. When you make suggestions, they are eager to work with you to help their fabulous child do even better. At the end of the conference they give you a beautiful letter of appreciation and stop by the principal's office to let him know that they feel blessed to have you as their child's teacher. After their child leaves your class, the whole family returns several times a year to donate funds to help the newer students buy important supplies.

Stop laughing. If you think you're reading a fairy tale, I have had students do everything described here. Having Kid One is a fairy tale, but it doesn't end happily ever after. Do you know why? Because just a few seats away is Kid Three.

KID THREE

Kid Three hates you. Actually, Kid Three hates everyone and everything. He misses more school than he attends. No teacher has ever been able to motivate him. He is mean, ominous looking, and a downright threat to anyone within his reach. Either with words or with fists, Kid Three can't be in a classroom for more than a few minutes before causing such awful distractions that he can ruin an entire day. Teachers dread having him in class. So do his peers. He smells bad and intentionally does disgusting things. One day during math class he intentionally sticks an M&M so far up his nose that an ear, nose, and throat specialist has to be called in to remove it.

Kid Three lives with his mother. He has not seen his father since he was a baby. You call his mother several times to try to sit down with her and come up with a plan to help her son. You remain positive and say everything professionally and positively. She hangs up on you but not until she has screamed two words into the phone. That's right, she has listened to your genuine concern and offered the universal suggestion.

But you are undaunted. When she refuses to come for a conference, you finally get her to agree to let you come over to her house to talk. Her nephew is there to help at the meeting. He is drunk and tattooed all over his shirtless torso with gang insignias. He gets in your face and threatens that if you ever bother his little cousin he will kill you and urinate on your grave.

You might be laughing in a different way than you did at the fairy tale known as Kid One. But the nightmare of Kid Three is no dream. It's a composite picture, but I have had all these things happen to me.

And this brings us to the point of the Man in the Middle—Kid Two. Most teachers spend practically all their time with Kid One or Kid Three. It's great to spend time with Kid One because it's fun. He's funny and smart and enthusiastic and appreciative and it can temporarily remove all the pain that can accompany a day of teaching. The usual alternative is to spend enormous amounts of time with Kid Three, because he is destroying the rhythm of the classroom and no one is learning and having fun. It is normal for a teacher to spend 90 percent of his time with Kid One or Kid Three. But I have learned to direct the majority of my efforts toward Kid Two. My favorite kid is Kid Two.

KID TWO

Kid Two appears to be average. He never raises his hand. He comes to school and completes his assignments without ever being noticed. He does not have behavioral issues. He does what he is told, but he does not engage you in a real conversation.

Kid Two has nice parents. At a conference, Mom and Dad listen, sign the attendance list to make a record of their participation, and are never heard from again. These parents do not go to the school office to complain about anything. If their child has a teacher who is clearly substandard, they tell their child to do the best he can. Kid Two passes his standardized tests, and is considered to be at grade level. His file describes him as a good kid, but no adult has ever inquired about his hobbies, favorite bands, or what he does when the school day is over. His essays are bland but basically grammatically correct, so a few comments are written until it's time to turn in another insipid piece of writing. He gets 70 percent of his math right, and is ignored because two kids who got 35 percent correct demand your attention. Kid Two gets passed through the system without raising any dust.

These are the kids I spend time with. There is a Kid One inside many of them. It's just that no one has ever developed him.

I talk to such kids a lot, both in class and during breaks. By week two, I might say the following to a girl as I hand back her paper: "Cynthia, has anyone ever told you that you are a terrific writer?" A silent head shakes no. "Well, you are on your way. This essay you wrote is much better than the one from last week. What did you have for breakfast? Whatever it was, keep eating it. You know, Steinbeck was just a kid once, too."

This is not false praise. I simply tell the child that her work is improving, and that I am excited because I believe her next bit of written work will be even better. I feign shock that other teachers did not mention that Kid Two sings well or is meticulous in her presentation of assignments.

After being a wallflower, Kid Two becomes so excited because someone has taken notice. Never underestimate the power of simply paying attention and offering honest praise. When this happens, the Kid Twos of the world begin to act and perform like Kid Ones. In the early part of this journey, many students are so happy that a teacher has noticed them that they fall into the trap of the third stage of Kohlberg's six stages of moral development. That is, they work hard to please the teacher. It's not catastrophic, but as the year continues, remind such students that you are simply a bystander. Eventually, these enthusiastic students will see that they are not working for you but for themselves.

Pay a lot of individual attention to these undiscovered jewels. In math, they often get from 70 to 75 percent of the questions right. Because they are considered proficient, their teachers have paid them little mind because the kids who are failing miserably need extra help and guidance. I tell the kids that if they are getting 70 percent of a test right, it indicates that they basically understand the material. In fact, I explain, if they understand most of the material, it indicates to me that they are closer to 95 or 100 percent than they believe. But I believe. I tell them I believe strongly.

I advise them to internalize Marion Wright Edelman's suggestion to "assign yourself." As I do not give a lot of homework, they could practice extra math at home. I ask them to recite to me some extra things they could do. Kids learn to say that they could do a few extra problems that are printed at the back of their books. They could redo some of the practice pages they have done. And, best of all, they realize they could make up their own problems to solve. Because such assignments are not forced upon them but created by the students, they work longer and with more purpose than they would on assignments that were shoved down their throats.

Just last year, when my students took the dreaded California standards test, I tracked all of my Kid Twos. It is said that if students improve from the year before by at least seven points, progress has been made. The Kids Twos increased their averages by more than *eighty* points. Many of them got perfect scores after two days of the math assessment. They are not Kid Twos anymore. Someone paid attention and that led to excitement, self-confidence, and measurable differences.

Most teachers have stood in front of a class asking questions and either thought or expressed, "Now, let's not always see the same hands." Usually, Kid Ones dominate class participation and discussion. This will change as the year goes on, and far more hands will be raised. The Kid Twos learn that you believe in them, and now they believe in themselves, too. Their arms get exercised and their voices heard for the first time in their school careers.

There is a bonus that comes with focusing on the Kid Twos: an aftershock affects the Kid Threes, who find themselves suddenly outnumbered. In the past, when Kid Three planned to disrupt the class, Kid Two was often the target or a reluctant collaborator. With the Kid Twos so engrossed in their assignments, the Kid Threes have nowhere to direct their negative energy.

With the three-kid approach, several positive things can happen. Kid Ones will continue to soar. These kids always do well, even if their brilliance gets a little less attention. Eventually they play a new role in class. While you are giving extra help to a Kid Two, have a Kid One work with a Kid Three. Kid Three learns that the classmates he used to despise are actually nice people who care about him. It is not the job of a top student to spend all his time being your special helper; great achievers need to spend most of their day going far beyond the basic assignments. But to spend a few minutes a day assisting someone in need helps both the top student and the one mired on the bottom. During this time, a teacher is freed up to address the Middle Man, who won't be stuck in the middle much longer.

There is a sad truth about Kid Three. Most students who are far behind did not get there simply because of a lack of ability.

Hostile and disruptive students usually bring all sorts of baggage to the classroom. Their lives of struggle did not happen overnight. A check of past records will normally show a pattern of scholastic failure for a long time despite the help of teachers who cared. With the Kid Twos showing what is possible, Kid Threes may begin to discover that they can do the work. The reality is that a Kid Three may do much better in your class, only to fall down in the future when he is in a culture that does not create the possibility of success. However, if a teacher can at least show a troubled youngster a glimpse of the possibility, there is still hope.

Some teachers love the challenge of rescuing a Kid Three from the depths of despair. The challenge to get a kid moving whom no one else seemed able to reach is both an admirable and an essential part of teaching. Just know that while you are spending many hours with a student who may be beyond your help, there is a Kid Two sitting quietly, saying nothing, and moving on toward an ordinary life. Kid Twos matter just as much. Go after the middle, and the odds increase that everyone in the class will do better as a result of your aiming your focus where few have looked before.

For Your Consideration

- Early in the year, take a careful look at the students. Find the kids with ability who are in the middle. Make an effort to call on them in class when you know they know the answer.
- Have a couple of private conversations with Kid Twos to make sure they know you believe in them.
- Make sure Kid Three knows he is one of many and will not get more attention than other children. He must understand that you care, but that other students matter as well.
- If a Kid Three confides his sad story to you, show empathy but explain that everyone has problems. You believe he can over-

come his situation, and you have seen many students do so. Be kind but firm.

- Try assigning a Kid One to be a guardian angel for a Kid Three. Make sure Kid Three has his phone number and access to him so that he knows he has somewhere to go at all times for help.

- Make sure your students measure their progress against their own past performances, not other people's. Teach them that there will always be a faster runner, better writer, or more accurate calculator of math. Show them by their previous work that they are getting better, and do not hold up other kids' work in front of them.

- Never give up. Your students will if you do. Have a goal that one day you will receive a letter from a student that will say "You believed in me before I believed in myself."

CHAPTER FOURTEEN

Leave Some Children Behind

Leave no child behind.

It's a lovely sentiment. It's one of those righteous expressions that belongs on the wall with *Clean water for all* and *Cancer is a bad thing.* No one wants to leave a child behind.

But we should. Some children need to be left behind. Not the ones who are struggling with the material, or whose problems make focused learning difficult, but there are students who have not earned the right to move forward.

We have created situations where children do not understand that actions have consequences. School systems, under fire from all corners, have become desperate to please everyone. In doing so, they hurt the very children they are supposed to be helping.

If we stand in the shoes of a child in today's school system, it is easy to see how a ten-year-old has internalized a sense of entitlement. He did not have to apply to go to his public school. His only requirement for admission was to live in the neighborhood. He wakes up in the morning and saunters into school, where he receives a free breakfast. When the 8:00 bell rings, he is rounded up to get to class. If he does not have materials, paper and pencil are frequently handed out. Books are free. Hopefully, he will do his best during the morning sessions, but even if he is rude to his teacher and mean to his peers, he is given a free lunch at 12:15 P.M.

Even the most incorrigible children get to keep coming. The most serious consequence for unacceptable behavior is usually a scolding from an administrator or a teacher. The effects of such punishments wear off quickly.

When it comes to tough love, I learned my lesson the hard way. When I was a very young teacher, I dreamed of taking my class to Washington, D.C. At the time, my school ran on a year-round schedule, which meant my students were on break from school in November. It's a fantastic month to take kids to our nation's capital. The weather is beautiful, the crowds are gone, and the kids spend glorious autumn days learning about their country and discovering the beauty of our nation.

My first attempt to take students seemed to get off on the right foot. A supervisor downtown even wrote my class a personal check to help make the trip happen. I made many mistakes on this initial adventure. Our itinerary was too full, and I had not yet learned to be flexible if the weather didn't cooperate. Still, I did a few things right. The kids were well prepared both scholastically and socially. They were ready to fly on a plane, stay in a hotel, and ride public transportation with courtesy and confidence.

But I made one huge mistake. My principal called me into his office a couple of weeks before the trip. A parent had complained because I was not taking her child. Ironically, this child had a biblical name, but I assure you, any connection between his namesake and his character ended there. This child was the terror of the school, refused to do the most basic of assignments, and berated staff and classmates with language that would be deemed inappropriate in a brothel.

I explained to my boss that this trip was taking place during my break and that I had followed district procedure in planning the excursion. I had filled out every form, received permission from all the right people, and pinned down every last detail. The district and parents had signed papers acknowledging that this was a private trip not connected with Hobart School, and that participation was based solely on teacher authority. However, my principal asked me as a favor to him to take the boy. I knew it wasn't a good idea. But when I took into consideration the dozens of times my school leader had supported, encouraged, and helped me, I felt that doing him a favor to help him out with a difficult parent was the right thing to do. I was dead wrong.

When we arrived at our hotel in Washington, I placed the child with all the problems in a room with three of my most dependable guys. They woke up around 2:00 A.M. to find their roommate going through their luggage and stealing clothing, wallets, and cash I had given them. Clearly, I should have listened to my own instincts and not brought this student on the trip. He had not done anything to earn it in the first place, and even if he had, he was obviously not ready to be on the road with his classmates.

To double my pleasure, I returned from the trip to receive a mild reprimand from my principal and a tirade from the boy's mother. They felt my punishment to the child was too harsh. Because he was caught stealing, I did not allow him to go into any of the shops in the national monuments and museums we visited. Although I never raised my voice to this student or humiliated him in any way, I told him that he was not ready to go shopping and would remain with me while his peers bought postcards and books. As the mother was cursing me, I couldn't help but think that something much larger was at play here. Is it any wonder that we have so many children who do not understand that actions have consequences? I was being yelled at for reasonably disciplining a thief.

The lesson I learned on this trip is hard but fair: some children need to be left behind. With experience, whether it is simply while they are playing baseball on the playground or spending a Saturday afternoon at an art gallery, my students know beyond a shadow

LEAVE SOME CHILDREN BEHIND | 163

of a doubt that their actions determine their participation. Once I incorporated this thinking into my classroom management, two things happened.

First, it forced me to be a better communicator. Before any activity, I make sure the students know the consequences of various actions. The science experiment or baseball game begins after students have been reminded that unacceptable behavior means exclusion from the activity. The lesson begins after the students, and not their teacher, explain what is expected of them. Yelling or insulting a teammate or the opposition means the player is out for that day. Playing around with science equipment means that child's team will have one less participant for that day's discoveries. I have had observers comment on this. A few have said that since Billy did not participate in the science experiment, he might not learn the important skill the other children learned. You know what? He might not. However, a far more important lesson was learned.

Almost a year before the trip to Washington, D.C., the students are invited to prepare for their week in the capital. Along the way, a dozen things might happen that will remove them from the trip. Obviously, they must do well in history and be outstanding citizens to get on the plane. Subtler still, the kids must demonstrate that they have the emotional maturity to make the cross-country voyage. If I constantly have to ask for a child's attention, even if he is a brilliant scholar he'll get a postcard and not a plane ticket. I explain to the parent that if her son does not listen all the time in class, failure to listen as we cross a street could be a very serious safety issue. I care about my students, and those who are still developing listening skills are not going to be safe three thousand miles from home.

There is a second outcome that will happen in class once a teacher has decided to leave children behind. A wonderful sense of calm will rain down over the class. Much of a teacher's stress is based on making sure each child is on task and achieving scholastic nirvana every day. A relaxed teacher does not panic when a student is left behind. I'm not advocating that we easily give up on a kid who is chewing gum in class or has missed an assignment; we teachers need to try everything and anything to engage and motivate every child to participate and take advantage of our valuable lessons. That said, when a student is not following the program, don't take it personally. Keep calm in the knowledge that your job is to open the door. If a child is not interested in walking through it, you must accompany the willing ones through and move on. Make sure the door is open for the difficult student every day, but you do not have time to coax and beg him along when thirty others have crossed the river and are ready to enter the Promised Land.

BOBBY, ISRAEL, AND CHRIS

I have been listening to students for three decades, and there is a pattern to their reasonable complaints about school. They are bored and disgusted with meaningless homework assignments. They think about (but are often afraid to question) those they perceive to be unfair teachers and ridiculous rules. Students despise being yelled at. But right near the top of their complaint hit parade is the frustration over waiting—the dozens of days their entire class sat in boredom because one or two students were behaving badly or not paying attention. This is what can happen if we literally adopt the concept of leaving no child behind.

On the first day of class I invite the kids to sit wherever they like. I often smile and ask them if their parents advised them not to sit with their friends. I laugh as most of the hands go up. I put them at ease and encourage them to sit with their buddies. "After all," I remark, "it's better to sit with your friends than with your enemies." The kids learn quickly that laughter is allowed in our class. I do caution them, however, that we have a lot of work to do.

I tell them I believe that they are capable of understanding that we cannot let friendships and chatter disturb our understanding of marvelous literature or precision in problem solving. I make sure the kids understand that their seats will be changed if sitting next to a friend prevents them from doing good work. The kids absorb that I am giving them my trust, but they know that with that gift comes a responsibility Over the years, this system of seat assignments has served the class well, resulting in an easy warmth in the room coupled with a tremendous focus.

But one year, I had a trio of boys who forced me to take action quickly. All of them were unwashed and unprepared. They had brought no materials to school on the first day. They sat together in the back of the room with their feet on their desks or folded beneath them on the seats of their chairs. By the time I had said good morning it was painfully obvious to me that thirty-two students knew the basics of paying attention and three did not. I walked over to Chris, who from his demeanor appeared to be the surliest of the bunch, and asked him his name. He told me he didn't have to speak to me "because you're not my fucking teacher."

"Actually," I said calmly, "I am your fucking teacher. My name is Rafe and I would like to know yours."

The first two or three days of class that year were hell. These three "little darlings" interrupted and did everything possible to ruin every lesson. We were far behind my plans by Day 4, and it was time to take action. During those first few days, my observations led me to learn a lot about the trio.

Chris was the leader of a small gang at the school. For the past several years he had spent far more time sitting alone in the school office than in his classroom. His previous teachers threw him out of their rooms most days because he was completely mean, rude, and out of control. When the final bell rang, he went to the after-school day-care group held on campus. The program supposedly helped kids finish homework and provided healthy activities until parents finished work and picked them up. But Chris spent his hours there running with his crew, punching and cursing smaller students.

Israel was the quietest of the three. He lived with his mother, who was rarely home. When I called on him to read, his decoding skills were low but not shockingly awful. However, his writing skills resembled a child who had barely learned the alphabet. He did no homework the first week of school. It appeared that Israel, like so many students, watched the clock and waited for the dismissal bell. He no doubt never thought about school past that moment until he was forced to go back the following morning.

Bobby was the most active, constantly wriggling in his chair. He was the type of child who some would quickly diagnose as having ADHD and recommend medication for. I checked his records to discover that several years ago a conference between our school counselor and his mother had brought up the subject of prescribing drugs, but Mom had turned down that idea.

Bobby and Israel were disruptive and rude in class, but Chris was clearly the ringleader. During a science experiment on the second day, Chris threw a compass at a member of his team. When sharp objects are thrown, it is time to leave a child behind.

Chris had to be separated from his classmates, but I did not want to throw him out of the room. Several things had to be established in his mind quickly and simply. I do not have long conversations with incorrigible youngsters. While it might be satisfying to get to the bottom of a child's anger, like teachers seem to do almost instantly in movies, this is a real book for real teachers. I worked with seventy other students each day, including those in activities I led before school, during recess and lunch, and after school. There might have come a time when Chris and I had a Hollywood moment of discovery/tears/solutions and living happily ever after, but for the immediate moment I had to get the classroom functioning smoothly. Chris needed to understand that he would not prevent that from happening. Yet he also had to learn that he was one of many; we were moving on with our work without him. Whether he would join us was his decision.

I set up a desk in the back of the room where he sat next to no one and could not easily make eye contact with others. Israel and Bobby were moved to the front of the room on opposite sides. By the third day, both boys were left behind in art. Their classmates spent their time after lunch making latch-hook rugs and having a lot of fun while learning about organization, patience, and following directions. Israel and Bobby had spent much of their morning fooling around and did not finish their work in math or history. They also were required to do their homework during art time, as they had not turned in any of their assignments. As they were unable to complete some very simple work at home, they were given class time to complete the work others were turning in daily. Israel expressed his desire to make a rug. I told him that was certainly possible, but first things first. Rug making was for students who had completed their other assignments. Each day the rug with his name on it sat in the corner of the room while others created their projects, and Israel sulked while slowly finishing work others had completed with relish.

The final piece to this strategy involved Chris. He was not allowed to go outside for recess or lunch due to his bullying of other children. I walked him to lunch with the other students but returned with him to the room. I told him that in our society when people cannot coexist with others they are separated. I never raised my voice, uttered a mean word, or used sarcasm. I was kind but firm. I told him he could use the bathroom during recess and lunch, but only accompanied by another student, who would make sure he caused no problems on his way there.

"When can I go out on the playground?" he muttered.

I told him that would be up to his classmates. When he was able to convince them that his behavior had changed they would be the ones to give him back the privilege of rejoining them for games and hanging out. And that was the end of the conversation.

By the fourth week of school, leaving these three behind had brought many positive outcomes for the boys and their classmates. Israel and Bobby always finished their assignments and were participating in class with positive attitudes. They saw the good times the other kids were having and made a decision that joining in was better than being left out. Their classmates complimented them, genuinely excited to see peers succeed when they had been previously known as bad influences. Better still, their antics and disruptive behavior disappeared. Their finished rugs were stunning.

And finally there was Chris. He was allowed back on the playground about four months into the year, when his classmates gave him one more chance. He wound up back in the classroom a week later, having reduced a girl to tears by calling her vulgar names. His mother promised to help her son by encouraging kindness, but that was the only time she came to school. She did not even come to his graduation ceremony.

But Chris did reach grade level in all his subjects. He still occasionally disrupted the class, but he enjoyed our reading sessions. Eventually Chris completed all his work, earning him the right to create art projects. His test scores improved dramatically, even in science, where he rarely participated because of his propensity to fight with other students. Simply being in the room and watching science from a distance was better for him than being isolated in the principal's office.

A terrific substitute once took my class for a day and told me when I returned that she could not believe the change in Chris. She said I had transformed him, but I do not believe this to be true. The harsh reality hasn't changed: the chance for Chris to be a successful, happy, and contributing member of society is still a long shot. But for one year he did learn and function in a classroom. He never missed a day of school and was at least given an opportunity to see an alternative way to behave. He was often left behind, but he was never left out. And it might ultimately make a difference.

Several years ago, a reporter from a national magazine came to do a story on Room 56, spending most of her day observing the class and visiting with the children. Early in the afternoon, I was at the front of the room going over a student's essay while others were working on various writing projects. She was standing in the back corner of the room talking with one of the girls about her experiences. The reporter suddenly fell down on her knees laughing hysterically.

When she had dried her tears and composed herself, I asked her what was so funny. It seems she had said to the girl, "I need to ask you something. You kids *really* focus on your teacher. Rafe doesn't raise his voice. In fact he has a very soft tone, but you all really tune in. What's the secret?"

The little girl answered, "Well, ma'am, you have to understand. Rafe doesn't yell or scream, but everyone in our class knows, Don't fuck with Rafe!"

For Your Consideration

- Before beginning an activity, make sure your students know that disruptive behavior will result in being left behind. You are not angry or frustrated. You simply have things to accomplish and cannot be sidetracked by anyone who is not with the program.
- Constantly invite students to comment on the rules of your class. Kids do not mind a tough teacher but they despise an unfair one. When students feel they are a part of the creation of the boundaries, they are more likely to stay within those lines.
- When leaving a child behind, always make sure he knows there is a way out. In the same way he must understand why

he is being left behind, he must just as clearly see that a change in his behavior will result in being part of the group again. If the door is not left open, the student has no motivation to do better.

- When a student has to be removed, always have an assignment or ongoing project he should be working on. Spend very little time discussing the situation with the youngster being left behind. He needs to see that you (and his classmates) have work to do.

- Never show anger or be sarcastic when leaving a child out of an activity. Smile, stay calm, and go on with your work. No student should believe he has that much power over your emotions. He does not run your class. You do.

CHAPTER FIFTEEN
Eyes Wide Open

There is never enough time.

As you have learned in your formative years teaching, it is truly impossible to effectively cover the curriculum given the limited hours and days allotted. Every teacher's situation is different, but for the sake of having a reference point, here is the official program of instruction at my elementary school. According to the Los Angeles Unified School District, teachers need to cover all the material for the fifth grade within this schedule.

8:00	School begins
10:45	Recess break
11:05	Students return to class
12:15	Lunch break
12:55	Students return to class
2:19	School is dismissed

A simple bit of addition will reveal that if every available second is used, teachers have five hours and nine minutes with their students each day. Of course this is not true. One day a week the students are released an hour early so the teachers can attend professional development meetings. Students are often out of the classroom for orchestra and chorus classes. Struggling students are pulled out of class for hours at a time to go to other teachers for remediation. There are assemblies, fire drills, and a dozen other interruptions. Realistically, many teachers actually see their entire class for two to three hours a day, and on many occasions less than that. In addition, there are at the very minimum seventy-five to one hundred hours of state testing during the year that interrupts instructional time.

Within this schedule, here is the district's proscribed daily curriculum for every teacher:

- Three hours of the school's reading program
- One hour of mathematics
- Twenty minutes of physical education
- Science
- United States history
- Health
- Art
- Safety
- Work habits and citizenship

And, of course, good teachers often go beyond the daily schedule to have lunch with a student, schedule an extra tutoring session, or write a letter of recommendation. But even when you don't go the extra mile, the numbers just don't add up. And because it is actually impossible to accomplish what is being asked of us, we must be careful to spend our time wisely and effectively.

This is where using caution can guide us. Think of a flashing yellow light on the highway telling drivers to slow down and beware of a hazard. This sort of caution can help us to use our time where we can do the most good. The flashing yellow lights are everywhere, but they get easier to see after experience sharpens our vision. Parents, fellow teachers, and the kids themselves can intentionally or accidentally shine a light on the best ways to direct your time and effort.

By the growing-up period of your career, you will have most likely taken a close look at your schedule to try to squeeze in as much teaching as you can. With the constant pressure of time, good teachers always fret about the quickening hourglass with its precious grains of sand slipping away. In my early years of teaching, I often missed or ignored caution signs and wasted minutes, hours, days, and even years trying to support a student who was beyond my ability to help.

AN UNNECESSARY DISASTER

An extreme but true example of ignoring a warning happened during my early years of teaching. One of my students, Susie, was well known for having a mother who was a classic helicopter parent. Mom was at school constantly, carrying her child's backpack and musical instrument, bringing her a special lunch daily, and gossiping with anyone who would listen about the brilliance and extraordinary ability of her daughter. Her child was a wonderful violinist.

Mom was constantly hovering at my door, but never to help the class. If the students were spending Saturday afternoon at an art museum because a terrific exhibition of Magritte was on display, Susie was the first student signed up. However, her mother never offered to help drive or pack some refreshments for the trip. Other teachers bemoaned this parent's behavior.

I did not want my dislike of a meddling parent to have any bearing on my work with Susie, a perfectly capable student. In fact, I foolishly thought that I might subtly rescue Susie from a life in the shadow of whirring chopper blades. The mother was of course an obvious flashing yellow light, but in addition Susie's peers gave her somewhat of a wide berth.

Mom created problems for me at our first parent conference. She was upset that Susie did not have a perfect report card. She told me that her daughter was not only the most talented but also the most popular child in the school. This was not even close to the truth, but I still wanted to include Susie in the after-school Shakespeare program. A child doesn't get to choose her mother, and she did play the violin beautifully.

The kids complained constantly about Susie. She would poke her peers offstage and even try to trip them up on entrances. My eyes were not wide open; they were practically closed to the obvious fact that this child deserved my best effort during regular school hours, but no more.

During a rehearsal in the middle of the year, a student tripped during a dance and hurt her arm. It was a sprain and required her to wear a sling for three days. Susie's mother went to the principal and complained that my class was a dangerous place and that I was not fit to teach. She also called every parent in the school to warn them of my incompetence.

We made it through the year. The show was terrific, but I paid a price that was too high. Susie should not have been in the show. I spent dozens of hours dealing with a mother who should have been avoided. Time is too precious. I fell into Richard II's dilemma: I wasted time, and it wasted me.

GROWING UP

The beauty of teaching is that we can learn from our mistakes. In my early years, I almost certainly missed signs of trouble, blind spots that sometimes prevented me from being an effective teacher. Cathy and Anthony were in my class years later, when I had become far more aware of warning signs, and it made a difference.

At first, a teacher would most likely notice Cathy before Anthony. She was tall, slender, pretty, and had an outgoing personality. She was a very good student who was always ready for school. Anthony glowered constantly and mumbled when spoken to. During our year together, Cathy quickly earned a lead part in our Shakespeare play. She had a fine speaking voice, and was also an outstanding singer. Anthony did not want to be in the play.

But being in a play or having natural talent does not mean a student is worthy of extra attention, no matter how dazzling she might be. As our year went on, two warning lights told me to use caution in giving too much attention to Cathy. One appeared when students went places after school or on weekends—Cathy was never invited. Even when some of the friendliest and most sensitive kids were simply walking down the street to the bakery after school, Cathy was not part of the group. As this was not my business, I never asked why. I simply observed. I thought it might be due to the fact that Cathy's mother was an extremely loud talker and school gossip. Perhaps the kids did not like her mother and Cathy was collateral damage.

Within the confines of school Cathy was always treated with respect. Her peers were friendly to her as they were to every member of the class. But they did not go out of their way to include her when the school bell rang. In time I learned why. Cathy did not possess that generosity of spirit that makes a person attractive to those around her. She followed her mother's lead in confusing reputation and character; Cathy was more concerned with what people thought of her rather than who she really was. The kids had known her for years and had seen too much self-centeredness to invite her into the inner circle.

On the other hand, Anthony flew under the radar at the beginning of the year. His father was the only parent in his life, the mother having fled the scene years earlier. It showed. There was hardness to this young man that a casual observer might have misinterpreted as rudeness or apathy. However, in the safe haven that the classroom provided, Anthony slowly warmed to the options around him. Eventually, he joined several of the extracurricular activities offered.

Cathy had much higher grades. I knew all about her life because she constantly began conversations with me and wrote letters as well. But Anthony would stay late to sweep the room. He never asked for recognition for his extra work. With glacial speed, he began to open up to me over the months. I slowly gained an understanding of his life, dreams, and frustrations. Cathy was a more gregarious student but experience had pried my eyes wide open. She was a good student, but a superficial one. Anthony may not have been as likable, but he planned to help his father in years to come, and quietly expressed care and concern for his classmates. If the time and opportunity presented itself, this was a young man with whom I might want to put in a little extra time and effort.

At the end of fifth grade, I make an offer to interested students to come back to class Saturday mornings to continue studying Shakespeare, vocabulary, and algebra. Most students do not do this, as they are moving on with other activities and interests. During the summer, I received a panicked phone call from Cathy's mother. Despite several meetings for parents offered by both our school and my classroom, Cathy's mother had failed to turn in a form to the school district that would have allowed her daughter to attend a magnet school. There was a particular school that would have been a good fit for Cathy, as it offered excellent programs and was a ten-minute bus ride from her neighborhood. Many of Cathy's peers had followed instructions and were accepted into the program.

During the phone call, Cathy's mother made two urgent requests of me. She asked me to call the school to see if I could use my influence to get them to allow her daughter in after the deadline had passed. She also asked me not to mention anything to her daughter, because she did not want Cathy to be furious with her. The mother's request of me to be secretive with her own child was enough of a warning light for me to help them as much as I could without going overboard. I made the call to a friend I had at the magnet, who found room for Cathy at the school without preventing any other student from attending. In years past, I might have also reminded the mother that Cathy had an opportunity to continue studying on Saturdays if she was looking for some advanced challenges for her daughter. I did not make the offer. Cathy had a good year with me, and I helped open the door for what might be other good years to come. But enough was enough.

Anthony finished that year and went to the local middle school, a struggling facility known for excessive violence and classrooms with weary teachers struggling to keep order. Two weeks into the year, Anthony showed up back in my class one day after school. When I asked him how things were going, he told me he missed fifth grade. When I pressed him, he told me that what he missed most of all was "nice kids." I mentioned to him that he could still work with our class on Saturday mornings, but he did not jump at the chance. It was not his style. Two years later, Anthony has never missed a Saturday morning. His work is extraordinary. He is not the leader of the class, but he is constantly invited to play soccer with the other guys, and his work in middle school is letter perfect. Both Cathy and Anthony are doing well in school these days, and that's a good thing. Better still, experience had helped me read the signs correctly, put some extra time in where it would be effective, and help a young man improve his lot in life.

He did not know it at the time, but Anthony caught my attention by passing what I call the Peter Mack test. You might like to try it with your students, as I do with mine. It helps me decide which student gets the extra fifteen minutes when fifteen minutes are all I have.

THE PETER MACK TEST

Peter Mack is a brilliant educator and mentor at Cate Boarding School in Carpinteria, California. He has a lovely wife and three beautiful kids. The students at his school are treated like his own children. They know him, admire him, and trust him. He is the sort of educator who makes you wish you were back in school in his class.

Thousands of kids apply to this elite high school, and Peter once told me about his personal litmus test for spotting students who would benefit from extra time. When he enters the lunchroom, he enjoys walking over to a table and simply sitting down with a group of students. At his school, practically all the students are bright and well mannered. He mentally divides them into two groups. Most of the kids engage him in polite and polished conversation. These kids are terrific, engaging, and headed for good things.

But some kids do more. They do not engage in conversation because they are polite or well schooled. Some kids are truly interested in an exchange of ideas. These kids show a real curiosity in what he has to say, and are equally interested in sharing their passions and beliefs with him. They argue, challenge, and laugh with him. They do not change their behavior or pattern of speech as he approaches the table. They are real. Anthony was like this. His demeanor never changed when I sat with him. He never turned on or off. And as a result, I was able to understand his needs better than some students who might have had more polish but less soul.

Before your efforts go beyond your best, think about the Peter Mack test. Keep your eyes wide open, and look for flashing lights that signal caution before you make the home visit or a call on behalf of a student. Your time is limited, and seeing things clearly help you make every second count.

For Your Consideration

- There will never be enough time to accomplish what you hope to do. It is usually impossible to carry out the curriculum assigned by the district. The unending problems and hurdles placed in front of a classroom teacher guarantee that you will not be able to help and reach every child to the degree you would like.

- Be very careful when you devote time to extra projects. It can be discouraging and even heartbreaking to spend your time trying to help a student with whom failure is a certainty. Stay alert for flashing yellow lights in your use of time.

- A student in need should be given your best efforts and attention. However, a student in need should not be given hours outside of your normal schedule unless you believe that your extra effort will produce real results.

- Use the Peter Mack test when deciding to spend extra hours helping a student. His need for your assistance is not enough. Look for a sign that the student is seeking help. Deciding unilaterally to save a student can result in not helping him at all, and possibly denying another student valuable assistance that could change his life.

- All teachers strike out. You will give extra effort unsuccessfully many times in your career. It hurts. But you still need to get up to bat and swing. Keeping your eyes wide open simply improves your vision to swing at better pitches.

CHAPTER SIXTEEN
The Soft Sell

There's a silly conversation the kids and I enjoy having in Room 56 in which they are constantly reminded to leave stage-three thinking behind. This refers to the third stage of Kohlberg's stages of moral development. Level-three thinkers behave in a way that pleases others. Kids are often trained to please their teachers, but this is a mistake. What they think of their art project is more important than what I think of it.

To make the point, once or twice a week a child will ask me for a favor. Before I say yes or no, we have a little conversation. Eugene might come up to me in the middle of a math lesson.

> **Eugene:** Rafe, may I go to the bathroom? I know we were supposed to go at recess but I didn't have to then and now I do. Can I please go?
>
> **Rafe:** That depends on your answering a few questions. Who is the smartest person you know?
>
> **Eugene:** (smiling because he knows what's coming) Rafe.
>
> **Rafe:** (The rest of the class has stopped working and giggles.)

Rafe: What is your favorite color?

Eugene: Rafe.

Rafe: Your favorite number?

Eugene: Rafe.

Rafe: What name will you give your first daughter?

Eugene: Rafe.

Rafe: Who was the first president of the United States?

Eugene: Rafe.

Rafe: Eugene, you are obviously a brilliant young scholar and you may go to the bathroom.

The class giggles some more, Eugene goes on his way, and everyone goes back to work. But the point is made. There are students who believe the teacher is the center of the universe, and it's ridiculous to think so.

And yet, I do have to be all things to all students, at some level—part of the job is to know what's best for them. During a typical day, one child might hear from me to keep his hands together as he swings a baseball bat. An hour later he might be hearing how his sentence structure should be changed to make his essay more clear. He'll be told that he needs to line up his numbers differently or use a different finger to play a lick on the guitar. During a day of school a student can expect to be constantly corrected by an authority figure who "knows what's right."

There's nothing wrong with this, of course. As professional explainers, we should be showing students the correct way to do all kinds of things. Sometimes, though, a subtle and important line gets crossed. It often happens too easily. There is a difference between teaching a child the right way to perform a skill and telling him who he should be. Giving students valuable information is good; shoving information, or ideas, or behaviors, or even values, down their throats is not. As we mature as teachers, we can see the difference, and in doing so encourage students to listen to our information and use it to form their own opinions.

I used to make this mistake all the time. For many years, I have offered my students an optional activity before school called Math Team. Four days a week students are invited to come to class forty-five minutes early to improve their critical thinking by solving complex and interesting problems. I know in my bones that it is very helpful to the students who participate. As with all quality activities, the kids are learning things that go far beyond problem solving. The very fact that a kid would volunteer to come to school early to do some extra work is a huge statement. He has decided that school matters and he wants to be the best student he can be. As the problems are solved in groups, friendships are formed. The kids learn to cooperate with one another. When students arrive at different solutions, they learn to listen to one another. It's time well spent, and students write to me years later that it was beneficial for them.

But when I began doing this twenty-five years ago, I would browbeat students who did not come early to school. I would say, "Luis, you're making a big mistake. Math Team is something that will really help you. You need to be here early. You should be doing this." If Luis did not show up early, I would remind him on a daily basis that Math Team was available to him and that he should emulate the other students who were taking advantage of this worthwhile opportunity.

While it is true that I often wore down students and convinced them to join, I lost sight of the bigger picture. One of the best things we can do for students is to help them control their own destinies. If we force them to do everything, even good things, how will they know what to do when we are no longer there to tell them? We need to provide a large menu for the kids, but it's best to allow them to order their own food. When I figured this out, I was then able to develop the soft sell, and the benefits this approach has reaped for the kids is incalculable.

These days the options for the students in my class have gone beyond Math Team. Our Film Club allows students to watch classic films after school on Tuesdays, and to borrow films from our extensive library on Fridays. Students can learn to play the guitar during their recess and lunch periods. After school, the biggest commitment of all involves being a part of the year's Shakespeare production.

In all of these offerings, the attendance grows enormously throughout the year with my use of the soft sell. On the first day of school I explain the options to the students and send a letter home to the parents. I never mention the activities again, but make myself available to any students who have questions. As in the film *Field of Dreams,* I follow the "If you build it, they will come" approach. It works remarkably well.

A familiar pattern emerges each year with Math Team. On the first day, about eight students out of a potential thirty-five show up. The team begins at 7:15 A.M. and ends about 7:55. This allows the early birds to stretch and go to the bathroom or get some water before school officially begins. As the kids exit the room to take a break they pass their classmates who are coming to school for the 8:00 A.M. starting time. The students who arrive later notice that the kids who came early had a terrific time. Math has become fun for them, no surprise as our practice avoids the drill-and-kill method presented in many of today's classrooms. Engrossed in challenging, team-oriented, and sometimes downright funny problems, it's a wonderful way for the children to begin their day. Rather than preach this to the students, I allow the team itself to sell the importance of the early session simply by being happy. As the days go on the students who come in early are easily the best math students in the class.

By the third or fourth week of school, dozens of kids have shyly approached me during a free moment and asked, "Can I still join Math Team?"

"Of course you can," I reply happily. The door is always open.

Typically, by the third month of school the vast majority of the kids come early. Best of all, it was a decision they made themselves. The kids feel in control of their lives. The room is filled with willing participants rather than prisoners watching the clock, waiting to escape.

With Film Club, many students do not stay after school on Tuesdays for various reasons. Some cannot because they have family obligations such as taking care of a younger sibling. Still others go to various day-care facilities at the end of the school day and need to leave campus immediately. In every case, I smile and calmly tell the student, "Hey, thanks for telling me. It's no big deal. It's just a little club. I completely understand." I do not extol the merits of the club, which are many. Participants will watch outstanding films while improving listening and writing skills. It's a fabulous party atmosphere every Tuesday afternoon.

On Friday mornings, before school begins, the kids in Film Club check out movies to take home for the weekend. Several of the kids borrow a film they plan to watch together. Whether it's *The Man Who Shot Liberty Valance, The Empire Strikes Back, The Wizard of Oz,* or *March of the Penguins,* the students who have not joined the club watch this activity as they enter to begin their school day

Almost immediately, kids come and tell me they would like to join. "What about your little sister?" I ask. Without exception, every student who felt he was unable to attend found a solution to the problem. Tuesday afternoons are packed with filmgoers in the classroom, and their viewing etiquette is impeccable. Indeed, they mention to me that they are discouraged by the noisy habits of today's movie theater audiences. Students who decide on their own to be a part of something are more likely to "own" good behavior because nothing was forced on them. I can leave the room for two hours while thirty children watch a film silently, and not because they fear getting in trouble or because of a rule written on the wall. They have created a culture by and for themselves.

The same casual offer is the centerpiece of motivation within traditional lessons. To be sure, I play hardball with some basic skills that must be learned. From the first day of class, the students are offered an enormous variety of learning opportunities, including art, music, science, history, and drama. However, they are told that these are not all equal. I certainly hope all students learn about Thomas Jefferson and the Louisiana Purchase. Realistically, however, a student going on to middle school will not suffer horribly if he does not understand Jefferson's contributions to the nation. If it comes down to Jefferson versus understanding how to read and write a paragraph, the language skills trump the author of the Declaration of Independence.

During the first few weeks of school several students simply do not do their work. These students fall behind and end up spending their day finishing their essential projects while others move on to Thomas Jefferson and building rockets. In most cases, it is the struggling students who come to me and ask why they do not get to play history games or build scale models of the solar system. They are informed that they *can* participate when their basic work is done. I never humiliate lazy students or use sarcasm even though the temptation is strong to do so. This takes a lot of patience, as there are times we want to scream at a lazy child to get off his rear end and finish his work. This might work in the short term, but with patience and a soft sell it is the student who will come to understand that good work will lead to even better times in school.

My first book, published many years ago, was called *There Are*

No Shortcuts, and that phrase still decorates a banner that hangs in the front of our classroom. When I ask visiting teachers what it means to them, they tell me that it's a reminder to students that nothing comes easily. Mastering a skill or achieving a difficult goal takes thousands of hours. They want their students to internalize the realization that in our fast-food society, good things take time.

True, but *There are no shortcuts* is not just a reminder to students. It is for teachers as well. Despite the pressure we are all under to get immediate results and to turn troubled kids around instantly, that is not going to happen. Children five years behind in reading are not going to become brilliant readers in one year. This is a long process and we should not be in too much of a hurry. Using the soft sell reminds us to take our time while helping the student make productive decisions. If we can get a student to truly commit to the joy of learning and self-improvement, the possibility of a successful journey increases exponentially. The soft sell is the cornerstone of how I help students take charge of their own lives. It takes more time and patience, but its long-term effect is worth the wait.

For Your Consideration

- The language you use is crucial when communicating with students. It's not easy, but make sure you are giving the student facts rather than your opinion. This is about his life and his decisions, so avoiding your personal opinions removes you from the equation. Think of Atticus Finch, who raised his children with "courteous detachment."

- Never close the door. If a student does not want to do something, make sure he knows that he can join something later. If the door is shut he has no motivation to follow the path you hope he chooses.

- As you mature and improve as a teacher, try to add options to your class every year, ranging from extra credit assignments to special field trips. The student is more likely to find something he wants to eat if there is more on the menu.

- Respect all the students who choose not to participate in extra activities. Students who do extra things should not be treated as special, or in any way differently, when regular class activities are going on.

- Make sure a student who chooses to do something extra is doing it because *he* wants to participate. Get to know your students' motivations. Many students join the after-school Shakespeare program I run because their parents believe it is good for them. Students who do extra activities for you, their parents, or their peers are destined not to reap the benefits you are working so hard to instill. Feel free to ask a student why he is joining an activity. If it is for someone else, make sure he knows it's only an option and he should not do anything because of outside forces.

CHAPTER SEVENTEEN

Tomorrow, and Tomorrow, and Tomorrow

Good teachers employ a secret weapon to help their students reach great heights. It is rarely mentioned at professional development meetings, and that's a shame. Every teacher who has taught for more than five years has this effective tool at his or her disposal, and best of all it's free. And I've got that secret weapon, too.

Room 56 is a successful classroom for many reasons. It has terrific kids, many supportive parents, and many professionals at the school site who have helped make it a fabulous place to learn, have fun, and develop character. But by far the most important factor in the success of the class is its many alumni.

Former students are the most powerful force at work in Room 56. The middle schoolers drop by several times a week to visit, help clean the room, and grade papers. High school students bring the kids candy on Halloween and return to watch the Shakespeare plays in June. Adults mentor the kids and make financial contributions. Former students are the glue that holds the class together.

As teachers, we have a vision for what our students can be. We believe they can develop a strong work ethic, use their creativity to change the world, and walk through doors that were previously closed to them. Often students do not share this vision. How can they? It's nice when your students have college-educated parents who sit down with their children every night at a family dinner. Such evenings can be the springboard that instills the values that shape and mold kids into future superstars. But the majority of our students do not have this luxury. Many students do not even have a family dinner, if they have dinner at all. Many grow up in neighborhoods where violence, drugs, and gangs are the norm. When the reality of their lives turns kids into young cynics, even a dedicated and interesting teacher is swimming upstream.

Chefs on cooking shows usually try to grab your attention by telling you that they are going to make something special and often show you the finished dish in advance. It looks fantastic. For the rest of the show, the viewer is taught how to get there. While ingredients are mixed and cooking techniques are demonstrated, we already have the vision of what the finished product will look like. We are willing to absorb all the information about the preparation of the food because we know that something scrumptious waits. We have seen the vision.

But many of our young students have never seen the vision. It's all well and good for a teacher to urge students to set a goal of going to college. But realistically, if that kid doesn't know anyone who's been to college and has no idea what college is like, it's hard for him to listen. To him it seems like a pipe dream.

Your former students *are* that vision for your current class. They give the pipe dream tangible form. My little fifth graders often hear from peers that school is a waste of time, but this is not the only message they receive. Not a day goes by without some of my former students returning from seventh or eighth grade to say hi and talk with the younger kids. When my current students hear around the neighborhood that nobody cares about school, they know this is not true. They have met students, who look like them and come from their streets, who care about school a lot. These young role models are a far greater influence on the current class than I could ever hope to be. For my current students, simply sitting around and talking with these older kids, or playing catch or strumming guitars with them, is a more effective lesson in life than anything I can show them in a textbook.

Mentors can help shape a new class without even paying a visit. Keep teaching and your collection of letters will grow into a vast wealth of observations that paint a picture of possibilities. Some of the letters might be sad tales, but even those might have a little lesson or some wise advice for those who follow. When a jewel of a letter comes across my desk, I make copies that students carry in their notebooks. This way former students are with the new class even when time and distance has separated them.

TWO CAUTIONARY TALES

Here are two letters you might like to read to your own students. Young adults wrote both of them. A college sophomore wrote the first, and the second was sent from a graduate of one of the nation's elite universities. Both letters, particularly the second, are tinged with some sad truths. When brave students share their mistakes or pain with others, it can help illuminate the road ahead for those who follow.

Cassie was a lovely young girl when she was a fifth grader in Room 56 many years ago. She had a supportive family, and came to school prepared and eager to learn. She was particularly strong in music and was also a good athlete. Friendly and outgoing, she had many friends and what appeared to be the strength of a young person who knows her own mind and would be able to face up to any problems in her future and solve them with ease. The good news is that today she attends a respected university and is quite happy there. However, like so many terrific kids, her adolescent years were not as sunny as she had hoped they would be.

Dear Rafe,

It's Cassie from nine years ago. I hope you are still doing amazing things with the class and that your health is in good condition. I just wanted to encourage you to keep doing what you're doing because you have made a huge impact in my life. In fact, I feel compelled to tell you the top two ways in which you have been a blessing to me.

The first blessing is that you showed me that being nice and working hard was possible, even in an environment where students don't believe in their capabilities. I remember that most of our class was in consensus about this goal, and it was easy to carry it out in the fifth grade.

However, middle school brought about some changes. There were so many people who were immature. So many talked out of turn, and often were just plain mean. I remember thinking, "Why can't we all be mature? We are in middle school, ready to become young adults. It should be the standard that we can follow the rules and be genuinely nice to one another." I was so frustrated that the world that was created for me in fifth grade was collapsing.

But I kept attending Shakespeare and SAT classes with you on Saturdays. I tried to hold on tight to the goal of Be Nice and Work Hard. I tried to stay nice and work hard. I must confess that there were times I did succumb to social pressures in middle school. Still, I made it my truth that being nice and working hard were things that eventually became rooted in my character. Thank you for showing me I could do both things.

The second blessing was to show me a combination of passion and stamina. I have met other teachers with similar passion or a great amount of energy. But none of the teachers I have known so far have both of those in a combination of those two forces working in harmony.

I want to be a teacher like you. I aspire to be a person of influence and help a large number of students keep hope alive in their potential and to grow to be great people.

> With love,
> Cassie

Hearing about adolescence from me is one thing, but reading the words from a student who used to sit in my classroom drives home important information for middle schoolers in ways that even a top teacher cannot.

For high school students going through the often agonizing and frightening college application process, reading a letter from a young woman named Celeste might help them keep their perspective on what really matters. Celeste was never in my class, but she joined the after-school Shakespeare program with her peers. During her middle school years she studied with me on Saturdays and was one of the most gifted writers I have ever had the pleasure to teach. Celeste devoured books and made brilliant contributions during class discussions. Math was a different story. She was not interested in numbers and her grades reflected her distaste for algebra and geometry. Still, her brilliant writing helped her win a scholarship to a private high school known for its artistic and creative teaching staff. Celeste eventually was accepted to a school frequently mentioned as one of the best in the country. I last heard from her in the tenth grade. Her friends told me about her acceptance to college, but Celeste dropped off the radar screen for about eight years.

And then last year I received this letter. It has become required reading for every high school student I know.

Dear Rafe,

Thanks for your last email, and sorry it took me so long to get back to you. And thanks for your offer to listen. I do feel like you of all people deserve to know what's been going on with my life.

What happened was the depression and other issues that run in my family got to me, and was compounded when I was overworked, overstressed, and didn't even realize it until I burnt out. It started in middle school, maybe even at Hobart, and it got worse in college.

I know you always encouraged us to talk to you if we faced any problems, but to my 10, 15, and even 20-year-old self, that offer never computed. Frankly, I had no idea what I was even dealing with, never mind asking for help about it. I didn't know how to talk about it. I never thought your offer even applied to me and my family issues because they never interfered with my academic life, which I could handle by myself. I thought that was all I existed for. My whole life revolved around school and getting good grades, and school hadn't been fun for me for a very long while.

I went to _____ because it was the best school and far from home—and with no debt. Once I got there and aced the first year, I kind of floundered because I'd "filled my life's purpose" (according to my family). I'd powered through all those years in an effort to get out, and college was my first chance to relax from the pressure. Except college was a place of work. I felt trapped in a perfectionist cycle of wanting to really experiment and learn things but felt compelled to "get the grade" and with rapidly decreasing energy—I felt like I was in a rat race all over again, where no success ever felt good enough.

After graduating, I moved back home to recuperate. I'm still trying to rekindle my passion, but I keep on trucking with a supportive network to help ground me. I have a tough time with self-doubt—whether my perception of the world is the right one when there are so, so many different sides to the same story (*Rashomon*!) and there's no real way to determine "truth" (or is there?).

Right now, life is very bumpy from trying to figure out how life works, how people function, and how I fit into it—and not to mention job searching in this economy when I'm not even sure what I want to do. I feel a little like I'm catching up on lost time, but you're right—for the first time, life feels like a journey: an uncertain one, sometimes perilous, but always exciting.

   Celeste

Both of these letters end with hope but are tinged with sadness. It is necessary and proper to share such information with young students. They need the truth, be it good, bad, or ugly. Fortunately, experienced teachers often hear from former students sharing wonderful news. A quick trip to the copy machine, and one student's success becomes hundreds of students' possibilities.

Damian was a first-rate student in elementary school. He not only studied with me on Saturdays during his middle school years but volunteered to help teach others when he was in high school. He was deservedly accepted into many outstanding universities. On his first day of college, he sent my class a postcard:

Hello Room 56!

It's been a long time since I was a fifth grader, but I found the beginning of college to be a lot like my first day as a Hobart Shakespearean. It was hard, but I told myself I could manage. I needed to be nice and work hard.

I owe it all to Room 56. The older I grow, the more I come to realize that there's no other place in the world like that tiny little classroom two blocks from my house. Thank you, Rafe, for making this happen.

Reading letters such as this makes an academic future slightly more plausible. Damian's connection of his elementary class to his present experience in college helps the current students see the possibilities. The door to an impoverished youngster opens just a bit wider when real success stories touch his fingertips every day as notebook pages are flipped.

It is a constant struggle helping young people prepare for a future they can barely envision. Whether it is the grind of college, the pain and pressure of adolescence, or deep-seated troubles that lie dormant only to surface in later years, alumni can provide a road map for the future like nobody else. With your guidance mixed with their real-life experiences, your current students' chances for happiness and success move from dreams to reality.

For Your Consideration

- Each year you will connect with some of the students. Make an effort to stay in touch with them, and urge them to do the same. Make sure they know how important they are to you.
- Don't be shy about asking for help. When a former student makes an offer of assistance, ask him to talk to your students about how your class has helped him to be successful.

- Create a pecking order in your room similar to the army. When former students return to class they are practically worshipped by the younger students. Fifth graders must listen to seventh graders, who in turn do anything asked of them by a high school student. This respect for older students is an important part of our classroom culture.

- Remind students that they are on a long journey. Their success cannot be tested at the end of the year with you. The real test for them is where they are ten years after they were in your class.

- As often as possible, talk to the kids about the future. Ask them where they will be next year. In three years. In ten years. Existentialism is terrific when studying Camus and Sartre, but help your students believe that what they do today affects what they will be doing tomorrow.

- Create a Wall of Fame in your class. Put up the names of former students who are now in college. Place the names under banners of the universities they attend. Remind kids that college is not the top of the mountain, but a place that they might want to make a part of their life's journey.

- If you've done a good job, your alumni have far more skills than you do. Our class Web site, musical scores, and foundation are all handled by former students.

CHAPTER EIGHTEEN

Thomas Jefferson's Big Mistake

Thomas Jefferson was wrong about something big.

That's a bold statement, considering Jefferson is widely regarded as one of the most brilliant men our nation has ever produced. Ever heard President Kennedy's great homage at a White House dinner honoring Nobel Prize winners? "There hasn't been this much intelligence at the White House since Thomas Jefferson dined alone."

But even geniuses can be wrong, and despite Jefferson's assertion in the Declaration that certain truths are self-evident, one of his claims has never been self-evident to anyone who has ever been a teacher.

"All men are created equal."

Really? I have never found this to be true. I often joke with the kids that if they ever saw Roberto Clemente and me play baseball, it would be pretty obvious that all men are *not* created equal. Clemente was so much better than I am, it's as though he came from another galaxy.

Of course all people should be *treated* equally. All should have equal opportunity and be subject to the same laws. But to make the leap and say that we are all equal is not true.

This does not mean that I should not be able to play baseball. Of course I should. But school systems are often built on the foundation of Jefferson's inspiring lines, and that is a foundation so shaky that any classroom built on it will surely collapse, to the detriment of the children.

The children are not equal. They may be the same age and come to you having had the same teachers, curriculum, and opportunities. Yet it is often the case that in the same group of students one is ready to write the next *The Great Gatsby* and another cannot even write a sentence. What do you do when there is a Grand Canyon of disparity in the ability of your students? According to the demands of our system, all the children should succeed because they are all equal.

Harper Lee addressed this problem in words she wrote for Atticus Finch in *To Kill a Mockingbird*. Much attention has been paid to Atticus's heroic dignity, yet often overlooked is the scathing attack on our educational system that is part of Atticus's closing argument in defending the innocent Tom Robinson. In making the point that in a courtroom all people must be treated equally under the law, Atticus claims that this is the only place where all men really are equal:

> One more thing, gentlemen, before I quit. Thomas Jefferson once said that all men are created equal. . . . There is a tendency . . . for certain people to use this phrase out of context, to satisfy all conditions. The most ridiculous example I can think of is that the people who run public education promote the stupid and idle along with the industrious— because all men are created equal, educators will gravely tell you, the children left behind suffer terrible feelings of inferiority. We know all men are not created equal in the sense some people would have us believe—some people are smarter than others, some people have more opportunity

because they're born with it, some men make more money than others, some ladies make better cakes than others—some men people are born gifted beyond the normal scope of most men.

Atticus Finch is a wonderful character but he is a work of fiction. In the real world, and in a real school, his point is being demonstrated everywhere one looks.

KARLA AND DIANA

Although I had read *To Kill a Mockingbird,* I had never internalized this important part of the book. As a young teacher, I had the Declaration of Independence hanging on the wall of my room and also believed that all men are created equal. But in my first year of teaching I heard a hilarious story from our orchestra teacher.

Karla and Diana were two lovely little girls who played in our school orchestra. Both were violinists who began their lessons the first week of school. Twice a week they spent about forty minutes a day learning to read music, play scales, and develop their technique. Each of the girls received a violin, and both were diligent in their studies by practicing each night at home.

For the first five or six months of their training, they played only with other beginning violinists. As the end of the year approached, the girls began to rehearse with other children who had been studying a variety of other instruments. Three months later, the orchestra was ready to play a year-end concert of music ranging from Bach to Hollywood show tunes.

The children had a dress rehearsal on the morning of their final performance that ended around 11:30 A.M. The concert would begin at 7:00 P.M. As the children packed up their instruments after the dress rehearsal, they received final instructions from their teacher.

"Children," she said, "I am so proud of all of you. You sound terrific, and we are going to have a great performance tonight. As you leave the auditorium now, don't fold up the chairs and store them as we normally do after a rehearsal. Just leave them set up along with your music stands so they will be ready for the show tonight. I'll be over at the piano for the next fifteen minutes or so if you have any questions. Pack up your instruments and leave them by your chair. Be here tonight at six o'clock for tuning. We'll warm up around six thirty and the doors will open at six forty-five. I'll see you all later."

As the sound of instrument cases being snapped shut and chairs squeaking on the linoleum floor filled the auditorium, Karla and Diana walked over to their teacher. They each had a question.

Karla said, "Mrs. C, I have a question. I have a small problem that I wanted to share with you. My grandmother is flying in from Mexico tonight to spend a month with our family. I am so excited that she will get to see my concert. But here's the problem. Her plane lands at LAX at four P.M. My family and I will be there to pick her up. I spoke with my parents, and we are sure we will be able to be here by six for the tuning. But just in case the plane is late or my grandmother has to wait in a long line at customs, I am going to leave my violin case open on my chair. I am sure I will be here on time, but if I am a little late, could you tune it for me so that it will sound good tonight? I am sure you will not have to do this, but I wanted to tell you just in case."

The orchestra leader told her that it would be no problem and complimented Karla on her thoughtful consideration and planning. Diana had waited patiently for Karla to explain her situation, and then stepped forward with her question.

Mrs. C said, "How can I help you, Diana?"

Diana had only one short, sincere question. "Mrs. C . . . do we need to have our instruments tonight?"

That's a true story. And of course Mrs. C explained to Diana that the orchestra would sound better if they had their instruments. Both girls played (Karla was on time) and both had a memorable evening.

But they are not equal. Hearing this story helped me immensely in creating a classroom that served more of the children, even though the kids have a variety of abilities.

Anyone who has taught for a couple of years has already figured out that clearly all are not created equal. Yet your school district has most likely assigned you a set of skills all of your students are supposed to master. To increase the pressure on the teacher, bureaucrats often distribute an absurd pacing plan. These plans are immaculately designed and proclaim that on such and such a date, every student will have mastered a particular skill. All real teachers laugh, and sometimes bitterly, over the futility of such goals. Certainly it is good to have a grand strategy, and class leaders should have a well-organized scheme as they prepare their lessons for the year. But experienced teachers use these district objectives only as a jumping-off place to begin teaching. Real teachers differentiate their classrooms in an effort to help as many of the students as possible. The goal, a very hard one, is to help struggling students do better while making sure top students are allowed to soar.

ONE SIZE DOES NOT FIT ALL

All children are not created equal, nor are they created *the same*. Eric and George were both in my class one year. They were born within thirty days of each other. They had attended our elementary school together since kindergarten and they were both boys. The similarities ended there.

Eric was one of the saddest-looking boys I had seen in many years. Depression drooped from his mouth and eyes. He never had anything to say, and my attempts to engage him in conversation were failures. At best I was able to get a syllable or two out of him. His test scores from the previous years were far below grade level. I did learn that his fourth grade teacher had called him "stupid and lazy" during a parent conference. He was particularly weak in math. He was ten years old, entering fifth grade, and did not even know how to add two-digit numbers. Multiplication tables had not been forgotten; they had never been learned. It took a week for Eric to finally understand that holes go on the left side of the paper when doing writing assignments.

George was a happy and bright young man, and I have no idea how he faced the world with such a positive attitude. His parents had divorced when he was two. Alcohol was a prime factor in his family's dissolution. His mother worked three jobs to support him and his two older sisters. He regularly came home to an empty apartment. The family of four slept in one bed.

And yet his infectious smile exuded confidence and happiness. He loved to learn and was a talented and enthusiastic student who excelled in music and consistently made valuable and astute observations during class discussions. He was loved by every teacher he had ever known and was always surrounded by a host of friends reveling in his company. He may not have had the easiest start in life, but there was no doubt that his future was a bright one. On the first day of class, he confided in me the one thing that bothered him more than anything else about school. He hated waiting. He complained that he spent hours in school waiting while the teacher explained a concept to a couple of students when the majority of the class was desperately bored and wanting to move forward.

The Los Angeles Unified School District proscribed a rigorous course of study for these boys for the coming year. The list included a series of grammar skills, reading comprehension, and the ability to add, subtract, multiply, and divide whole numbers, decimals, fractions, and integers. They were supposed to be introduced to geometry and algebra, as well as earth, physical, and life sciences. Eric was not fluent in English, so part of our year together would be spent developing his English competence to pass a test at the end of the year. And let's not forget that these two boys were also supposed to cover the material in a two-hundred-page health book, have one hundred minutes a week of physical education, and cover United States history from the days of the Native Americans through the end of the Civil War.

For those teachers who live on planet Earth, it would be painfully clear that Eric would never finish this course of study. George might not either if too much of my time was spent getting the slower students to master some of the most fundamental concepts of English and math.

What does a teacher do once he realizes that Thomas Jefferson was mistaken? Both of these boys matter. Both of these boys (and their thirty-one classmates) deserve our best efforts. In Hollywood movies, both boys would wind up at an elite university after a magical fifth grade moment when they discovered that they were geniuses and destined to become the next Thomas Edison. But this is a real book for real teachers, so let's try to be a bit more realistic.

DIFFERENT STUDENTS, ONE OUTCOME

In Eric's case, a decision had to be made in terms of what was most important for him to learn in his year in our class. The experiences of being humiliated by some of his teachers and laughed at by many classmates had completely turned him off to school. He was far behind, particularly in math, where his previous test scores were abysmal.

Eric's reading was below grade level, but as I got to know him it became apparent that most of his poor test scores were the result of his attitude rather than his ability. While he was no genius, he clearly was better than his previous lack of accomplishment indicated. Still, he was so far behind in his subjects, there was not enough time to cover the entire curriculum while simultaneously plugging the many holes in his knowledge. The strategy here was to put together a plan that allowed Eric to master certain skills that should have been covered long before while ignoring other lessons that were not as crucial in the long run to his success in school.

Some of Eric's previous teachers had tried to help him catch up by burying him with homework worksheets. This resulted in Eric losing sleep and coming to school exhausted, making it impossible for him to focus on important lessons teachers were trying to get through to him. Worse, the homework was ineffective, as Eric rarely understood the material and had no one at home to offer assistance.

Our class spends enormous amounts of time covering United States history. In Eric's case, I set out on a slightly different but deliberate course of action. Realistically, if Eric did not understand the Compromise of 1820, he could still be a successful student. However, if he could not do basic mathematical computations, many doors would be closed to him. When students are far behind, it's a good idea to prioritize what things they must know. Multiplication facts take precedence over memorizing Mohs' Scale of Hardness in geology. Writing a basic paragraph correctly is more important than learning how to latch hook a rug. While other kids were working on rugs, I worked with Eric on his math. He could work on a rug at home, but he needed individual attention to help him understand important concepts. The kids making rugs did not have to wait, and Eric was able to work on his rug at home rather than falling asleep over a worksheet. He smiled more in class. I gave him needed individual attention and support, and other students did not resent the attention because they were involved in an exciting project.

George had a wonderful year in class. He often said that it was his best year in school because it was his most challenging. He easily completed the assigned curriculum for the year, but this was only a beginning for him. George starred in our Shakespeare play, learned three additional instruments, and was able to do several other activities. He was able to accomplish all this because no time was wasted waiting for other students. It is admirable when a teacher tries her best to work with a struggling youngster, but George should not have to suffer because of another student's lack of progress. Ironically, it can happen that outstanding students can be the most neglected of children.

Eric and George were not equal in either ability or family situation. But both of them felt their fifth grade year was a good one—and they were right.

Eric had an outstanding year. It is true that he did not learn as much history and science as would be hoped in a perfect situation. But Eric, with an individual learning plan designed by a teacher and supported by his family, made enormous progress in language and mathematics. His skills had previously been considered far below the basic level of proficiency, but by the end of the year his language and math skills were as proficient as that of many of his peers. Eric discovered the crucial truth that he was a perfectly capable young man who, like so many kids, had for one reason or another simply lost his way. A year of differentiated study had helped him discover that he could be a good student. By the end of the year he was volunteering to read difficult works of literature. Best of all, he was one of the most respected kids in the room. Students who had known him for years as someone who was lazy or slow were as happy as Eric was to discover that this was not true. Middle school beckoned, and Eric left elementary school with the knowledge that he had the tools to continue to do well and open doors for his future.

George had never been happier. He was in a class that recognized his talents and allowed him to soar. He was delighted to learn that when he asked to read ahead or begin work on the next chapter, no one told him to slow down. He not only scored brilliantly on standardized tests but played three instruments, sang in a chorus, and became the shortstop and captain of a baseball team. Previous teachers who had liked him a lot commented that they had never seen him so happy. His face beamed not because he was any smarter than before but because he was in a class where diversity was not simply a word but a reality. He was allowed to be different, and began his journey, which is still going on to this day, to discover the size of his extraordinary mind.

Two different students here had one thing in common. They were treated as individuals. Both were given an opportunity to learn. No one ever gave up on them. And this is the challenge to all teachers. High school English teachers can recognize that while some of their students might be able to dissect *Brave New World* brilliantly, others might not. Yet all of them can be shown the beauty of reading. It would be nice if Thomas Jefferson had been correct and all men were created equal. But they are not. And it is both a blessing and a curse to teachers that we have a chance to try to help students rise to the best each has in them. And this is where a classroom can approach Jefferson's ideal. The kids are not equal, but with dedicated teachers they can be given equal opportunities to discover their personal bests.

For Your Consideration

- All students are not created equal, nor are they all the same. While it is impossible to create individual assignments for the students, try to create assignments where one size does not fit all.

- Pacing plans and edicts such as No Child Left Behind force teachers to teach as though all the kids were preprogrammed learning units that advance at the same pace at the same level in the same way. Recognize that many well-intentioned people who create these plans do not actually work with students on a daily basis.

- With experience, create lessons where students of different abilities have the opportunity to make progress. Students who are behind will be more motivated to work if they see reachable goals.

- Have your students measure their progress against their own past work and not the accomplishment of other students.

CHAPTER NINETEEN

The Price You Pay

Most good teachers I know agree that working with young people is joyous. However, a nagging truth never goes away. Teaching hurts. There is a price to pay, and often an unfair one.

It hurts because of the outright cruelty that can come from all corners. There will be students who do not like you. There will be colleagues who are rude to you. Parents, administrators, and even complete strangers can be so mean that it's easy to become despondent. As Mark Twain had Huckleberry Finn observe, "Human beings can be awfully cruel to one another."

Outstanding teachers are very sensitive to the needs of their students. They have radar that picks up on what makes children hurt or afraid, and this sensitivity is to be commended. Ironically, however, this same sensitivity also makes them susceptible to the slings and arrows that come with the job.

I have never found a solution to this particular problem. Some problems do not have solutions. Like certain diseases, they can be managed but never cured.

It's an intimidating prospect, one that leads many good teachers to stop trying. During the growing-up years, teachers are at

special risk for giving in to the incessant cruelty and disappointment. The initial shock has worn off, but so has the burst of resil-
ience triggered in response. At five years or more, the pain can start
to slowly chip away at a teacher's humanity, when she realizes that
it will be a constant presence throughout her career. These teachers
have enough experience to get through the day and have decided
to do it by following the path of least resistance. They never participate at staff meetings because they do not want to upset anyone.
They never take any risks in their classrooms because they might
fail, and failing is painful. They do not have meaningful conversations with parents for fear of upsetting a mother or father. These
teachers are fine people who have simply been defeated by the sad
fact that being a good teacher hurts. And who in their right mind
would walk into a classroom daily looking to make things difficult
for themselves when it is easier to avoid the agony of defeat?

It can get nasty on a campus. Recently two teachers at my
school got into such a heated argument that our principal basically
locked them in a room and would not let them out until they had
settled their differences. Given the potential grief that goes with
teaching, it's a wonder more teachers don't turn into ostriches and
bury their heads in the ground.

PEAKS AND VALLEYS

For every peak there's a valley. As the failures and bumps in the road
add up, the scars can turn dedicated teachers into boring ones.

Many years ago my students were invited to give a history recitation at the United States Supreme Court. On the surface, this
was a most successful day. The students performed speeches
and music for an hour in the nation's holiest chambers of justice
and brought the house down. The kids had researched famous and
history-making speeches from across the political spectrum. The
show included tributes to Barry Goldwater and Ronald Reagan,

but also had plenty of time for Clarence Darrow and Malcolm X. It was not evident during the weeks of preparation, but one of the pieces the kids performed would be forever burned on the brains of the fortunate crowd that attended the show, entitled "Freedom Is Not Free."

A young man named Wayne was set to recite a touching letter written by Union soldier Sullivan Ballou before the first Battle of Bull Run. The kids had first heard it when they watched Ken Burns's award-winning documentary *The Civil War*. Ballou wrote a moving love letter to his wife, Sarah, before the battle, but he was killed during the fighting and Sarah never received the letter. As Wayne recited the beautiful words, a few of my students played "Ashokan Farewell," the haunting melody that provided much of the emotional background for the Ken Burns film. During the recitation of the letter, Wayne did something he had never done in rehearsal. As the letter spoke of a young man's complete devotion to his wife, Wayne began to cry. It was a moment so unexpected and brilliant that everyone in the audience began to sob along with him. You can see the clip of Wayne's speech at www.hobartshakespeareans.org or on YouTube.

The success of that day should have been one of those achievements that keep a teacher above water for years. Famous people in attendance mobbed my students and congratulated my work, though, truth be told, all of the brilliance was Wayne's and not an ounce of it mine. Late in the afternoon we found the Blue Line back to King Street Station and boarded the Metro with our guitars and violins to return to our hotel in Virginia. Walking into the Embassy Suites lobby that day was wonderful. The hotel serves free sodas and chips to children during their happy hour, and the kids politely waited in line, got their goodies, and sat around the indoor fountains and foliage to toast one another and celebrate a day they would never forget.

I sat there nursing a Coke when a well-dressed gentleman

walked over to me. He sat down next to me and asked, "Are you the teacher of all these students?"

"I certainly am," I said happily. I was sure news of the Supreme Court performance could not have reached the hotel so suddenly, but figured this man would be like so many other strangers who stopped by to compliment the students on their decorum as they munched on their snacks.

"Well, you make me sick," he snarled bitterly at me through clenched teeth. "Teachers like you are what is dragging the country down. Where are you from? I plan to write a letter to your school board to make sure they fire your ass."

I was stunned into a confused silence, which turned out to be fine because this man was on a roll and ready to elaborate. That morning, the kids went down to breakfast around 6:45. We were staying in eight rooms on the same floor of the hotel. As is our classroom routine, the kids were careful to modulate their voices when they were in their hotel rooms and did not talk at all when they strolled down the hall to the elevators. They had, however, made a mistake that was entirely my fault. I had not taught them about hotel doors. Because of important fire laws, the doors at the hotel were quite heavy and closed forcefully to prevent potential fires from spreading rapidly. The kids had opened the doors that morning quietly and walked to the elevators quietly, but they had not taken the time to hang on to their doors and close them carefully and silently. That morning, eight doors had slammed shut, to the disgust of this angry man. Obviously this triggered some terrible memory or reaction in him, and now this stranger was cursing at me mercilessly with a vulgarity that had everyone in the lobby staring at me as if I were public enemy number one.

It is not an exaggeration to say that thousands of people have been inspired by Wayne's beautiful performance that afternoon at the Supreme Court. This should be enough to make a teacher carry on when the going gets tough. Yet when I remember that day, all I can see is the angry man who wanted me fired. Whether it was the degree of his anger or the fact that the style of presentation was unfair and uncouth, it scarred me. I understand that the problem was largely with him, not with my kids, but the memory is with me every time I see a child open or close a hotel door.

DEVASTATION

There are bumps along the road that weaken one's resolve to teach with passion. Fortunately, many of them can be brushed aside or attributed to flaws in the system or the ignorance of another person. However, when failures force a teacher to consider that he might be completely ineffective, it can be so excruciatingly painful.

I like to travel with students. Both my wife and I work hard to use the road to teach young people life skills. Our favorite trip with kids is to Ashland, Oregon, home of the Oregon Shakespeare Festival. We spend about ten days there every summer, and hundreds of students have told me how much they loved their time in this small town, and how much they miss those days even years later when they are raising their own families.

It takes a year to get ready for this trip. After the students graduate from elementary school, some of them return to study with me on Saturday mornings. The kids work on their reading comprehension, algebra, and geometry, and study Shakespeare. We read about five of his plays over the course of the year, in preparation for watching them the following summer in Ashland. During the year, much of our class time is devoted to character development. All of these students are involved in community service beyond the work we do inside the classroom, and have developed a reputation as the kind of kids who make our nation stronger.

When summer arrives, my wife, Barbara, flies with the students to Medford, Oregon. There, a private bus picks them up and makes the final twenty-minute trip to Ashland. When the students arrive at the hotel, their bags and all sorts of equipment are waiting for them. I drive a van almost seven hundred miles from Los Angeles to Ashland the day before. It's a long, tough drive, but these students are worth it. The van carries not only their luggage but also sports equipment and all sorts of games and puzzles that make their stay at the festival even more fun. These are beautiful summer days for the children, filled with swimming, soccer, baseball, Frisbee, ice cream parlors, and, of course, Shakespeare.

Even though they are well-mannered students, taking care of about thirty of them for ten days is not easy. Each morning I drive them in groups to a local market where they shop for food. They learn about budgeting money and choosing healthy food. They take care of their own rooms, get enough sleep, and have the pleasure of meeting thousands of theatergoers who all have something to teach them. It's a splendid way to spend part of summer.

One summer, our stay had ended and the kids were catching an early morning flight back to Los Angeles. I left around 5:00 A.M. with their belongings. The plan was to get back to L.A. by dinnertime. I would then drive the suitcases back to the students' homes. It's a lot of work and a very long day, but when I think about how hard they have worked over hundreds of hours of study, and about the quality of their characters, it's worth it.

Only this summer it wasn't.

About 8 P.M. I was finished, in more ways than one. Mission accomplished, I left the last student's apartment and headed for home eagerly awaiting a good night's sleep. My phone rang, and when I picked up a lovely woman from the hotel was on the other end of the line. She had worked with my class for years, and, like everyone else, had nothing but praise for the students and wished other school groups could be like them.

"Rafe, I am so sorry to call you, but I really have no choice. Things were stolen from the hotel."

I was shocked. Numb. Speechless.

On the final night three of the girls decided to steal hair dryers that were connected to the walls of their bathrooms. They yanked one out from the wall, and then used the connecting door to enter the room of their sleeping neighbors. A second dryer was also stolen. One of these girls had been studying with me for four years. She had received a scholarship to an elite high school. All three of them had incredible opportunities and doors pried open for them to have better lives. And now they were stealing from a hotel.

It wasn't about adolescent rebellion. This was just stealing, and the incident shook me up in ways nothing had before. I called their parents and met with the families individually to share with the parents that this was a serious matter. In addition to the felony committed, it meant that these girls did not for a moment consider the larger consequences of their actions. Their dishonesty placed in jeopardy the chance for future children to have some of the experiences they had. Their actions were unconscionable and I could not find an answer to why this had happened. There were no warning signs in the past and none of the girls had been going through any sort of crisis that could have forced them into a desperate cry for attention. It was simply greedy, awful, and wrong.

One of the fathers was upset with me for asking him to come to the conference. He rolled his eyes at me and said, "Everybody steals. It's just not that big a deal."

You look for solace. Three kids stole. I have brought almost one thousand students to the Oregon Shakespeare Festival and no one else has even littered. But those three haunt me still. It was a wake-up call reminding me that despite every effort possible, there are kids who will make terrible decisions and thumb their noses at you. As teachers, we like to think we can have an effect on the kids, and we do, but not always.

Every setback brings a teacher closer to throwing in the towel, or at least to simply going through the motions. Teaching hurts. Teaching is pain. Disappointment comes with the territory.

Angry people and incorrigible students are only part of the problem. Recently, one of the class patrons spent some time with the students and me on our annual trip to Washington, D.C. Inside the National Air and Space Museum, the kids excitedly entered the Wright Brothers gallery, where the original Wright Flyer sits, along with the dramatic story of Orville and Wilbur. As the children read with fascination the notes made by the brothers during their test flights, the patron asked me one of the most frequently asked questions veteran teachers hear.

"I get it, Rafe. The kids are having a ball. But you have probably been in this gallery twenty-five times in your life. Don't you get sick of it?"

It's a fair question. A mixture of pain, disappointment, and repetition does not exactly sound like a formula for pleasure.

Watching the kids joyously looking at the Wright Flyer, I was reminded that it's not their twenty-fifth time. It's their first. And they haven't stolen anything from the hotel. They haven't even slammed a door. Looking at these young scholars motivated me not to burn out but to burn brighter. But before that, let's acknowledge the fact that teaching hurts and it's tiring. And we limp forward.

But then we reflect. One sleepless night, I figured out what the three girls who had stolen from the hotel had in common: I had felt sorry for them. All of them had overcome personal difficulties and were doing fine in school, but in reality, they should not have been on the trip. I had invited them only because I felt sorry for their circumstances. Although they were decent students, none of them had really distinguished herself as extraordinary in the same way her peers had. I learned from my failure not to ever again do something extra for a student out of sympathy. Feeling sorry for a child is not enough of a reason to raise a grade or buy a plane ticket.

The following summer I brought the students to Oregon again, and it was the best trip we took there in thirty years. When pain comes, it is an opportunity to reflect and grow. I'm sad about what happened a few years ago, but I no longer limp. I look forward to sprinting up to Oregon next summer with another fabulous group of kids.

For Your Consideration

- Teaching hurts. Get used to it.
- If you are criticized or treated meanly by someone, consider the source before you take it too seriously.
- Remember that Joe DiMaggio ran out every ground ball because the kids in the stands might see him play only once. We cannot let past disappointments affect our attitude with the current class. The children deserve our very best effort.
- Discuss your pain with other teachers. Colleagues can give you strength because they understand your suffering more than anyone else.
- Try to stay strong and upbeat. Your students need a positive person, and dwelling on past disasters helps no one.

CHAPTER TWENTY

The Undiscovered Country

I t's only Tuesday afternoon and you're already tired. You care just as much as you did when you began teaching. How do you keep the fire burning when all the problems that go with the job conspire to sap your strength? In your first years of teaching, Friday afternoons seemed to sneak up on you suddenly, but now the weekend seems light-years away. And there was a time when you were sad the weekend came because there was so much to do. Now there are days when you can't wait for Friday night.

Here is a suggestion. Every year you teach, add one new activity to your class.

It does not have to be some show-stopping, spectacularly inventive lesson. Your new activity does not have to require you to dress up in a costume or dance on top of your desk. No one, including the students, needs to know that you have added to the menu and made your lessons tastier.

But you'll know. Your students have only a snapshot of their days with you. It's the difference between two-dimensional paintings and cubism. You are Picasso or Braque, and the changes you make in your program will add shadings and views appreciated by perhaps only you over many years. But those subtle changes can make your days more enjoyable, effective, and invigorating.

Every year I add at least one new activity or lesson to the class. Here is one idea I added to my classroom after I had established our basic rhythm after five years of teaching. It may not sound interesting or relevant to you. You are the artist of your classroom and will enhance your program with ideas you feel will make the class more exciting and you more committed than ever.

HISTORY BOXES

During my first few years of teaching, I was moved from kindergarten and third grade into a fifth-and-sixth-grade combined classroom. The fifth graders were supposed to read a textbook that covered United States history from the days of the Native Americans through the end of the Civil War. The book was rather dry. It wasn't a terrible book, but I discovered that when teaching history it is often better to use a variety of sources to make the subject more interesting and the students more well rounded.

After adding a variety of interesting workbooks, coupled with the viewing of many excellent historical documentaries from the History Channel, I noticed something interesting. Even the students who enjoyed history rarely retained many of the facts that had been covered. In student terms, the kids had rented but not bought the knowledge.

That's when I came up with the idea of history boxes. I designed an activity that would reinforce many of the lessons incorporated into our basic curriculum. The goal was to help the kids "connect the dots" of history permanently and understand their future in relation to our nation's past.

Here's how it works. I order index card boxes from an office supply company. These are cheap plastic boxes that hold three-by-five-inch index cards. A set of alphabetized dividers for the boxes and about five hundred lined cards for each student will be sufficient for an entire year.

Each week the students receive a list of fifteen to twenty terms, places, or people that we will be studying that week. Next to each entry is a description or definition. The students take an index card and on the blank side write the subject. It might be James Monroe, or the Whiskey Rebellion. I gather people's names and terms from the various books we read, but if you are looking for a quick and easy way to start, go to the Internet and search for "SparkNotes history study cards." For between fifteen and twenty dollars you can get five hundred history facts. You won't use them all, but they are a terrific foundation for a student, ranging from fifth grade to high school.

The students write a name or fact on one side of each card and a short description of the person or event on the other. The cards are filed in alphabetical order in the boxes (Hobart Shakespeareans are organized) and neatly written (Hobart Shakespeareans understand the importance of presentation). The students often practice with these cards during free moments or at home with one another. Without a doubt, this simple addition to the class helped my students learn a lot more history and comprehend it better, and because of this, it made teaching more fun for me.

New ideas do not have to be colossal. Simply reading a great book with a group of students can help keep your fire burning bright for your entire day. There is nothing sacrilegious about a high school teacher who occasionally shelves the official list of reading to try something new. Be bold. Perhaps one year your students will howl with laughter as you read Douglas Adams's *The Hitchhiker's Guide to the Galaxy*. So as Adams taught us, don't panic and carry a towel. Trying new things makes the job more enjoyable and you a better teacher.

TRADITIONS BEGAN AS SOMETHING NEW

A nice result of trying new things is that some of them will be so successful they will become classroom rituals. Early in my career, I noticed that most of my students knew very little about the Thanksgiving holiday. They certainly knew they got four days off from school, but that was the extent of their knowledge. One year I thought it might be nice to have a small meal on Wednesday night before the kids went home for the Thanksgiving holiday. Our first dinner consisted of getting some sliced turkey from a local delicatessen and the kids having a turkey sandwich and a drink. It was a nice hour. In fact, I was surprised at how many of the students constantly mentioned that little meal as one of their favorite moments of their year.

Over the last quarter of a century, this adding on of something new has grown into a major event. On the Wednesday evening before Thanksgiving, more than seventy children crowd Room 56. This includes both current students and former students who return from middle and high school to help serve food and share an evening with children following in their footsteps.

When school ends that day, the children watch the terrific film *Planes, Trains & Automobiles*. Their parents are notified about the profane language in the movie, but we have never had a parent request that their child not view it. It's a wonderful piece of cinema, as the hilarious moments take a sudden twist and inspire the audience to reflect on the true meaning of Thanksgiving.

Before this day occurs, during our history lessons the students learn both the real and the fabricated stories behind Thanksgiving. They even hear Jon Stewart's bitterly ironic quip "This year my family is celebrating a traditional Thanksgiving. We are inviting our neighbors to a great feast. Then we are going to kill them and take their land!"

My wife found a restaurant that will prepare an entire take-out Thanksgiving dinner for the children. Before the meal is served, each child from the current class stands and tells his peers something for which he is thankful. Family members are often mentioned, but so are members of the United States armed services, past and present. It's an emotional hour, and more than a few tears flow. The room is filled with genuine feelings. It's an hour very well spent.

Dinner is then served to the current students by the returning alumni. Music and laughter fill the air, and the kids eat a very hearty meal. Before the evening is over, many students express that they can't wait to return next year to serve others. Clearly, the activity that once began as a simple meal has evolved into something more meaningful and important.

As a veteran teacher, the question before you is, what is the one thing you will add to your program this year? It may become an event that will reenergize you and bring astonishing opportunities for your students to grow into the kind of people you will want to spend time with for many years to come.

For Your Consideration

- Adding one thing a year to your program can make you a happier, more engaged teacher.
- Not all new ideas work. Projects that flounder are fine and even necessary to build a great classroom. Real failure is defined as never trying anything new. We ask our students to try new things, and we must lead by example.
- If possible, make sure your special or new ideas are those that can be conducted within your own classroom. The moment your project leaves your walls, the chances increase that your activity might interfere with another school program and

make problems for you. New activities are supposed to make your day better and not bring you more headaches.

• Watch as many great teachers as you can. Many ideas that have been added to Room 56 came from fabulous teachers I observed who were happy to help me implement their lessons in my classroom.

CHAPTER TWENTY-ONE

One of a Kind

Doing something new each year can keep things fresh for both the teacher and the students, but doing one thing really well over many years is just as important and revitalizing. Many of the outstanding veteran teachers I know have been able to sustain their passion and output by creating a unique project. These quests all have something in common: they take an entire year to complete. It springs from the teachers' own love of something that they enjoy passing on to others. Such projects take an enormous amount of energy, and yet to these teachers it is not work at all.

I know a marvelous high school counselor who has helped students for more than a quarter of a century. He is very good at his job and well respected at his school. And despite all the students who go on to college or simply make good decisions listening to this man's sage counsel, it is only a part of why he is recognized as a school leader who makes a difference.

This man loves to run. The only thing he loves more than running is to teach young people the joy of the sport. Each summer before school begins he invites students to be a part of his running club, with the ultimate goal of participating in his city's marathon at the end of the year. This is serious business. It is a commitment, his students learn, that encompasses a complete way of life.

The kids run, but they learn so much more. They change their diet, sleeping habits, and eventually their lives. They live by the clock, learning to balance their important academic work with their running schedules while still finding time for play and relaxation.

Not all the students who sign up at the beginning of the year have the discipline to reach such a high bar. But many do. When they cross the finish line at the marathon, they have completed one journey but have begun so many others. And, more likely than not, their journeys will be happier and healthier because of what they learned by running. The discipline, courage, sacrifice, teamwork, and struggle will be with each student forever. Their lives have been changed forever because of the year they spent with this counselor.

But the kids aren't the only ones who benefit. The teacher's passion for exercise keeps him young physically, and the one-of-a-kind club he created keeps him fresh when others succumb to the grind of teaching school for many years. He is literally the Marathon Man.

THE LONG AND WINDING ROAD OF THE HOBART SHAKESPEAREAN PRODUCTIONS

The special activity that has kept me engaged for three decades is the annual production of a Shakespeare play. It did not start out this way. Many good ideas evolve slowly, taking shape over many years and constantly getting better. I share this story with you not because you need to teach Shakespeare but because the backstory of our productions might give you a notion of how your special idea might take shape and become a unique force in the life of your students.

I began teaching at Hobart Elementary School in 1985. Even the greenest of teachers could see that most of the students there were far below grade level, and the common factor in the rate of failure was poor language skills. Many of the children were still learning English, so they were not behind because of a lack of ability. Grasping grammar and basic reading skills could help these children catch up, but I thought that if the students were given the opportunity to stay after school and learn about Shakespeare, it might make things more fun for them. Of course old Will would be very challenging for even fluent nine- and ten-year-old kids, but with my help and enthusiasm, I thought we might give it a try. Naturally I faced the typical roadblocks teachers encounter when they try anything original, but eventually the school district was kind enough to allow me to stay after school and teach some of the students for free.

It was a lot of extra work, but there was an important upside to this madness that I had not considered. Because the program was voluntary and held after school, I was surrounded by true believers. During regular school hours, rude students and other problems are basic to any room full of youngsters who, by the grace of the state, are a captive audience. But this is not the case when you create a voluntary extracurricular activity. The students who come to Shakespeare want to be there, and also are quite aware that if their behavior and work ethic are not exemplary they will be shown the door. As a result, the forty or more students in the shows always paid attention and gave their best effort for the entire rehearsal. For a teacher, it really was heaven on Earth.

Better still, the positive energy created in the Shakespeare plays carried over into the classroom during regular school hours. The students in the shows had spent more time with me, and as a result were more attentive during daily lessons. Their positive attitudes helped shape our class culture, and even the apathetic students were more likely to make an effort in class because so many around them were behaving.

Within five years the kids were performing rudimentary

Shakespeare plays right in Room 56. They were messy, fun, and the students learned a lot.

Simultaneously, I began classical guitar lessons for interested students during their recess and lunch breaks. I thought music lessons would be fun while helping the kids improve their work ethic and concentration. The focus, discipline, and practice involved with learning the guitar were sure to benefit the students beyond music, and they did. As the years went on, I improved as a guitar instructor and received a lot of help from the music teacher at the school. Eventually, the kids were good enough to warrant a concert.

At first, our terrific instrumental music teacher allowed the guitarists to play a piece or two at the orchestra concert. One thing led to another, and within a few years the classical guitarists had added some keyboard parts, vocals, and drums to their songs. Soon they were holding their own year-end concert while the kids studying Shakespeare staged a play in our class to finish their days with a wonderful memory.

I was making a mistake, however, during those early years. The plays and concerts became so popular with the kids and the neighborhood that I forgot the original reason I began doing them. For a little while, the play became more important than the lessons I was supposed to be teaching. Part of the problem was that I had not clearly defined in my mind or the minds of the students a specific set of objectives. Sure, the students were learning tons of language and becoming accomplished musicians, but there was too much focus being placed on the final product. It would be better to place the emphasis on the journey and not the final creation. Realizing this helped me correct my course. Such is the beauty of developing something over a long time.

Another mistake was that we held the concerts in the school auditorium. This tradition had begun because our school orchestra had their concerts there, so my class followed suit. Yet the orchestra needed to use the auditorium because there were one hundred musicians playing; we had only thirty. It dawned on me that being in the auditorium shifted the emphasis to pleasing a big audience. It was nice hearing the applause, but it did not improve the students' musicianship and work habits, the supposed reason I had started teaching music in the first place. The mistake was confusing the final product with the process of learning. I was wasting time worrying about how many people would see the concert that could have been spent helping the kids become better musicians and people. It was time to take two good ideas and fuse them into something magical.

I listed the objectives of both the Shakespeare and the music programs and found that many of the goals were the same. When your special program takes shape it's a good idea to spend some time really defining the mission. Each objective of the Hobart Shakespeareans centers on a skill that will serve each student for the rest of his life and not simply for the show:

- The students will learn large amounts of new vocabulary through Shakespeare.
  With a larger vocabulary, students will improve their reading, writing, and speaking.
- The students will increase their ability to focus for long periods of time.
  A student who learns to focus and pay attention will be better equipped to handle all his future classes, from physics to art appreciation.
- The students will improve their patience.
  Reinforcing the concept of There are no shortcuts, students will learn that true excellence takes thousands of hours of disciplined practice.
- The students will learn to work as a team.
  In our productions everyone matters. Students not in a scene or song are silent while others rehearse, because those onstage deserve their moment in the sun.

- The students will learn to stand up and speak confidently in front of others.

  Overcoming shyness will benefit students in professional, social, and, of course, school situations. A child who can confidently recite hundreds of lines in front of a live audience will have no problem with nerves on his next oral report or college interview.

- The students will learn not to be afraid of making mistakes.

  Everyone in the production learns that when a music cue is missed or a line dropped, the show goes on smoothly. They come to realize that when we lose our fear of messing up, we make mistakes far less often.

- The students will be supportive of peers who struggle.

  When an actor has trouble memorizing his lines or a pianist keeping time with a song, others help by rehearsing with him. Empathy is a valuable character trait. It helps both the giver and the receiver.

- The students will practice independently to perfect skills.

  There are no deadlines given to the performers. No one tells them to have certain lines or songs ready by a particular date. Instead, the students go home and rehearse. As certain students show up to rehearsals with their parts ready, others are inspired to do the same. This showing of initiative is crucial to future success in life.

- The students will make a yearlong commitment to a project and finish what they start.

  Many students give up too easily. By internalizing a value that we finish what we start, these students finish classes, assignments, and, eventually, college.

Notice that there is no mention of the Shakespeare production in the objectives. We rarely talk about the show itself. Instead, we focus on the important skills we will learn over a long journey of discovery. These goals are discussed with the children almost on a daily basis.

What began as an attempt to make school more fun and challenging to the students has evolved into the foundation of Room 56 and all its activities. As I stepped back and clearly defined the objectives of the production, everything got better. The students became far better musicians and singers. The actors began to own the language in ways they had never done before. I became a better teacher. No rehearsal was ever about the show. Instead, ninety minutes a day was spent with all the children finding their rhythm as they spoke Shakespeare's language. And the better they spoke, the more they wanted to improve. Sir Ian McKellen has remarked that "the best thing about the Hobart Shakespeareans is that they know what they're saying, and that can't be said about even professional actors doing Shakespeare."

THE GREAT FOCUSER

As you'll read in the next chapter, many music experts came on board and helped the Hobart Shakespeareans. Within a few years, the students went from being a good group of singers playing basic music to a sizzling band accompanied by dynamic vocals and harmonies. As the singers would gather close together, literally looking into one another's mouths to make sure their harmonies were tight, their concentration was inspiring. This skill had a direct effect on their precision in math and the way they meticulously presented essays and reports. The Hobart Shakespearean project taught me that in an era when adults fret about students who cannot pay attention, music is the great focuser.

The final piece to the puzzle fell into place after I attended an opera. I knew little of this art form and wanted to learn more. One of the many great things about opera is how more than once voice can tell a story simultaneously. While performing Shakespeare, if two actors spoke their lines at the same time it would certainly confuse the audience and ruin the story. But opera is different. Two different voices can sing and enhance rather than hurt the tale.

During our shows, we mix the Shakespeare with music and neither suffers. The Shakespeare the students speak is recited with the precision of a McKellen or an Olivier. Yet in the middle of much of the text music is inserted to help tell the story, and the songs are played and sung with a professionalism normally associated with adults. Helena's woes about being left behind by her love in *A Midsummer Night's Dream* is mixed with Donovan's beautiful ballad "Catch the Wind." More than a dozen children now perform a scene originally intended for one actress. Four singers create magnificent harmonies. Other students play guitars, bass, and even harmonica. Their listening skills are extraordinary, as every student onstage must be aware of Helena's lines, the bass guitar's cues to sing, and one another's voices to sing in three-part harmony.

After thirty years of growth, the shows are amazing to witness. Yet the mission remains the best part of the Hobart Shakespeareans, and the real assessment of the worth of such an activity cannot be measured for many years. Here is a letter from a former student, now a college freshman, who is on his school's water polo team.

Dear Rafe:

Before I get back to work, I just wanted to share something with you.

Recently I've been really busy with school. Finals are coming up next week, and the swim season has just begun for the team, so practices are really wearing us out!

But every time I have had hard workouts of underwater kick sprints without breathing, Henry V's words start to pour out of my memory. My whole body shakes and trembles, my lungs feel ready to burst, but the mighty voices of

Timothi and Rudy propel me to hold on and finish with might. Out of our 25-person team, I'm one of the few who can successfully complete the set without taking a breath. The following words have eternally radiated might and tears into me every time I hear them, ever since the day I first heard them roared in Room 56.

"We few, we happy few, WE BAND OF BROTHERS! For he today that sheds his blood with me shall be my brother.

"Be he ne'er so vile this day shall gentle his condition. And gentlemen in England now abed shall think themselves accursed they were not here. And hold their manhoods cheap whilst any speaks that fought with us upon St. Crispian's Day!!!!!!"

Thank you so much Rafe for doing what you do. My thoughts grow happier when I remember the happy few that still say these words every day in Room 56. Can't thank you enough Rafe!! Now back to my essays!

A special program you create can sustain you in a profession that causes so many to leave feeling bitter and defeated. Better still, the lessons learned sustain the youngsters who carry useful skills that will serve them long after the applause dies down. Like Shakespeare himself, a good program helps children not for an age but for all time.

For Your Consideration

- Pick something that you love to do and create a project with your students that will frame the entire year. Whether the students make quilts, become Scrabble experts, or learn to surf, a special project will make all parts of your day better.
- Make sure that the objectives of your project are clear both in your mind and in the minds of the students.

- Students need to know they are lucky you are making a supreme effort. They must pay for your efforts by doing their best at all times.
- Students who participate in your extra project must exhibit outstanding character at all times, and not only when they participate in your program.
- Always move forward. Make each year special by adding things to your project or perfecting things that need improvement.

CHAPTER TWENTY-TWO

All for One
and One for All

Teaching can often be a profession of isolation, but it doesn't have to be. No one is an expert at everything, and it takes a team of people to help students accomplish things that might seem impossible. If you can collaborate with others, your classroom and your life will be happier and less stressful. After almost three decades of teaching, I have a team of people around me who are amazing at a variety of specialties, and their knowledge and skills have found their way into Room 56 opening doors and improving the lives of thousands of students.

It can take years, but for teachers who come to believe that staying in a classroom is their best destiny, time is on their side. The group of people who help my students became part of the Hobart Shakespearean family one at a time, and none of them has plans to ever leave.

Many teachers team-teach, of course, and that is often a terrific strategy to reach students. By sharing the often impossible task of reaching hundreds of students in increasingly smaller amounts of time, working with other teachers can be very effective.

However, I am writing here of a different type of team. With years of experience under your belt, you will have developed your personal vision of what you hope students take away from having been in your class. The unfortunate reality is that while you might have the noblest of goals for the kids, you might not have the range of actual skills or talent to help students reach the heights you envision for them.

I work with some amazing colleagues at my school, but even they do not always have the time, talent, or knowledge to help students in my class with particular skills. There may be times when you must look outside the world of your school to meet people who can help. I have been fortunate to connect with several brilliant people who have elevated Room 56 from a fine little public school classroom to a unique place of learning and fun This team of people has made all the difference.

They were not easy to find. In fact, when I realized that looking for help was a good idea, I did not have a clear understanding of how to be sure if someone could be of real value to the students. Eventually, though, I came to define what I was looking for in a person in a single word, one that has become essential not only in my own vocabulary but for my students as well.

Running the risk of sounding like a Howard Hawks movie, I work only with people who are *professional*. Let's face it—even on our college campuses we have all seen teachers who are not professionals. A professional is on time. He takes his work seriously. A professional choreographer approaches lessons with the same care and intensity whether he is working with a movie star or a ten-year-old child. A pro dresses appropriately. If he has a disagreement with a colleague, it is handled in a mature and friendly manner. Allow me to introduce some extraordinary professionals who have signed on forever to make Room 56 a better classroom, and maybe it will give you some ideas about the talent that's waiting just around the corner for you.

RIGHT IN YOUR OWN BACKYARD

When I began to understand that everyone could use some assistance, I began to look for help. As Dorothy taught us, I really didn't have to look beyond my own backyard.

One day I saw a third grade classroom singing a song. They did a good job, but no child in their little choir would have been mistaken for the next Ella Fitzgerald. However, the amazing thing about the song was that the children were using sign language as they sang. It wasn't a modified version robotically performed. These kids were signing language with a fluidity and confidence of the level one sees at public gatherings or at political rallies.

Their teacher, Barbara Hayden, was fluent in sign language and brilliant in teaching it to children. I asked her if she might be interested in helping my class, and Ms. Hayden was thrilled to assist us. The question itself taught me two valuable things that have been instrumental in helping my students. First, I discovered that when a fellow teacher has a passion, she does not feel put upon if a colleague asks for help. Good teachers love to share their knowledge, and Ms. Hayden has been working with my students now for more than fifteen years, donating hundreds of hours of her time to teach them. She never feels that anyone owes her anything except a good effort during the lessons. Ms. Hayden is knowledgeable, clear, and has high expectations of the children while remaining patient with them. They love learning sign language with her. She is a professional.

Second, by going to Ms. Hayden for help, I was modeling the exact behavior I hoped my students would internalize. All teachers struggle at times to get their own students to ask questions. Because of the ever-present fear that grips so many youngsters, some of the kids would rather remain ignorant than risk embarrassment in front of their peers. When my students see me acknowledge my ignorance or lack of talent and go to an expert, it encourages them to do the same. As the team of experts in my class has grown, so has the trust between my students and me. They are much more willing to come to me because they have seen me go to others.

The second member of the team that elevates Room 56 to the highest peaks is a man named Kurt Ingham. Another fellow teacher at my school, Kurt stopped by my class years ago to see one of our Shakespeare productions. He and his wife, Heather Harris, enjoyed the show immensely, and afterward noticed some of the pictures I had hanging on the walls—photographs of happy children in places like Washington, D.C., and the Grand Canyon. They asked if it would be okay with me if they photographed a future performance of the play.

When I said yes, I had no idea that both of them were brilliant photographers who had taken some of the most iconic photos in pop music history. You have probably seen some of their shots of Jim Morrison, Bob Marley, or the Rolling Stones without knowing who was behind the camera. Kurt and Heather suggested that they begin taking professional photographs of our Shakespeare casts and making posters of the productions. Like true professionals, they have signed on forever. The students love working with them and are fascinated by the complex equipment the duo brings to Room 56. It is no wonder that many of my students go on to take photography classes in middle and high school. The pictures taken by Kurt and Heather adorn our classroom and even the children's homes. The photos capture a spirit and happiness my poor camera efforts could never have achieved; in doing so, their work has defined what Room 56 looks like, and helps new students have a vision of what opportunities are in store for them.

Professionals show a commitment to their work. Just last year, Kurt received the awful news that he had stage-four throat cancer. It was a terrible year for Kurt, and the treatments were painful and frightening. Thankfully, he has courageously beaten the disease and is back at school. Amazingly, while he was at home recuperating from months of awful chemotherapy, Kurt contacted me and said not to worry. He was designing new ideas for the class photograph he was planning for my current students. When the students heard this, they were motivated to work harder than ever. Kurt's a pro, they told me. If a man recovering from cancer can still show a commitment to excellence, they would follow suit.

SEARCHING BEYOND THE SCHOOL

It took many years to get there, but Room 56 rocks. Each year the kids play a variety of music ranging from Vivaldi to Radiohead, and they play the music well. Members of the Los Angeles Philharmonic have attended performances and been astonished by the musicianship of ten-year-old children who at best have played in our school orchestra for a year and very often had not previously played music at all.

I had been teaching interested students how to play the guitar for almost fifteen years before I realized that my amateurish ability was holding the class back. There were songs we wanted to play, and through sheet music from the Internet the kids' playing was tolerable. But they could have sounded much better. I was holding them back. They were being instructed by an amateur and needed more.

Enter Dan Ciarfalia, a professional guitarist and teacher as well. I signed up for lessons with Dan, hoping to improve my skills and then pass on the knowledge to the children. Dan, however, knew what the students needed. In me they had someone who could show them how to play the guitar but lacked a real understanding of how music is put together. So rather than teach me directly, Dan started writing professional scores for the guitarists in the class. He taught me that much of the sheet music posted on the Internet is simply wrong. Those who post guitar music may mean well, but their mistakes are passed on to other young guitarists, who miss an opportunity to be precise in their approach to music and develop an advanced understanding of being a member of a band.

Each year I submit to Dan a list of about sixteen songs the students will be performing as part of their Shakespeare production. Using computer technology and almost a half century of musical knowledge and expertise, he writes precise scores for each song. The students learn to read the music, and see on the page how bass, rhythm, and lead guitars work together. When these young students perform The Who, they do not merely sound like The Who but actually *become* The Who, as the kids channel John Entwistle and Pete Townshend with fabulous enthusiasm and skill.

The beauty of having a professional guitarist onboard helps us in other ways as well. As our band was coming together, Dan brought to our team someone from his network of friends.

THIS BEAT DOES NOT GO ON

After Dan solved our guitar problems, we slowly put a band together and I bought a cheap set of drums. Able to play only the most rudimentary of beats and even less able to teach them, I sought help. One of the students was already taking drum lessons with an instructor through his church, and I got his name and number.

For about a year, two of my students went to this man on a weekly basis and I paid for their lessons. I was quite happy in that the kids were clearly learning more than I would have been able to teach them, and the class band produced a garagelike sound that was not brilliant, but not awful either.

But the following year a little girl came back to me unhappy after her first lesson. She did not like this teacher. Her complaints rambled a bit, but as I pieced her rant together, it became clear that while the drum teacher was no doubt a nice fellow and a talented drummer, he was not the best fit for our class. The little girl told me he was late for the lesson that was conducted in his own store. They worked for an hour but he never asked her name. He showed no interest in who she was or why she wanted to play the drums.

In later years, I recognized this syndrome. He was a hired gun, but not a professional. When I choose someone to help my students, I know that he or she probably won't have the same emotional investment that I do, yet there must be some real interest in the students or the work will be superficial in ways that prevent them from maximizing their potential.

Fortunately, when you build a network of friends helping your class, you have a place to go when problems arise. I called Dan to explain the problem and asked him if he knew a drum teacher who might be a good fit for our class. He told me about a man named Mike Clarke but he cautioned that Mike was a serious teacher. He did not teach drummers; he taught musicians. He required that his students have an outstanding work ethic and a real commitment to the instrument. I was sold instantly.

So were my students. Mike, as the kids love to say constantly, is a professional. He has been written about in drumming books on display at the Smithsonian Institution. When my students take lessons from him, their improvement on a weekly basis is so exponentially huge it is hard to describe. More important, Mike begins each lesson simply by talking to the child about what is happening in her life. He comes to the shows and often brings gifts like gig bags to help his young protégés with their craft. Again, asking for help and having a network of experts has made a huge impact on the achievements of the students in Room 56.

CHOOSING THE RIGHT PEOPLE

Bringing the right folks into your classroom is key, but just as important is knowing how to make a change when things aren't working. Many people are quite good at what they do but may not be the right fit for your students. Sometimes an instructor's philosophy will not match the goals of your classroom.

Under the heading of "Try something new every year," I decided to include dance segments in our Shakespeare productions. Shakespeare himself calls for a dance in many of his plays. For several years, I tried to insert dances by copying moves I had seen in films, and to say I did it badly would be an understatement. I needed help.

I went to a dance school and was very impressed by some of the classes I watched, and got to know a dance teacher who was interested in working with my students. She was excellent in many ways. Her ideas were outstanding, and the following year the class production was far better than anything we had done before. The dance sequences were fantastic. But something was definitely missing behind the scenes. Her philosophy of teaching was not in sync with the mission of our class. Her goal, a fine one, was to create spectacular dances for the show. In doing so, many nice kids had their feelings hurt from being left out of sequences because they were not good enough dancers. In our class, everyone who is nice and works hard always participates in some way, whether the child dances like Gene Kelly or has two left feet.

The students talked to me and I tried to work with this teacher for another year, but clearly the kids were not as happy rehearsing the dances as they were when they rehearsed their Shakespeare or music. The lesson here is that this woman was a fabulous teacher and good person, but she wasn't a good fit with our class. While it is a good thing to expose students to different people and different methods of instruction, at the end of the day it is best when all the adults working with the students paddle together. This was not the case here, and a change had to be made.

Lost again, I asked my network of friends if they knew of

anyone. Kurt and Heather, the shutterbug duo who photograph the kids every year, introduced me to Sarah Scherger, whom they had met while horseback riding, one of their passions.

The first thing Sarah wanted to do was to come and spend time with the children to understand who they were and what they wanted. Bingo. She knew very little about Shakespeare but a whole lot about teaching dance. She has choreographed professionals all over the world, but as a pro herself, she works with the kids with the same enthusiasm and push for excellence as if she were designing a scene on Broadway or in Las Vegas. The kids adore her and actually applaud spontaneously every time she walks through the door. They love rehearsals with her.

She's tough. After the kids work with Sarah for an hour, the floor is covered in sweat. But in Sarah's world, every child matters. If you are not a great dancer but make an effort, she will find a spot for you front and center. She represents everything our class is supposed to believe in, and watching her work with the students is inspiring. She does not know more about dance than other choreographers, but she is the best fit for our shows and mission. She is so in tune with the shows that she can practically finish any sentence or idea the kids and I suggest before we even complete a thought. No one in our class can even imagine doing a show without her being a part of it.

MOMMY LIGHTING

Sometimes, luck plays a part in finding someone to become a member of your support system. I was signing books for a group of teachers one evening when a young woman named Lindsey asked to speak with me. She told me her boyfriend would be able to help my students. I nodded and smiled but thought, *If I only had a nickel for every person who thought they could be of assistance.*

It turned out that Lindsey's boyfriend and eventual husband was Craig Housenick, a brilliant lighting designer whose work includes lighting for the Los Angeles Kings at the Staples Center, television shows like *American Idol,* and even the Jabbawockeez dance troupe in Las Vegas. Craig came to one of the shows, loved what he saw, but gently criticized me later for using "mommy lighting."

"What is 'mommy lighting'?" I asked him.

"Mommy lighting is when you have lights that light up the children's faces so their mothers can see them. Your performances and music are far ahead of your technology. I would be happy to help you."

Craig and a host of friends came the following year with all sorts of equipment I could not possibly understand. I had some concerns, but Craig is a professional and said the magic words. He warned me that he would not come to the shows and light them. He would design the lighting but wanted the kids involved in the production of the show. I was ecstatic but still worried.

"This is great," I gushed, "but what about next year? Once the kids do a show that looks like the Royal Shakespeare Company, what happens when you and all the equipment disappear?"

"We'll be back next year, and every year," he assured me. "We are in it forever. We love what you do and will never let the kids down."

Craig was better than his word. Once again, beyond the expertise he brought to the students, he set an example of commitment that kids need to see to understand the importance of loyalty and dependability. Craig likes to work in silence, and I invite the kids to leave the room when he is working at night or on a Saturday designing spectacular effects for the show. No one leaves. The kids love watching him. When they grow up they want to be like him. This is the type of person you want to invite into your classroom.

BUILDING MEMORIES

Craig is the gift that keeps on giving. When he saw me struggling to create seating for the audience, he laughed at my renting risers from a local company. Craig introduced me to Matt Scarpino, a brilliant carpenter, designer, and professor of stagecraft. Matt not only builds comfortable and efficient seating for the show's audience but cleverly creates props and effects that help the children tell the story. Whether we need a door with an alarm for *The Comedy of Errors* or prison cells for *Measure for Measure,* we call 1-800-Matt. He is like all the other members of our team—kind, hardworking, dependable, and professional.

There remained one missing piece of the puzzle. We were now able to produce shows that rivaled professional companies. However, we had no way to capture these wonderful memories for the children. The final member of our team is the award-winning documentarian Alex Rotaru. After filming our class years ago for a PBS documentary, Alex loved the kids so much that he returns every year with his camera to immortalize the productions. These clips help teachers who want to see the method behind the madness; they also provide the children with a tangible memory I could not ever give them. I can barely point and shoot a camera, but Alex is a professional filmmaker. The students in Room 56 remember their Shakespeare days forever, and Alex is the expert who makes that possible.

THE BEST TEAM MEMBERS OF ALL

Building a team is a winning scenario for all involved. Having a fabulous support system helps you and your students and brings enormous joy to the individuals who become so important to the success of your program. Some of your team will be fellow teachers and others might come from outside the school.

But no one can help you more than those secret weapons I've mentioned before—your former students. I've already suggested some of the valuable things recent graduates can do, but adult grads can pitch in in different but equally powerful ways. Nothing will make a teacher smile more than receiving assistance from a successful adult who you knew years before spilling paint or forgetting homework.

For Room 56, Matthew Parlow, now a law professor at Marquette University, created a foundation that allows us to raise money for our productions and trips. In Yong and Hwi Yong Song, engineers from the University of California, Berkeley, created and maintain our Web site, where people can learn about our class and make contributions. And Joann Cho, a graduate of Northwestern with a Ph.D. in music from the University of California, Santa Barbara, writes all the keyboard parts for our band and returns to teach piano and arrange all vocal harmonies.

E PLURIBUS UNUM

As you find your voice in the classroom, remember that there are talented and caring people who want you to succeed. Please take a moment to go to www.hobartshakespeareans.org or YouTube to see two clips. First watch our class band perform the classic song "Riders on the Storm" by The Doors in our production of *Macbeth*. Then go to the clip of *A Midsummer Night's Dream*. Keep the following in mind when you are smiling.

I had the idea to put on Shakespeare productions each year, but these clips are on a Web site because of In Yong and Hwi Yong. I may have taught the guitar pieces, but it was Dan who wrote the score and gave all of us a road map to follow. Isn't John's solo on "Riders on the Storm" incredible? Joann wrote it and taught it to him. Look at the stunning lighting design for the "Venus and Mars" section of the *Midsummer* clip. That is all Craig Housenick. How funny is it when the kids are dancing to Randy Newman's "Short People"? That is Sarah at her best, challenging the students who have no fear looking silly for the good of the show. Matt Parlow made it possible to raise the money for the instruments and equipment. Mike Clarke is the reason the band rocks so steadily. The Web site is filled with pictures of the plays taken by Kurt and Heather. Everyone paddles together.

For Your Consideration

- As you grow as a teacher, ask for lots of help. Slowly but surely, find people who are able to help your class in ways you cannot. We all can use assistance.
- Experts are not enough. Character is the litmus test. You want to build students who have integrity, and that is best done by surrounding them with people who are admirable even without their field of expertise.
- Talk to your students about why you ask for help. It's a wonderful chance to model behavior that will help the kids for the rest of their lives.
- Stay out of the way. Let the experts do their thing. I rarely question one of Sarah's dance moves or Dan and Joann's musical ideas. I brought them onboard because they know more than I do. Check your ego at the door, and let the professionals lead your students through doors that are closed to you.
- When your team members are not around, lead class discussions about what the kids admire about them. Help the kids discover that these are admirable people who have developed a field of excellence, but that the fact that they are terrific human beings is what is best of all.

PART III
Master Class

CHAPTER TWENTY-THREE

Getting Better All the Time

Experience can be a beautiful thing, but being a veteran teacher does not guarantee excellence. We have all had teachers who should have retired long before we sat in their classrooms. But those who hang in there and continue to grow by learning from mistakes and taking risks might discover that their passion for teaching waxes rather than wanes. Like Bill Murray's character, Phil, in the film *Groundhog Day*, teachers have a chance to improve and even perfect lessons that were once mediocre.

It's fun when you are good at what you do. Being a master teacher is exciting. You get the pleasure of helping students and fellow teachers. Master teachers do not get stuck in a rut. With the confidence that comes with years of practice, a good teacher can challenge himself to do more in the same way that he raises the bar for his students.

Vision usually decreases with age, but it can sharpen in the classroom. You see so much more than you did in your early years. You anticipate problems before they happen. The students feel good about being around someone who clearly knows what he is doing. They know a pro when they see one.

In Thornton Wilder's masterpiece *Our Town*, Emily wants to

return to the world of the living after she has died. The Stage Manager grants her request to return for one day, and Emily wants to choose her birthday or another special occasion. The wise Stage Manager tells her to "choose the least important day of your life. It will be important enough."

He's right. Every day in a good classroom is special. When you are a master teacher, you get to double your pleasure. First, you get to help many children have better lives. That's why good teachers sign up in the first place. Second, you get to see yourself improve. By perfecting lessons that were once only adequate or good, you surpass your previous efforts, and that is a tremendous feeling.

Let's say my morning science lesson is about solar energy. Students are going to try to increase the amount of solar energy in water in an aluminum container by using reflective shields to gather more of the sun's power. The kids have always loved this experiment. It involves materials previously foreign to them, working in small groups with friends, and even going outside to set up their stations.

It's always been a good lesson, but with years of experience, it is far better than it used to be. It used to take me hours to collect the necessary materials, and I spent many weekends driving from one store to another to purchase items we would use. Today I make one phone call and everything is delivered to the school within two days. Previously, the experiment was successful but often ran longer than expected, cutting into the children's reading time. Now I know how to structure the timing of measuring solar energy so that they understand the science concept more quickly. Not only is the lesson better, but so is the reading hour to follow. As the kids work successfully and efficiently, one of the class maxims is being reinforced: *Hobart Shakespeareans are aware of time and space.*

It's not about working harder. Experience and growth help master teachers work smarter.

During the afternoon, we usually do art projects. But instead of everyone doing the same thing, a portion of the kids will instead work on writing assignments. By dividing the class into different projects, with only ten or so students writing on laptops, I can circulate among the writers and edit their stories as they work. I want everybody to complete their latch hook rugs and also write wonderful stories. But in my early years, my evenings and weekends were eaten up editing earnest tales written by students with poor language skills.

Not anymore. I never have to edit stories outside of school. And because I work with small groups of students, their work is far better than that of the kids of previous years. I am able to devote time to talking with the writers, helping them develop their ideas as they write, and not staying up past midnight with a pile of thirty-page disasters in front of me. Instead, I am in bed far earlier than I once was, getting the necessary sleep to help me be at my best the following day.

The rugs are more beautiful than before because I have found that some companies produce better raw materials than others. The kids are better organized with their materials, using a variety of sorting techniques I did not know when I started out.

Actually, during my earlier years, some of the kids didn't finish their art projects. These days everyone finishes. Previously, some of the kids wrote decent stories good enough to be illustrated, bound, and published in a volume they would keep forever. Nowadays everyone publishes. Experience can make a teacher more effective.

It works this way all day long. Experienced teachers have a fantastic sense of timing. History and geography lessons not only run smoother but far more kids enjoy the lessons and internalize their value. A calm confidence means that you will have far fewer classroom management problems, because more students are willing to listen to what you are teaching. And when they don't, your experience will help you reach difficult kids who were once beyond your grasp. More of your goals will be reached. In Room 56, the goals of being nice, working hard, showing initiative, and all the other postulates are not empty slogans that look good on a classroom wall. They are real skills that are the center of every lesson, and they are skills that the students are eager to acquire. It wasn't always that way. Great classrooms take time to build. Master teachers are artists, and it is a thrill every day to walk into a room that through your efforts is even better than it once was.

I have to spend only about two hours each weekend preparing for school (I'll give you the details in chapter 25). The rest of my weekend is my time off; I do things with my family and friends. And I never worry about school as I watch a play.

In *Groundhog Day*, early in the film Phil can't wait to get out of Punxsutawney and return to Pittsburgh. By the end of the film, he wants to live in the place he once detested. With things running smoothly and children learning real skills that will help make their lives extraordinary, why would a teacher want to leave? It's not always a wonderful life, but it's an awfully nice way to live one.

For Your Consideration

- Veteran teachers do not have to be stuck in a rut. Teaching the same lesson each year is *not* the same lesson if improvements are made.
- Make a stand. Be steady and reliable. Staying in a classroom for many years and creating joy and excitement is terrific role modeling for the students. They will more likely care about your class if they know that you do.
- There is nothing wrong with being a teacher for thirty years. Many teachers want to "move up" and become administrators, and that's fine. But if we can develop hundreds of thousands of master teachers who want only to teach, that will help public education more than the latest trend or set of standards.

CHAPTER TWENTY-FOUR

Looking Out My Back Door

I t's a wonderful feeling to come to school when you are a master teacher. Gone are the days when you worried about breaking up fights, covering the curriculum, or dealing with the everyday madness that goes with the job. You're not cocky, but you carry the easy confidence of one who knows what she is trying to achieve and has the tools to meet certain objectives. Life is good.

A first-rate veteran teacher who runs an outstanding classroom is a thing of beauty indeed. But teaching within four walls has its limitations. Some teachers want to teach outside the box, or room. Taking your students on field trips can help them and you reach greater heights. Consider two quotes from Henry David Thoreau:

> The deepest and most original thinker is the farthest travelled.

> During the berry season the Schools have a vacation and many little fingers are busy picking these small fruits. I remember how glad I was when I was kept from school a half a day to pick huckleberries on a neighboring hill all by

myself to make a pudding for the family dinner. Ah, they got nothing but the pudding—but I got valuable evidence beside.

Most schools provide students with field trips. They range from a morning at a museum to a trip to Washington, D.C. Although such excursions can be valuable for the kids, they are too often badly planned activities that fall far short of the objectives they are supposed to meet. Many of the same systemic mistakes that prevent schools from achieving real excellence derail the school trip train before it ever leaves the station. The assumption is wrong that all kids must attend. Not enough prep is done by students or teachers. The result: a boring and pointless expenditure of energy.

Master teachers can step in and create excursions that will make a difference for the students who have earned the privilege of hitting the road. But whether you take students to the capital or a museum in your hometown, a look at the planning and organization of the trip is beneficial to master teachers who want to go the extra mile.

The first step forward is to step back and reflect on why you are taking your students on the road. When your objectives are clear in your mind, you can frame all the preparation with the students around your goals. Here is what I hope to help children learn when we prepare for and eventually embark on a trip.

OBJECTIVES

— The students will learn skills that will be useful to them for the rest of their lives.

— The students will learn to be independent and take care of themselves.

— The students will become more organized.

— The students will learn to be more considerate of other people.

__ The students will improve their work in the classroom.

__ The students will return home as better sons, daughters, brothers, and sisters.

These objectives are made clear not only in my mind but also in the minds of the students. A close look at the list reveals that such lessons can be applied even while playing Frisbee at the park. Students must make sure that they do not interfere with families that are there. They have to focus to catch and throw a Frisbee well, the same focus that will help them solve math problems next week. They have to share with one another, just as they need to do as members of a family. They need to bring food and drink and sports equipment, and carefully pack things up when the day is over. Actually, I tell the students, we haven't left the classroom at all. We just moved it to another place.

WHO GOES

Ask any good kid who has been on a field trip ranging from a day at a museum to a month in Europe, and he'll tell you some of the kids on the trip had no business being there. Bad behavior can ruin other students' days and damage the reputation of the school. This problem is widespread because many people have the mentality that all children should go on trips. Going on any field trip should be a privilege that is earned. Being invited on an amazing journey like one to Washington, D.C., should be a ticket that is hard to get. One of the problems facing teachers taking students on the road is selecting which children should go—and recognizing that it may not be everybody in the class.

Below are some details about our annual Washington, D.C., trip, but the spirit of what is listed can be easily applied to taking kids to a play or movie. The ground rules are the same for a trip across town as for a trip across the country. Reasonable expectations must be clearly explained to the students and their parents. These trips are not a reward dangled on a stick to get the kids to behave or work hard. Trips are simply an extra opportunity for kids to learn, provided they have shown themselves to be ready to get on the bus or plane.

Students and parents receive information about our trip to Washington, D.C., at least six months before we leave. A letter and subsequent meeting detail the dates and purpose of the trip. Parents of children who have gone on this trip in the past come to the meeting to verify the safety and value of the trip, as many of my students have never been on an airplane or stayed in a hotel. Most important of all, the parents learn that their children must earn a spot. Although scholarship and good work in school are an essential part of the offer, character traits and behavior are stressed far more than test scores.

There are two other keys to the selection process. First, I do not run the Washington, D.C., trip as an official school activity. Everyone's situation is different, but it has been my experience that to do things outside of the school district has its advantages. When a trip is a sanctioned school activity, you lose control over key components, such as deciding on the final roster. By making this a private outing, from the word *go* the parents understand that I have the final say as to whether their child participates. Our trip to Washington, D.C., is done during a vacation period, so students do not miss school.

The second part of selecting students revolves around the reasons a child might be left behind. If a student is doing poorly in school, he does not get to go. That's a reasonable issue to explain to a disgruntled parent. If the initial meeting clearly lists a certain grade point average as one of the requirements to attend, a review of tests and work will help a parent to understand your decision.

However, the most difficult part of rejecting a student is recognizing bad behavior that should prevent a student from attending. With these students, I use a bit of language that might help you. I tell the parents that the child is being left behind for safety reasons. My number one job on such trips, I explain, is to make sure all students are safe all the time. I document countless occasions when a student was not listening in class. I report to the parent that because their son frequently does not pay attention, I can't run the risk of taking him. I like their son a lot; enough to care about his safety. What might happen if he was not listening as we were crossing Pennsylvania Avenue and did not hear me call out instructions to ensure his well-being? I never tell parents that their child was not chosen because of bad behavior. I tell them he will not be safe at all times, and he is too valuable to take such a risk.

I do not take improvement "projects" on the road. The road is too dangerous a place to try to help a struggling youngster find himself. Going to Washington, D.C., should be a privilege reserved for young people who have consistently demonstrated the emotional intelligence that shows they are ready.

This reasoning is applied anytime I take students on the road. Recently, I took sixteen students to Yosemite National Park for a week. It was a wonderful trip. In Yosemite, one of the most popular hikes begins at a place called Happy Isles, where people can ascend to Vernal and Nevada falls. The truly adventurous can even make it up to Half Dome.

At the Vernal Fall bridge, there are signs everywhere telling people to stay away from the river. It's beautiful and inviting, but deadly. When we were there, we saw countless families and their children ignore the signs and go down near the raging waters. The students looked at me in disbelief, because I had told them they would see such foolishness. The kids hiked several miles that day up to the top of the waterfalls and listened carefully to me to keep safe. There were many students in my class whom I would have liked to bring, but they had not yet developed the listening skills required to participate. The students who earned the trip had a fabulous time hiking and returned to our cabin that night without a scratch.

Just two weeks later, two children were killed right where we had been hiking. It was a horrible tragedy that should not have happened. They were playing by the river despite clearly posted warning signs not to do so. Every student in my class that year received a copy of the story of the accident, as will every future student of mine as well. I read the news today, oh boy, indeed.

When my students travel, I take out liability insurance. I also have parents sign the proper forms with the Los Angeles Unified School District, making sure they understand that this is not an official school trip but one for which I accept all responsibility for keeping the students safe. Forms, however, are merely legalities. The best liability insurance you can take out is to select the right students before the trip begins.

AN OUNCE OF PREVENTION

A trip to Washington, D.C., may take a week, but our class spends months preparing. The students cover American history and pay particular attention to information about presidents and events that they will encounter while in the capital. Most of their preparation, however, focuses on life skills that will be beneficial to the kids on the road and beyond.

Each week we spend an hour or two after school preparing for the trip. The word *rules* is never mentioned. The students do not learn rules. Instead, they discuss and agree that there are ways to do things, and by the time the plane is boarded, the kids have adopted and internalized valuable knowledge that makes the trip efficient and fun.

In my previous book *Teach Like Your Hair's on Fire,* I outlined in great detail the planning steps we take before our Washington, D.C., trip, as well as a schedule of our actual activities. I'm summarizing the categories and giving you a few of the steps here.

THE PLANE

The students already have their bags tagged and know how to check them. They've practiced going through security, safeguarding their boarding passes, and making their way quietly and in an orderly fashion through the airport and onto the plane. Students know the configuration of the plane before they board.

During the flight, they read or work on history puzzles that they carry with them in their notebooks. They know how to order food on the plane. They make eye contact with the flight attendants and thank them for their service.

Students know how to deplane, waiting patiently for the row in front of them to leave first.

THE HOTEL

We have already worked out roommates and shower schedules, and the students bring their own dirty laundry bags. They know how to use electronic room keys, and they are very quiet in their hotel rooms. They're nice to the maids, and write thank-you notes and leave a tip. Their rooms are tidy, too!

Students go to bed by 8:00 P.M. When they are ready to go to sleep, they call my room and let me know. No one leaves the room after this call until breakfast the following morning. Many schools place tape on the doors of students to prevent kids from leaving their rooms at night. That is not necessary for Hobart Shakespeareans. The kids all stay inside because they believe they need to be safe and not because they don't want to get in trouble.

THE METRO

The students all carry their own Metro passes to ride the trains around Washington, D.C. The pass is always kept in the same pocket, so it is never lost. They know how to get on and off in an orderly way, and they let any elderly person standing have their seats. They also know what to do if they miss a train or get separated from the group, and they know the routes we'll be taking.

MOVEMENT AND ORGANIZATION

The students practice the use of a *rallying point*. When exiting or entering an area, the first student seeks a spot at least fifty feet from the door in an open space. Students gather around this leader to make sure they are not in the way of others.

The students plan to use certain pockets on their person or backpack to separate cell phones, Metro passes, and room keys. That way nothing gets demagnetized or lost.

The students practice the art of *consolidation*. When holding information brochures from a national monument along with a camera or other items, it's easy to lose things. The students learn to consolidate many items in one bag to keep themselves organized.

The students learn to cross streets in silence. All focus needs to be on traffic and potential danger. No one steps into the street without audio confirmation from their teacher. Green lights are ignored. No one moves into a danger zone without instructions from a group leader. The students do not take pictures or talk on cell phones when walking.

No student goes to the bathroom alone. We use the *rule of four*: groups of children enter and exit a bathroom together, even if some of them do not have to go.

RESTAURANTS

The students have practiced reading menus and ordering food in our classroom. They are ready when their server asks what they want.

The students drink only water during meals and make healthy selections. Each child orders fruits and/or vegetables with every meal. They also know about eyes being bigger than stomachs. They order small portions, knowing they can order more if they have not had enough to eat. We do not waste food, and everyone washes their hands before eating all meals.

The students learn how to bus their tables in museum restaurants.

The students practice placing salads on a scale, as they'll do when they pay for it in a museum.

The students learn how to gather together when paying for food in line in a museum. By placing their trays together, the cashier can tabulate one bill rather than twenty.

The students love the training sessions in which we pretend we're on an airplane or in a restaurant. Rather than memorizing an abstract set of rules forced down their throats, they can see how the rules work out in practice. They also discuss everything they practice and understand that there is reasonableness to the way we do things.

Some of my former students now go to a very fine private school that takes its students to Washington, D.C. The kids enjoyed their trip, but told me they liked our time there better. Some things bothered them. As an example, cell phones were not allowed. This rule was enforced because several years earlier one of the boys was sharing pornography with some of his friends on a phone. This caused the school to ban all cell phones from future trips. I understand the school's concern, but a different approach would have been to recognize the fact that this is a problem for today's teenagers, discuss the issue with the students, and teach them to use cell phones properly.

If the kids buy into the rationale behind the way you do things, your trip will run beautifully. Take time to explain the methods to your madness, and there won't be any madness during your field trip.

For Your Consideration

- As coach John Wooden often taught his students, failure to prepare is preparing to fail. Readiness is all.
- Avoid using travel companies that "do all the work for you." It might be convenient, but a private bus prevents students from becoming independent and using public transportation. Teaching the students to do things on their own will be more beneficial for them in years to come.
- The single most important decision you will make will be drawing the guidelines for who will go on the trip. Always err on the side of caution.
- Do not be married to your itinerary. Be flexible. Weather and other unpredictable factors might force you to change the order of activities. Teaching students to be flexible will probably be a better lesson than the activity you had planned.

CHAPTER TWENTY-FIVE

Stairway to Heaven

I'm pushing sixty.

Becoming a master teacher takes more than hard work and talent. It takes stamina. I was reminded of that recently when an assistant principal came up to my room, panting and sweating profusely. The man was about thirty-five years old.

"I've gotta get in shape," he was able to express during bouts of gasping for air.

"Yes," I answered. "Twenty-one steps to get up here."

And those steps are a daily reminder that sixty isn't thirty.

It's not easy bringing high energy to a classroom for three decades, but it's not an impossible dream. Now in my thirtieth year as a teacher, I can still show up revved up and ready to go. Many terrific people understandably get burned out, so I would like to share a few practices I use that help me show up with my batteries charged. The first two are no-brainers, but the third confronts the foe that empties the gas tank of many fine teachers.

PHYSICAL STAMINA

I intentionally do not have a desk in my classroom. I practically never sit down; I am on my feet for about eight straight hours every day. Circulating about the room, encouraging students to aim higher, and creating a positive and safe classroom environment is exhausting. Added to this, the very real energy sapper of remaining calm at all times is wearisome. Keeping cool when dealing with an incorrigible youngster is probably more tiring than running a 10K. I can completely understand why a teacher comes home and crashes on a sofa in front of a television. If he has children to feed and a spouse to care for, his last ounce of spirit is spent during the evening. Do this for thirty years and those twenty-one steps seem like Mount Everest.

But it doesn't have to be that way. My son-in-law is a pediatric orthopedic surgeon. His normal day consists of two surgeries every morning, an afternoon spent seeing patients, and evenings taking care of his wife and daughter while reading medical journals. And yet he still works out every night. He must stand on his feet every day for six to eight hours in surgery, he explained to me, and he better be fit, and if evenings are the only time he can hit the gym, so be it.

You need to be fit, too. Park the car or skip the bus and walk for a couple of miles every day. Hit the treadmill. Shoot some hoops or play tennis. This will actually increase your flow of energy. Once you get into the habit, getting in an hour of physical activity each day, even in the evening, is worth fifteen more effective years in the classroom. On the road, I can still easily outpace teenagers while sightseeing.

Also sleep! It takes discipline to get the necessary amount, and I learned that lesson the hard way when I became very ill several years ago because of lack of sleep. Turn off the television and close your eyes. Never underestimate the value of rest.

Finally, bring a bag of fruits and vegetables to school every day to eat as you grade papers in your room during a break or your lunch hour. If you can do these things, and refrain from smoking and a variety of recreational drugs, the twenty-one steps can be a daily reminder that you are still going strong.

SOCIAL STAMINA

Young teachers often complain, or grin and bear the fact, that they have no life. Some young teachers work an outrageous number of hours each week to try to make a difference. Nights are spent making copies, grading papers, planning lessons, or going to students' homes. These growing pains (and the scrambling that goes with them) are inevitable, but the sad thing is that because of them, so many teachers leave the classroom after just a few years.

If you want to continue to grow but also survive, you need to have a life; that takes time. If you want to raise a family, that takes a *lot* of time. But it's possible. A master teacher can have children, grandchildren, and friends while simultaneously doing a great job in class. Realistically, a good social life means you will do a better job in class, coming in daily with a happy and positive temperament.

Master teachers do not have to scramble. They teach more effectively even though they spend far less time getting lessons and supplies ready. Grading papers takes less time for experienced teachers.

Because of experience, I can plan an entire week and shop for supplies in two to three hours on Sunday morning. I know how long it will take to teach a math concept or set up a science experiment. Our school copy machine never works, but I can do everything I need to early Sunday morning at Kinko's. I never have to plan lessons at night. I never spend my evenings desperately running to a store because I forgot some material crucial to a project being made the following morning. My days of earnest desperation are over. This is the joy of having experience. I still care deeply about doing a good job; I just don't have to kill myself to do it.

Evenings once devoted to looking for two extra calculators for impoverished students can be spent with family and friends. When you are organized and have taught for three decades, your room is better stocked than an Office Depot.

Grading is easier these days, and technology is a big help. Many teachers, including me, use systems such as engrade.com. It's fantastic. I grade papers during lunch breaks and right after our Shakespeare rehearsal in the afternoon. I can also enter grades on a computer site that the students and parents can access the same day an assignment is turned in. This improves teacher/parent/student communication and adds hours to your day. I can't remember the last parent conference I had when a parent was surprised or disappointed with her child's performance. They have the information almost as soon as I do.

I am an early riser, so Sunday morning is when I plan, but I've already graded my papers at school. My evenings are focused on my wife, our children and grandchildren, and friends. My colleagues often comment that I have a positive personality. It is easier to be positive each day in school when the previous evening was an enjoyable one. Young teachers will certainly sacrifice enormous amounts of time to get their classrooms together. You have to pay your dues. But once they are paid, you reap the terrific rewards of that sacrifice. You get to enjoy your life and have a great time in the classroom.

EMOTIONAL RESCUE

You have to stay in shape, physically and psychologically. Experience can help you manage time better, become a top teacher, and have a life outside the classroom. But there is a harsh truth that does not get discussed often enough: teachers burn out because of the emotional toll of the job.

Here's the rub. The greatest killer of a teacher's emotional stamina is the system itself. Physical strength and social balance help people cope, but even these two defenses are often no match for an educational system so dysfunctional it would require George Orwell to give it a proper description.

Great teachers need to feel wonderful about the work, but that's a tall order. Emotions get rubbed raw over years of dealing with hundreds of young people who come to school unable to read or write at the most basic level. The schools themselves are a mess; roofs leak, floors buckle, and the drinking water is unsafe. Hysterical parents barge in and accuse you of shortchanging their little darling and are in complete denial that their "perfect" child has serious issues. Orchestras and libraries are being cut back and even eliminated. And every couple of years, a movie comes out with stereotypic representations of bad teachers who are demonized as the root of all our educational problems.

The system allows this to happen. Rather than encourage and support you, it actively works to discourage you. Every few years a new "game changer" is announced as the newest set of standards are introduced, but the system never really changes. Veteran teachers know that these standards are no different from the old ones. Taking a page from the politburo, leaders stand in the front of the room at professional development meetings making demands and predictions for their "New World Order." Good teachers don't know whether to laugh, cry, or quit. The most recent sermon on the mount has come to us in the form of Common Core Standards. I am not making this up: the presenter at our first training explained that our job as teachers was "to prepare the children to be a part of the international workforce." We were also told that the emphasis on imaginative literature was going to be scaled back because children need to read more nonfiction.

Mark Twain, John Steinbeck, C. S. Lewis, and dozens of Newbery classics would not be on the test deemed essential in the New World Order. I immediately thought of how many times I would have to go up and down those twenty-one steps to get rid of hundreds of books—thirty years' worth.

To steel your resolve and keep your emotional stamina strong, may I offer two suggestions? First, keep in mind that when George Orwell attacked government systems, he was exposing human hypocrisy and the corruption that power always seems to bring to the table. After all, let us not forget that we live in a country founded by slave owners who signed a declaration demanding freedom from oppression. Keeping this perspective might help you to remember that what is happening to teachers today is nothing new. A night with Orwell will make you feel less lonely. You are not the only one who sees the absurdity of it all.

Real teachers know that real teaching is not based on the Common Core, or blended learning, or the newest notebook of rules and regulations handed out at the Tuesday staff meeting. Given the ridiculous belief that all children are going to leave school ready for college (another handout at last week's meeting), master teachers, now more than ever, must keep things real. Recognizing that the system is seriously flawed helps one to remain emotionally strong.

Many have forgotten what good teaching looks like. It is tragic that current reformers are forcing teachers to base their entire day preparing students to bubble in circles on standardized tests. These exams have little to do with success or happiness in the future. Such thinking is killing the emotional stamina necessary to develop into a master teacher. Recognizing that this direction is wrong will help you keep your emotional stamina strong.

My second suggestion is to watch the film *Searching for Bobby Fischer,* which was written and directed by Steven Zaillian and based on the memoir by Fred Waitzkin. In the movie, young Josh

Waitzkin is participating in a chess championship, and in the final match he is up against a very tough opponent. Bruce Pandolfini, one of Josh's teachers, played by the outstanding Sir Ben Kingsley, watches his protégé on a television screen in a separate room. Josh is losing, but then, surprisingly, his opponent makes a mistake.

Bruce watches Josh survey the chessboard. A series of difficult moves will win the match, and he hopes Josh will see what he sees. Suddenly, although Josh says nothing, the teacher stands a little straighter, smiles, and says, "He's got it." Even Josh's father does not know it yet, but his teacher knows Josh is about to win the match.

A teacher knows. No computer or system or standardized test can look into a child's eyes and recognize true understanding. A teacher does that. A teacher can read body language, offer a sympathetic ear to a kid having a bad day, or show a child an open door that might change a life. If you ever feel that you do not have the emotional stamina to climb those twenty-one stairs, remember that you can do that. Someone is waiting for you at the top of the stairs, and a look into that student's eyes and beyond is the difference the system will never understand.

But real teachers understand. Stay emotionally strong and continue to make connections. That is the most important data of all.

Judy is a former student and now a junior at a top university. She is currently studying abroad in Istanbul, and I received this note from her.

Hi Rafe! (or as you would say in Turkish, merhaba!)

It sure is great to hear from you! I am very sorry for the delayed response but my Internet in Turkey has been on and off. I know that you must be very busy and it really means a lot to me that you would take the time to write and think about me. I'm sure that the play is coming along great. Have you fully cast The Tempest yet? I can't wait to come and watch it in just a few months!

I left last Friday and even though I have only been here for a few days, the journey and experience have been nothing short of amazing. I have met some great and hospitable people and made friends from all over the world. I'm sitting in my room now drinking some tea with my three other Turkish roommates. It's a little hard because I have no idea what they're saying but I know that once I begin classes, having them around will improve my speaking abilities immensely. As I sit here I can only think of how fortunate I am to have met you. I know sitting in your class nearly 10 years ago was the turning point in my life, and without it I am absolutely certain that I would not be where I am and who I am today and I only have you to thank.

I would have never imagined myself here. I could have never imagined leaving Koreatown but now I call the East Coast home and I've even managed to make it across the Atlantic over to Istanbul.

If I need anything, I know that I can always trust you. I will keep you updated on my trip and experiences here. Take care!! And please send my warm regards (from Turkey) to Barbara and your fifth grade class.

All the best,
Judy

You, the master teacher, help change lives. You are the turning point. Your skill and expertise are passed on, and the world is a better place because of your wisdom, hard work, and dedication to the craft of teaching.

You have learned that a great classroom is not about teachers *talking*. It's about students *doing*. Students should not merely take a test on *Hamlet*. They should act it.

Rather than play Guitar Hero, they should play the guitar. And they should not just study history. They need to experience history. They must live history. And with your guidance, your students will make history.

Students need master teachers now more than ever. And because they do, you must maintain the emotional stamina to help the next Judy and climb those twenty-one stairs for thirty years. Stay strong and those steps are not Mount Everest. They are the stairway to heaven.

Epilogue:
No Retreat, No Surrender!

The more things change, the more they stay the same.

We teachers can change. With perseverance and courage, we can look back on a long career with mixed emotions. There will be scars from too many failures. But these wounds can be soothed by other memories, of children who have better lives because of our efforts. The courageous teachers who remain in the classroom to grow and become masters of the craft have every reason to feel pride in a job well done.

But some things do not change. We will never be given our due. It's the sad reality all of us must come to accept.

Many years ago, I was asked to give a speech to young teachers. It was a great honor to be flown to another city to inspire some outstanding beginners. I do not consider myself a high-maintenance person, but I must confess that I was shocked when I was taken to my "lodgings" the night before the speech. I slept on a small cot in a garage under a Ping-Pong table. With my legs hanging over the edge of the cot and fresh cobwebs hanging above me, it was not a pleasant sleep.

Well, I figured, things had to get better. Eventually, dedicated teachers will be given their due. But maybe not.

Almost thirty years later, I was invited to a conference to give a speech for teachers in a beautiful city on the water. I wasn't expecting a suite at the Ritz, but I had to laugh out loud when the taxi that picked me up at the airport pulled up to a retirement home.

I am not kidding. The organizers of the meeting selected a retirement home for my stay with them. The room was a tiny cell, but I had a ceiling over my head instead of a Ping-Pong table. Progress! But as I went to sleep that evening, I knew one thing to be true: I am not ready to retire. And I hope you are not planning to give up either. There is too much to do, and too many good days to enjoy. There are kids who don't know how to cover second base. The next Eric Clapton sits in your room ready to play his version of the blues. There are science lessons to be taught. One of the students who learns those lessons might cure cancer. There are students waiting for you who have never heard of Mark Twain. My own class has never performed *Cymbeline*.

They can put me in a retirement home, but after thirty years, I am not ready to retire. Barbara still needs a new kitchen, and too many kids need all of us.

No retreat. No surrender.

APPENDIX A

A Day in the Life

Many teachers write to me or call to ask me to take them through an entire day with the class. Below is a day I jotted down from a Thursday in March 2012. Every teacher—and every day—is different, but I hope the following diary is an example of how major themes of the class are a constant presence in everything the students do. Hopefully, my sharing of a typical day will inspire a few ideas to make your good days even better.

5:00 A.M. It's a Thursday, and I am awake before the alarm goes off. I went to bed early the night before and feel well rested. I roll over and kiss my wife before shaving and hopping into the shower.

5:20 A.M. Thank goodness for supportive wives. Barbara has put out a good shirt and tie for me. It's important to set an example for the students. My clothes are pressed and in good condition. My Stan Smith Adidas are ready. I wear tennis shoes to remind myself that good teachers are on their feet all day long.

5:22 A.M. Over breakfast, I begin to go over my mental list of what has to happen today in school. Priority one is that the students understand the irony of Ralph's situation in *Lord of the Flies*. They identify with his desperate desire to be rescued from the island, and do not understand William Golding's point that there is no rescue. Today the students will hopefully recognize that lesson with a little help from me.

5:50 A.M. It takes about fifteen minutes to drive to school. It's pitch-dark in the parking lot. I take a minute in the car to breathe and focus on the tasks of the day. I want to cover situational base running when we play baseball. I need to check Bobby's work carefully today. He told me yesterday that he wants to start a string art project but he does not finish his work. I have told him that he will have to earn the privilege by completing his reading assignments.

6:05 A.M. The main building is locked up. Budget cuts mean that no secretaries are in the office until 8:00. Fortunately, my room is in a different building and I can get in. The room is a bit messy as a result of yesterday's dance rehearsal that finished after 4:00. Tables and chairs are askew and need to be straightened to keep the room orderly.

6:15 A.M. I organize several papers to pass out to the students to supplement today's curriculum. There are special word problems for this morning's Math Team. History terms covering the Civil War will be handed out at 8:30.

6:35 A.M. A math review test from yesterday that I have not yet graded sits on one of our keyboards. Next to it sits a music score for David Bowie's song "Changes." There are twelve copies, for the students who play guitar and piano. Three students, the earliest of birds, enter the room with a cheerful good morning. Hugo grabs a broom and starts sweeping the debris left from thirty-plus kids who danced at yesterday's rehearsal of the Shakespeare production, now four months away. Rosa and Angie get Big Bertha (our top-notch hole puncher) and prepare the various papers on students' desks. This way no class time will be wasted passing out work. Every second matters.

6:45 A.M. There are now about a dozen students in the room. It is still dark outside. Luis and Alexis borrow my math book and quickly grade yesterday's math work—a multiple-choice test on the multiplication of fractions. The grades are entered in a grade book and the papers left on students' desks. More than half the class had perfect papers. These students have earned bonus money in our class economy. Leo, one of the bankers and early birds, takes a pile of class cash that looks like Monopoly money. He places the bills on the desks of the deserving students and returns the remainder of the money to the ledge by the whiteboard. The money is in plain sight but no one in the class ever touches it except our four bankers. *Hobart Shakespeareans are honest.*

7:00 A.M. There are thirty-four students in class this year. By this time twenty-five have already arrived. Some are looking through bins of colored string, selecting the hues they will use for their afternoon projects. They are excited. Three days earlier they had been told that this was the day actual stringing would begin. The kids have worked on their projects for about a month now, so their excitement level is high as they begin the final and most fulfilling step in creating their designs.

Other children are cleaning the walls of the room. Several are practicing Shakespeare lines in small groups. Today we are working on act 4, and a few of the performers are going to try to go "off book" and run their scenes from memory.

7:15 A.M. I sit down with Emily, a fourth grader who is going to play lead guitar on the song "I'd Love to Change the World," by the band Ten Years After. It's a tough piece. I teach her one measure of the song, an eight-note riff. She's doing well, and learns the difficult licks step by step. By the end of the year she'll play the piece like a pro. Karen, one of our pianists, sits at the keyboard and plays her part slowly so that Emily gets down her timing. All the musical parts begin this way. It is best to start playing a piece of music slowly but accurately instead of at full speed and badly. The speed will come later, but for now, playing the piece in time is more important. The kids learn that the count in music is actually more important than the notes.

7:25 A.M. Math Team begins, and twenty-five students are in the room. It's a voluntary activity for kids who want to come in early and improve their problem solving and critical thinking skills. Today we are solving a problem involving the strategy of making charts and tables. The students have to find a pattern to complete their charts. We review the steps of problem solving. First, we understand the problem by collecting relevant data. We then choose an appropriate strategy to solve the problem. Next we solve the problem. And finally, we analyze our work to see if our answer makes sense. The kids go through these steps every morning. Once they have shown that they understand the problem, I leave them alone in groups of three or four to make their charts and come up with solutions. This morning's problem is a particularly complicated one but fun for the students. They are buzzing with chatter as they work together.

7:40 A.M. The phone in the room rings. A couple of teachers from Illinois are coming today to observe. Two of the students have the job as hosts in the room. They go down to the office, greet the visitors, and bring them back to the room. It will be these children's job all day to make sure our guests have materials and guides through each of the lessons. They also make sure the visitors have access to bottled water, juice, soda, and the bathrooms.

7:44 A.M. One of the groups announces that they have a solution. They call out their answers but the rest of the class finds errors in their work. Everyone goes back to the drawing board.

7:49 A.M A group has solved the problem. I ask them to wait a couple of minutes to see if others can also find the answer. The kids who are finished wait patiently for their peers to complete their work. Everyone matters in this room.

I ask all the groups to share their answers. All but one group solved it and completed their matrices correctly. The four kids who did not come up with the right answer understand their mistake. The kids clean up. The official beginning of the school day approaches.

7:57 A.M. The kids who came in early go to the bathroom before school begins. No one goes with them. They are independent and know they should go before a long morning commences.

The class is now full. The kids who do not come early for Math Team have been waiting outside the room for about ten minutes and enter as the early birds take their bathroom break. Several kids go to the closet where our baseball gloves are kept. They take them out and place them on the floor near the door, where players can select the one they'd like to use this morning.

8:00 A.M. The bell rings. Within fifteen seconds, the class is out the door and walking down the stairs to the playground. Other classes are lining up outside and being picked up by their teachers. We burn from the word *go. Hobart Shakespeareans make good use of time.*

By 8:01 A.M. all the students are running a mile. By the end of the year about three-fourths of the class will be able to run a mile in under eight minutes. We do this because it is good for us.

They are independent. I do not have to monitor their ten laps around the playground. I am on the other side of the field. There is a volleyball court with poles for the net and lines painted on the blacktop for the boundaries. Unfortunately, our school never puts up a net. They have stopped doing this because the students tear them down. While the students run the mile, I take a ball of string and tie it across the poles so the kids will have a line that the ball must clear when they play.

8:12 A.M. The class is divided into three teams. Today, the team that calls itself the Black Dragons will be playing volleyball with six on a side while I work with the other two teams on the baseball diamond. I will not have to monitor the volleyball game. The students play well with one another. They learned at the beginning of the year that poor sportsmanship means missing the game. No one wants to miss the fun.

Brian took a piece of chalk from the classroom when the students left to run. The work crew that recently resurfaced the playground painted the bases incorrectly. The distance between the bases is usable only for children in the first grade. They were supposed to paint a second set of longer bases but forgot, so Brian uses the chalk to draw in bases appropriate in length for a fifth-grade baseball game.

The game between the remaining two teams begins. The Gods are up first, having played volleyball yesterday. The home team, Call Us What You Want, won the game yesterday and gets to play again. If a team plays twice in a row, it will play volleyball the next day. This way all three teams rotate and play both sports.

I pitch for both teams. These kids have generally had no physical education for their first five years of school. With the day shortened from a 3:00 P.M. dismissal to 2:19 and a curriculum that is completely centered on standardized testing, most of the teachers never take their students out for sports and games.

The kids love playing a three-inning game in the morning. They are not very good yet, but they know how the game is played. Their sportsmanship is admirable. All the kids cheer for one another. Teams like to win, but no taunting ever occurs. The mission of *be nice* is alive and well.

8:22 A.M. Omar makes the mistake of being caught off base on a fly ball. He is doubled off because he does not yet understand situational running. I do not stop the game or lecture him. He got on base for the first time in weeks today. Learning about tagging up can wait until the game is over.

8:26 A.M. Valerie makes a terrific play by covering second base on a ground ball to third. Her team makes a force play. The students are learning how to cover the right base, depending on the situation.

8:29 A.M. Dana strikes out. She still cannot keep her eye on the ball but always tries hard. All her teammates give her a high-five as she returns to take her spot behind the backstop.

The game ends. I compliment Omar for reaching base. We then have a one-minute lesson on tagging up. The kids learn to go full speed on a fly ball when there are two outs, but to hesitate in other situations. Some do not fully understand this concept, but the foundation is laid for future pointers on situational running.

8:35 A.M. The kids take a moment to look behind them as they leave the diamond. A jacket is retrieved and the kids begin to leave the field. Across the way, the volleyball players see that the game is over and trot over to join us. Jonathan has remembered to bring the ball of string that has been used for the net.

8:37 A.M. The students chatter noisily as they approach the school. Once they cross the gate that separates the playground from the classroom area all talking stops. *Hobart Shakespeareans are aware of time and space.*

8:38 A.M. The students will go to the bathroom by themselves to clean up and get ready for United States history back in Room 56.

8:41 A.M. The guests talk to me about the independence of the students. They ask if students ever make mistakes or misbehave. Of course they do. They're kids. But if we do not allow them to be on their own and even make occasional errors in judgment, how will they ever learn to think for themselves?

I am drying my hands as I leave the teachers' bathroom The students see that I wash up the same way they do. The kids climb the stairs to the room and stay to the right. There are no other students on the stairs, but their good manners are internalized. They always keep to the right.

8:40 A.M. The television is already set to play a short segment of Ken Burns's film *The Civil War.* The students watch scenes of the third day of fighting at Gettysburg. They are astonished at the bloodshed and the size of the armies.

8:50 A.M. The kids take notes from the list placed on their desks earlier that morning and file them in their history boxes—the index card holders in which they store their information. Frederick Douglass, Stonewall Jackson, Gettysburg, Vicksburg, and thirty other terms will become a part of their knowledge within a few days.

9:02 A.M. I announce that they need to put away their history boxes because our science experiment is about to begin. Within thirty seconds, boxes have disappeared and everyone has taken solar energy records out of their folders. *Hobart Shakespeareans make good use of time.*

9:04 A.M. The students have already learned how to use solar collectors. Today's lesson involves testing whether the angle of a solar collector can increase the amount of energy captured.

Groups of four have taken solar collectors outside, and down the stairs, and placed them on a tiny patch of grass near the playground. They pour water into the collectors from bottles I have brought to school. The district has forbidden any water to be used from our classroom sink because it is contaminated. Three of my strongest students carry the two-liter bottles downstairs for all the teams to use. The teams of students fill their solar collectors and use thermometers to take the temperature of the water without guidance from me. *Hobart Shakespeareans show initiative.*

9:25 A.M. During the last quarter of an hour, the kids have written down their observations neatly. *Hobart Shakespeareans understand the importance of presentation.* They tabulate the final results and draw their conclusions. They carry the materials back to the room and put them back in their proper places. Quietly, and without instruction, the students take out their copies of *Lord of the Flies.*

9:30 A.M. The students cannot get enough of this frightening book. Today's chapter will shock them with the death of Simon. I need to make sure they recognize the vast amount of irony in this chapter.

Leo makes an excellent observation—that Simon's wounded head (he bumped into a tree) is reminiscent of Christ's wounds from the Crown of Thorns.

9:58 A.M. Valerie volunteers to read a passage. She rarely likes to read aloud but is feeling more confident. Other struggling readers have tried this week and not felt the sting of their peers laughing. This room is a safe haven. *Hobart Shakespeareans are nice.*

10:20 A.M. Luis is one of the best readers and thinkers in class, and it is no surprise that he makes the observation I have hoped the kids would discover. The character Ralph constantly expresses his hope to be rescued, but Luis points out that the boys are on this island because of a nuclear war. "There really isn't any rescue, is there?" asks Luis. The students gasp. "This is really depressing," comments Angela.

10:25 A.M. The character Simon discovers the truth that the supposed beast that has frightened the children is merely a dead parachutist who was killed in the war. It is dark, but he wanders down the mountain to tell the others. The room is as silent as a tomb. The kids brace for the awful action that they feel is going to happen. Thirty-four kids are glued to the book and have been reading for almost an hour. *Hobart Shakespeareans are focused.*

10:40 A.M. Simon is killed by the boys. Some of the kids cry. No one says anything. It's an awful but wonderful moment. This is what reading is supposed to be like. The room is silent for more than a minute. Then the kids will not stop talking, worrying about what is going to happen next. I tell them it is going to be amazing. And then I tell them we have to stop because it is recess. The kids groan audibly and beg to read more. Some suggest we skip recess. I tell them they will read more . . . tomorrow.

10:45 A.M. Some kids go to recess while others stay in to practice guitar. Today's session is synchronizing the piano and lead guitars for "The Seeker" by The Who.

10:46 A.M. to 10:49 A.M. The student hosts take the guests to the bathroom.

10:55 A.M. Joey nails the lead licks perfectly, but he and the keyboardist, Karen, are still not together. The students play the same song three times in a row and it is better each time. *Hobart Shakespeareans work hard.*

11:00 A.M. Four vocalists join the session to practice their harmonies. The first two verses are outstanding but the final verse is shaky. No one is worried. We have made progress, and the polishing will take place over the next several months. *There are no shortcuts.*

11:05 A.M. Recess is over. The guitarists put their instruments and cases away in the proper place. Kids from the outside enter the room and take out their math materials. The guitarists go unsupervised to the bathroom, which is ordinarily forbidden at school. But these musicians have told me that they have to go and did not have time during recess, as they were practicing. I believe them. *Hobart Shakespeareans are honest.*

11:06 A.M. The students in the room take out their Marcy Cook math tiles to warm up. Their favorite mental math problem of the day is this one: Take the number of senators from Pennsylvania. Add that to the number of justices on the U.S. Supreme Court. Multiply by the number of weeks in a fortnight. Add the number of feet in a yard. Take 10 percent of that number. Add 6.5. Show me the square root of that number. Almost every child correctly holds up the number 3.

11:10 A.M. All students are back in the room and their books are open to page 284. I wrote the assignment on the board early in the morning and it is also in my lesson plan book for all the students to see. Today we are introducing the skill of dividing mixed numbers.

I will not collect or correct the problems from today. There is no time. By this point of the year, I know that twenty-seven of the thirty-four students in my class pass every math test with at least

80 percent of the answers correct. About half of the class gets 100 percent. It would be a waste of time to review their practice work. I know they know.

Instead, I review the common mistake of mixing up reciprocals when converting mixed numbers to fractions. I call mostly on the struggling students during the session to check their comprehension.

Before practice problems begin, I have the students switch seats. All students who have struggled sit next to a top student so that questions can be asked and work can be checked immediately.

11:30 A.M. By now the students are working quietly and attacking the fifteen problems I have assigned. There are more than one hundred problems in both the book and supplemental materials, but I assign far less than the maximum. If a child can do fifteen there is no reason to do one hundred. If he cannot do fifteen, he certainly will never do one hundred!

Not all the students have finished, but everyone is far past the halfway point. Students are called on to share their answers. Questions are asked. No one ever laughs or makes noise during the question period. It's a safe haven. *Hobart Shakespeareans are never afraid to ask questions.*

11:55 A.M. Many of the students have finished. They have assigned themselves a practice test that they find on their own in the back of the book. *Hobart Shakespeareans show initiative.*

11:57 A.M. A check of Sharon's work shows progress. She is improving, as she finally has her multiplication tables down cold. She likes working with Janet, a top student who is very patient with her. I compliment Sharon and she glows. Janet has spent the last several weeks helping Sharon get her act together but says nothing. *Hobart Shakespeareans are humble.*

12:12 P.M. Two students have struggled during the period. They are given the option of eating lunch with me and finishing their work or completing the assignment during art. They choose to stay in and finish during the lunch period.

Our visitors are shown where they can buy some food for lunch at a restaurant down the block. They will rejoin me in the room to talk about questions they have from their morning observation.

12:15 P.M. The kids walk to the lunch area. Most of the students have rejected the free lunch that is provided and bring their own. The food they bring is healthier and tastes much better. They do not bolt their food but eat quickly and quietly because they want to get back to class for guitar. They do not want to waste any music time. As they walk back to the classroom down the hallway corridor, they stay to the right to allow other students space as they walk in the opposite direction. *Hobart Shakespeareans are aware of time and space.*

12:27 P.M. It takes me about four minutes to collect my mail at the office and make a stop at the bathroom. At the same time that I arrive back in the classroom to eat some fruits and vegetables, at least ten of the kids storm back into the room. They want to practice their music. During this lunch period the band is working on "All Apologies" by Nirvana and "Nude" by Radiohead.

12:36 P.M. Lydia, a fourth-grade cellist, has finished lunch and joins the rehearsal. She has been practicing a cello part for the Nirvana song. My former student Joann wrote the cello score. Lydia has the chops to play the piece, but is not ready yet. Other alumni who play the cello in middle and high school will coach her. During rehearsals, one of the keyboardists plays the cello section along with Lydia to help her feel the timing of her part.

12:40 P.M. Three singers work out some harmonies on the song. They ask the band to stop playing, and the kids gather and sing a cappella. The band sits in absolute silence to allow the singers to concentrate and do their work.

12:42 P.M. The adjacent room is empty because the district closed it off due to a hole in the roof. Two guitarists are working in there on the Radiohead song. They are getting the bass and lead guitars in sync because the rhythm of the song is complicated. The students know the room is safe because they've observed workmen hanging out there and playing our guitars without permission. The room has been vacant for almost two years now without any attention from the district.

12:45 P.M. My guests have terrific questions. Several students who are not practicing music join the discussion. These teachers are most interested in the literature we read in class and how we "get away" with reading controversial books. I explain that the best way to beat the system is to play its game. After lunch the kids will do some brief but effective test preparation, and that is how any argument is won. High test scores carry the day.

12:48 P.M. The bass and lead guitarists have finished the song without any help from a teacher. No one assigned this work. They just wanted to perfect the song and are now excited about playing it for the class. *Hobart Shakespeareans show initiative.*

12:52 P.M. The singers on the Radiohead song sound wonderful, as do the two guitars. Keyboard and drum parts are not ready yet, but the kids are satisfied. Additional instruments will be added later, and the students are not in a hurry. *There are no shortcuts.*

12:55 P.M. A bell signals the end of the lunch period. The guitarists pack up their instruments and put them in cases that are labeled for each guitar. The cases are lined up against a wall in order. *Hobart Shakespeareans are organized.*

12:57 P.M. Kids who played outside during the break enter the room. Cleiver has found a twenty-dollar bill on the stairs leading to our room. He brings it to me and asks if I know who lost money. No one is missing money, so Cleiver takes the cash to the office. *Hobart Shakespeareans are honest.*

12:58 P.M. The students engage in a short test-prep session to assess reading comprehension. They have done this for months and are getting quite good. It's a one-page story about kelp in the ocean followed by five questions. Almost everyone gets four or five right. The most common mistake is on the third question. Students discuss the fact that they fell for a trap. They are reminded that many potential answers repeat phrases from the passage without actually answering the question. The students who missed the question are open and forthright in reviewing their mistakes. It's a safe classroom, and no one is ever ridiculed.

1:20 P.M. Our string art projects continue for most of the students. Three students will not be working on projects because they have not passed their spelling tests and must finish additional vocabulary work before they can participate. Two other students will be working on their latch hook rugs. We finish what we start, and these two students must finish their rugs before making string art.

1:23 P.M. The students are now separated into four different areas. Some are sanding wood for string art outside the room to prevent dust from collecting in the class. Others are hammering nails into their boards on tables outside. They are not directly supervised. All the students have been briefed on our safety rules.

1:30 P.M. Other students are in the room painting their backgrounds. Finally, groups of three kids work together to tape patterns on boards that have already been painted. They use rulers and T squares to make certain the patterns are centered precisely on the wood. *Hobart Shakespeareans understand the importance of presentation.*

1:45 P.M. Valerie has a question about placing the dots on her board before hammering nails. She comes to me but I do not know the answer. I ask her if she can give me a few minutes to look it up in a book I use. She puts down her project and goes to help another student without being asked. *Hobart Shakespeareans show initiative.*

2:00 P.M. The students painting their boards are finished. They do not tell me they are done. They clean their brushes, cover their paint cans, and put the paint back where it belongs. These kids search for other students to help because their own projects must dry before work continues tomorrow.

2:09 P.M. I step outside and call out to the students on the field to clean up their sanding and hammering. Students inside who have finished cleaning go outside without being asked to help their classmates bring in their supplies. They also check the ground to look for any nails or scraps of sandpaper that may have been left behind.

2:15 P.M. All students are back in the class and ready for the traditional dismissal. We play the Compliment Game, where students volunteer to say something nice about a classmate. Several thank others for helping with their string art project. One of the students has a compliment for a student with behavior problems who has been kinder on the playground. It's a nice way to send the kids home.

2:30 P.M. Forty students are packed into the room and ready for a Shakespeare rehearsal. A little more than half are from my class; the others are fourth and fifth grade students from other classrooms. The rehearsal is divided into three parts. Today we are blocking act 4, scene 1, from *Measure for Measure*. The speaking parts are reviewed and recited by the actors, with all students following along. Everyone is involved in learning the vocabulary. The kids must understand the language if they are to act it properly.

2:50 P.M. Once I am satisfied that they know the meaning, we walk through the scene to decide who stands where and cover all exits and entrances. The students who are not in the scene are absolutely silent and do not move. They are considerate of their fellow actors. *Hobart Shakespeareans are nice.*

2:55 P.M. I notice Hugo sharing a book with Miguel and ask him if he has lost his book. Without hesitation Hugo tells me he left it at home. He assures me that he knows where it is and that it will be here tomorrow. It's not a problem and the rehearsal continues. *Hobart Shakespeareans are honest.*

3:10 P.M. The scene looks good. All the principals know their blocking. They are not told to go home and memorize their lines.

There is no deadline for when they will rehearse without their books. But they will. *Hobart Shakespeareans work hard.*

3:15 P.M. The second part of the rehearsal is a review of act 2, scene 1. The students have practiced this for more than two months. All the actors know their lines. Today we are synchronizing a wild dance choreographed by Sarah to weave through the lines of Angelo and Elbow, the constable known for his malapropisms.

3:20 P.M. The band is good; the acting is good. But we are not in sync. We slow things down to make sure the actors hear the bass guitar; certain notes are their cues for when to speak and when to dance. Fifteen minutes later the scene looks fantastic and the kids know it. They remember their struggles with this scene two months ago, and now, with disciplined practice, they have it. *There are no shortcuts.*

3:25 P.M. Elvin, who plays Elbow the constable, practices changing the position of his feet to make sure the entire audience will be able to hear his misuse of English. The other children simulate the audience to help him practice making eye contact with people on both sides of the room.

3:30 P.M. The new dance, to "Jailhouse Rock," is rehearsed. The kids have worked on it for only one week so it is raw. Sarah showed them a difficult move yesterday in which couples are dancing. Each girl performs a complete 360-degree flip over her partner's arm. There are four couples, and all are able to complete the move with two spotters to make sure the girls are safe. Once this move is practiced, the kids work on a finished number, "Cream," by Prince. It's particularly raunchy, but this is *Measure for Measure,* a play intentionally designed to offend.

3:40 P.M. As the kids dance, the doors open and a dozen or so middle school students enter the room. They have stopped by to say hi, watch the kids dance, and help clean the room and grade papers. Cynthia has come with her piccolo and will give Sion a lesson at 4:00 when the Shakespeare rehearsal ends.

3:47 P.M. Eileen, the lead guitarist for the Prince song, is having some trouble with her timing on the riffs. I am able to help her because Elsa, one of the returning students, runs the mixing board, freeing me up to teach.

3:56 P.M. Every child in the room has participated. The kids are reminded that we will be finishing act 4 tomorrow. Some of the kids have to dash out the door to waiting parents while others begin to clean the room. Many of these youngsters have been in class since 6:15 A.M. I tell them to let the room wait, and shoo them out the door. Leo asks if he and his friends can borrow some of the baseballs and gloves. Of course they can. How wonderful for a child to begin and end his day in school playing baseball!

Some of the kids walk the visiting teachers to their cars and make sure they know which way they are going. They have been gracious guests, and it's fabulous for the students to meet caring teachers looking for ideas to get better. I always think visitors bring more to the class than we ever give them.

4:05 P.M. Most of the Shakespeare cast has gone home or is outside playing. They usually leave the playground by 5:00, when the neighborhood becomes unsafe for little ones to be hanging out.

4:15 P.M. Inside Room 56, Karen and Angie spend time at the keyboards working on the Bowie song "Changes." They stay until 5:00, when their parents pick them up. In the next room, Sion is practicing her piccolo with Cynthia's help.

4:22 P.M. All the papers for tomorrow are sorted and collated by the former students. They are left on one of the desks for the early birds to pass out tomorrow morning.

Heather and Elsa, eighth graders, tell me about their day in middle school. Heather was tackled in the hallway by a boy she was supposed to escort to the office because he was behaving badly. She then got knocked down trying to get on the bus to come back to Room 56. Middle school is not easy.

4:57 P.M. I leave. A few of the kids who are still in the room rehearsing turn off the equipment and lock up. I say good-bye to the alumni and tell them I will see them Saturday. I know they are all busy, and I don't want them to feel obligated to come around. They never listen.

5:00 P.M. Homeward bound. I get to spend about four hours with Barbara and various family members. I will not spend more than thirty minutes tonight working on the play. I'll call a few teachers who want advice, but the evenings belong to my wife and family.

9:15 P.M. It's time for sleep. The students in Room 56 got to play baseball, experience history, conduct a science experiment, consider the darkest side of the human race while reading great literature, improve their mathematics, play music, create art, and perform Shakespeare. And they did it in an environment where people were nice to one another. It's been another productive day.

APPENDIX B

The Play's the Thing

Many drama teachers or others who would like to begin using drama as a classroom activity ask about the pacing of a Hobart Shakespearean production. Here is a Year in the Life of a play production in Room 56.

"We are such stuff as dreams are made on."

Making those dreams a reality takes a lot of hard work. Getting students to understand that there are no shortcuts is an essential part of spending a year putting together our annual production of Shakespeare. The bar is set high, but we are not in a hurry. Hard work. Joy. Patience. Teamwork. Risk. Improvement. These are the themes that will be a part of every rehearsal. The journey is everything.

June

The Hobart Shakespeareans who've been rehearsing since the previous July perform *The Comedy of Errors* for the month. During the day, third and fourth grade classrooms are invited into Room 56. The seasoned performers do a few scenes for the children. The audience is dazzled by the lighting and sound equipment in the room. Most of the little ones ask if they can learn to play the drums. The kids are told that next year's play, *A Midsummer Night's Dream,* will begin rehearsals in July. Prospective students receive information about the class schedule in addition to how to sign up for guitar lessons.

July

School is closed in July, but we have access to our room, and the after-school program for Hobart students is open during the first six weeks of summer. The new Hobart Shakespeareans are invited to come to Room 56 for two weeks of the month. The Shakespeare class will run from 8:00 A.M. until 3:30 P.M. There will be lunch and snacks for the children.

About twenty-five students show up. More will come in September. There are children who cannot come in summer because their parents have other plans for them. In that regard, this summer session serves another purpose. There are students during July who reveal themselves as extraordinary young people; they are eager to try new and difficult challenges. On the flip side, there are students who are dropped off at school because their parents are looking for baby-sitting. The two weeks in July is when I see the hand I am being dealt for the coming year's production.

During this month, the kids learn about William Shakespeare's life. We play games in which the kids have to try to remember the names of all the plays. They also are introduced to Elizabethan England, including the filthy conditions and the fact that men played all the parts of a play.

Marchette Chute's excellent *Stories from Shakespeare* begins their introduction to this year's play. All the kids get a copy of a summary that we read out loud for an hour or so on our first morning together. Then it is time to jump into the script. All the students receive a Folger Shakespeare copy of *A Midsummer Night's Dream*. We use Folger editions for two reasons. Each scene has a simple summary before it begins. Also, the notes explaining the language are conveniently located across the page being read. It is easy to clarify a passage without losing one's place in the text.

Many teachers prefer using SparkNotes or the Shakespeare Made Easy series. These texts have the original Shakespeare on one side and a modernized "translation" on the other. They can be very helpful. I do not use these texts because my goal is to teach the kids to recite Shakespeare as it was meant to be spoken. Having a modern translation can distract the students from the more difficult, original text. Modern translations are terrific if the goal is only to learn the story of the play. This class is about language, so we stick with the original.

We do not read the play during these two weeks. We download an audio recording of it from the Internet, and the students listen to each act as they follow along in their texts. I stop the audio frequently to explain certain passages. The more difficult speeches get a cursory explanation from me. We have an entire year to get to know the play well. These first two weeks are just a beginning. Still, by the end of July, the students know all the characters quite well and can identify them if I read a speech.

This is also the month when guitar lessons begin. Fifteen students volunteered to begin the optional lessons. They will stay for an extra ninety minutes and go home at 5:00 P.M. There are enough classical guitars for this group to learn to read basic notation and play simple chords. Not all of these students will finish what they started. Many saw the band the previous month and are dying to play exciting music. However, some will find out they're not willing to pay the price. This is going to be hard work. The month of July reveals which students are ready to fly and which ones are learning to walk. It will be my job to find a place for all of them.

On the final day of the session, the students are given an August schedule. We will meet for only one week, as I will be on the road with last year's class and have also planned vacation time with my wife. The kids have done a good job in July, and all promise to see me in a few weeks. Time will tell.

August

We meet only the first week of August. The school completely shuts down after that until the new school year begins after Labor Day. Even so, this five-day period is very important.

Almost all the students who attended in July have returned. Three have not, and at this point I do not know why. They may have quit, or not be able to get to school this week, or moved, or even left the country. However, some new students have shown up. In most cases kids who came to class in July have contacted friends and encouraged them to join the fun.

During this week each returning student receives a CD of all the music we will perform for the play. The list of songs includes Bach, Elvis Costello, Queen, the Beatles, the Beach Boys, Randy Newman, and The Kinks. The kids receive the lyrics to the songs, and we spend part of each day singing them and learning how they will fit into the play. For example, when Helena and Hermia get into a hilarious argument filled with jokes about Hermia's diminutive stature, the show will have a dance number to Randy Newman's "Short People." When the Master of the Revels, Philostrate, is urged by Duke Theseus to "stir up the Athenian youth to merriment," we will have a wild street dance to Elvis Costello's "Pump It Up."

An important part of this week of singing concerns creating a culture where the kids do not laugh at one another. As the songs are memorized, kids are invited to sing at one of our four microphones to showcase the quality of their voices. Some of the students are confident with good reason, as they sing easily and well in front of their peers. Others give it a try and have trouble staying on beat or remembering the lyrics even when reading from a printed page. When no one laughs and such students try to sing again, lessons far more important than learning Shakespeare are being internalized. We don't laugh at one another. It's a safe room.

For the first time, a few brave students begin to read the text they have heard. We try speaking a few scenes. Once again, fear is removed when kids who stumble over difficult passages are encouraged and not mocked by their peers. I learn that some of the students have strong voices, and these are the children who might be chosen for leading parts in the play. The kids want to cast the play immediately, but that won't happen until October. "We're just getting started," I explain to them. "This is a long journey."

September

School officially begins this month, and we have to change our rehearsal schedule. We meet four days a week from 2:30 to 4:00 P.M. A few of the students who came in the summer have quit. Their parents had other after-school plans for them.

However, another fifteen or twenty students show up. Many were not able to come in the summer. The problem is that half the class has already read this year's play, and the new students can't even spell *Midsummer*. So we have a lot of catching up to do.

During September, we listen to the play again but also watch the film. As we are doing *Midsummer,* we have the luxury of watching three versions of the play on film that we can use to augment the children's understanding of the play. There is the 1935 Max Reinhardt film with Mickey Rooney and Joe E. Brown. They will reference him again later on in the year, as some will watch *Some Like It Hot* as part of our Film Club. The 1999 film, with Kevin Kline, contains more technical excellence as far as the production values of the film. And there is my favorite of the three, Peter Hall's lovely 1968 movie, with Diana Rigg, Helen Mirren, Judi Dench, and Ian Holm. It is perhaps the best-spoken *Dream* ever recorded.

Each rehearsal is divided into three parts. We spend half an hour singing two or three songs from the play. Children get a chance to sing into microphones if they like. As the band is not yet ready to play the songs, I strum a basic rhythm to keep the music going. September is the month when we discover the six or seven voices that will do most of the singing in the show.

We then listen to a couple of scenes from the play and continue to understand the material. A key technique I use here is that I do not explain everything. It's only September. When Oberon speaks of oxlips I show them a picture of the flower so that the children understand his speech. But I might skip over Titania's mention of Nine Men's Morris. Eventually, the kids will know it's a game played by children, but under the heading of "Too much information," there is only so much that nine- and ten-year-old kids can process in a day.

Finally, we watch the scenes on film. The students learn that there is not one "right" way to perform Shakespeare. They view the same scene done three different ways. They notice that one Puck is very different from another. Their key lesson here is to realize that eventually it will be *their* Puck that matters. They will learn language, observe others, and finally filter all that information through their own personalities and beliefs to create something that is their own. It's a challenging and exciting road that each child travels.

Wednesday rehearsals are devoted to dancing with Sarah. The students respect and love her. She does not choreograph dances for the first rehearsals. Sarah gets the kids moving, demands that they try their best, and expects them to approach their exercises as young professionals. The students are eager to oblige.

I spend this month thinking about casting the show. There are plenty of students who will be terrific as part of the fairy world. Janice, a student who participated in last year's show as a fourth grader, will be perfect as Titania. A new student, Evan, has a marvelous voice and I am thinking of having him play both Theseus and Oberon. Puck is easy. I have a boy who actually *is* Puck in real life. The lovers are also going to be easy to cast, as I have several boys and girls who have shown themselves to be confident, willing, and talented.

A fifth grader not present last year will be a fantastic Nick Bottom. But I have one worry. I can't see many students who will be a good fit for the mechanicals. It's not easy being funny. At this point, I go to bed at night fretting about producing *Midsummer* without a lot of laughter. But time is on my side. As I get to know the students better, I may have a better cast than I think.

October

By October we have the rhythm of the class down. School ends at 2:19 P.M. and the kids go to the bathroom before Shakespeare begins. That way there is no interruption of flow (literally) during our ninety-minute rehearsal.

Fifteen students began playing guitar over the summer. A few have dropped out; one moved away. I asked one student to stop because she never practiced and it showed. She is still in the Shakespeare program, but being in the band requires a commitment of time she did not want to sacrifice. The others quit because they thought the lessons were too difficult. Ten are still playing every day at recess and lunch. They are still taking baby steps, but all of them know basic chords and can read music slowly. The guitarists can play some simple folk songs, and, for the first time, this month we will see Dan's scores for the production. We will begin with Donovan's "Catch the Wind" because the bass line is very simple.

October is the month we cast the play. All the students try out by filling out a sheet detailing what they want to do. Playing a part is only one of the options. Kids can request that they be in the band and ask to play specific instruments. The guitarists are set, but we will also need keyboards, harmonica, drums, cello, flute, triangle, and some exotic percussion instruments to be used in a Moody Blues song.

The cast members can also be in charge of the technical aspects of the show, including lighting and sound design. Many of the students place dancing in the play as their top priority. Still more kids favor sign language as the skill they want to learn and contribute to the production.

Students may request a combination of these choices. It is not uncommon for one of the performers to act, play two instruments, sing, and do sign language accompanying a song. These are Renaissance children.

Students who want speaking roles try out by picking a part and reading it from their text. At this point of the year acting skills are not important. I listen to the volume and clarity of the speakers.

By Halloween, the play has been cast, but I have stressed the point that this cast is temporary. There will be many changes as the year marches on. Some students who have been quiet in October become bold performers by February and replace students who have not worked hard or failed to live up to expectations. Nothing is in stone when the initial cast list is announced.

My fears of the players to be Bottom's crew have not been assuaged. Quince and the hard-handed men of Athens have been chosen, but I cannot see these six children creating the earnest but awful efforts that make the mechanicals so lovable. Their first scene will be blocked in November, and I'm hoping these children will rise to the occasion.

November

As November begins the class is in a particularly good mood. It's a glorious time of the year. The students have just attended a Halloween party at my friend Mary's house and had a lot of fun. There is wonderful warmth in the room as the students become more involved in the rehearsal process.

With the play tentatively cast, this is a month when we can build the show with the foundation now in place. Sarah knows who is playing what parts, so we can begin serious choreography. On Wednesdays we start work on the raucous Elvis Costello song "Pump It Up" to follow Theseus's instructions to "Turn melancholy forth to funerals; The pale companion is not for our pomp." As always, Sarah has great ideas, and the street scene will feature boys and girls competing against one another for space before they all come together and light up the city.

November is also about act 1. There are two scenes in this act, and we will spend the month blocking them out so that all the performers will know where they are supposed to be at all times. This is more complicated than it sounds. The play is done in our tiny classroom. We put tape on the floor so that the students can visualize their space once the audience and equipment are in place. With about thirty-five guests watching the show from the seating Matt Scarpino has constructed, the area to act, dance, sing, and play music is tiny. The students learn a valuable lesson in November. Their movements offstage are just as important as those on. Moving silently from place to place shows respect to the actors onstage and the audience.

During the first week two students are talking offstage. They are immediately asked to leave the rehearsal. There is no discussion or general reprimand. They're finished for the day. The rest of the cast nods at me. They get it. These are perfectly good kids, but we do not talk during a scene. Both students will get another chance tomorrow. But if they return to rehearse, they have to understand that there is silence when others work. There is no compromise on this issue, and students who internalize this huge amount of respect take a sense of pride in their deportment. We're a professional company.

By the Thanksgiving dinner the kids are on schedule. Act 1 is finished being blocked. All the kids know where they are supposed to enter and exit. The principal actors know what lines to speak and are beginning to find the Shakespearean rhythm. All the actors still hold their books when we run scenes. There is no deadline regarding the memorization of lines. The students rehearse so often, the entire class will memorize everyone's lines by the end of the year.

The first two songs are particularly hard, but the band is in place and working on Dan's scores. Although they are trying, the singers cannot duplicate the intricate harmonies of the Beach Boys' "Wouldn't It Be Nice," but no one is worried. Joann will be down from college next week and all will be well.

During the Thanksgiving party, the kids are not concerned, but I am. Act 1, scene 2, is not funny and it should be. The kids playing the mechanicals are trying their best, but they are not a good fit for their parts. As I stand in the back of the room listening to the kids laugh hysterically while watching *Planes, Trains & Automobiles,* I feel a tinge of regret. This year's class has several authentically funny boys who have not joined Shakespeare. They are good kids, but they have not bought into the idea that school can go beyond the traditional dismissal bell. Like the rest of the class, these boys are at the Thanksgiving dinner, and I wish that somehow a few of them would decide to join the Shakespeare program.

At the end of the evening, as the kids wish one another the best and head out to the parking lot, six of these boys approach me. Miguel, their appointed leader, says, "Rafe, this was a great night. Is there any chance we can still join Shakespeare when we come back?"

What a night. Christmas came early this year.

December

The addition of six playful boys is just the spark the cast needed. Rehearsals had been going well, but these students have made them even better. They are silly at inappropriate times, but they have good hearts. As they watch other kids run scenes, they begin to adopt the quiet respect for others that has been established in the previous months.

December is all about act 3, and that means the fairy kingdom is the center of attention. Janice will play Titania, and she is the recognized leader of the cast. As a fourth grader, she participated and played Adriana in *The Comedy of Errors*. As a result, she speaks better than the other students. They recognize that it is not only talent but also experience that makes Janice so commanding on the stage. Several students from the *Midsummer* cast were in the show last year, and they provide a concrete example of what Hobart Shakespeareans should look like.

Each rehearsal now includes a half hour of dancing. This serves two purposes. First, Sarah has taught the kids the importance of "the space between rehearsals." She sees them once a week and teaches them moves for a particular dance. Sarah expects the kids to be far better each time she returns. The kids spend some time each day perfecting their steps and learning how to be in sync with the music. They want to be able to show Sarah that they are different from the children she worked with just seven days earlier. This internalization of the need to practice diligently is the core of the group. At night, without my assigning it as "homework," actors run their lines, musicians practice the latest phrase they learned, dancers play the music in their bedrooms and imagine themselves back in Room 56. Every day kids see the improvement in one another, and that excitement makes them work even harder. The mission of the class is to be nice and work hard. They are and they do.

However, there are occasional bumps in the road. December is also the month of report cards and parent conferences. One student who joins us from another fifth grade class is not doing well with his daily schoolwork. He does well in Shakespeare, but his classroom teacher is not happy about missed assignments and a general apathy to class activities. We talk to the student and there are a few tears. He doesn't want to miss Shakespeare, but he must understand priorities. Basic schoolwork comes first. We all decide that the young man will miss Shakespeare class in December, and that if his work improves, he'll be welcomed back in January. The boy's parents agree with the plan, and now it is up to the young man. The door has been left open, but he's the one who must walk through it.

December presents the problem of less rehearsal time because of the vacation break that begins on the seventeenth. In past years this was not an issue because we had access to the school, but, as I explained earlier in this book, my keys were taken away. We are able to schedule an extra week of practice because the janitors will be on site until Christmas Eve. The kids are excited, as we can get in four or five full days of rehearsals and make huge strides in the production.

But the rains come and we are asked to leave the campus. The kids have the previously mentioned rehearsal in the storm, and we all agree to throw in the towel for December. It's a very nice cast, and the loss of potential time is disappointing, but that happens a lot to teachers and students. A few steps forward and then some force pulls you back. Still, the spirit of the cast is good. Everyone goes home for the holidays and will get back to work the second week of January.

January

The plan is to finish the blocking of act 2 and begin act 3. I have been worried that the three-week break might stop the momentum and produce sluggish rehearsals. I was dead wrong.

The beautiful thing about giving students trust is that they will surprise you. Many of the kids come to the rehearsals and are off book. They have memorized their lines, even for scenes we have not yet mapped out. As they perform a scene, if someone forgets their part, the actor gleefully shouts out "LINE" and the kids offstage remind him, as they are all holding their copies of the text. In this way, all the students are learning lines and language. There might be three or four actors on the stage, but in truth everyone is performing the scene. This collaboration among the students both on and off the stage brings them very close together, and they root for one another when a performer shows improvement. They are the safety net, and the comfort level they create allows the kids to soar to incredible heights.

Perhaps the most marked change comes from Stephen, who plays Francis Flute but is also the drummer for the band. He's been working with Mike Clarke, and although Stephen keeps a marvelous beat, his stamina was an issue. Many beginning drummers find fast rhythms tiring. It was common to hear Stephen slow down on fast numbers like "Pump It Up" or Queen's "Crazy Little Thing Called Love," the latest dance number Sarah has been putting together. For the first months of rehearsals, the dancers had to dance to a CD because they were ahead of the band.

But in January Stephen found his speed. A combination of his work ethic, Mike's great teaching, and forty peers cheering him on for months produced a first-rate drummer. The band that just months before could not play three chords is now a runaway train. The kids are excited because the sound that has been in their heads is actually being produced.

With the band now functioning, the dances take off. It's amazing how one student's progress affects so many aspects of the show. The band now improves its playing right in front of our eyes. The dancers are no longer looking at one another when they are on-stage but following their cues from the beat of the music. This leads to a uniformity that makes the scenes spectacular.

Everything speeds up. Having been through the blocking process for act 1, we are able to complete acts 2 and 3 by the end of the month. Practically every day, a different student surprises the cast with a marked improvement in his performance. There is a quiet confidence in the cast that was not there last July. What few of them actually believed would happen is becoming a reality.

February

This is the month when new instruments bring flavor to the show. The sitar is the biggest star of all. The show is done in two parts, and part 2 will open with "Norwegian Wood" by the Beatles. George Harrison played the sitar on the original recording of the song, a beautiful John Lennon tune. The problem is that I have no idea how to buy or play a sitar.

Dan, the guitar man, thinks buying one might be a mistake. They are expensive, he warns me, and when the show is over, the best use of it might be as an end table for plants. He suggests that we might get a similar sound by placing paper between the strings of our acoustic guitars. He's right on all counts, but the challenge and mystery of tackling such an exotic instrument is intriguing for both the students and me.

I buy one at a terrific music store, and begin to tinker with it. Janice, who plays Titania, is an accomplished musician. She is a first-rate violinist, cellist, and guitarist. She asks to be the one to play the sitar, and all the kids think she is the one for the job. The fact that the instrument is bigger than she is presents a challenge, but in time she gets comfortable sitting and holding the sitar correctly as we have learned from the sitar books we are studying. Janice's month of practice is a microcosm of everything this play is about.

It's new. It's challenging. It's a risk. But Janice is not alone. Other kids remove the sitar from its case, make sure she has a comfortable spot, and place it in her hands so she can use all her energy thinking about playing it. She works at it for about thirty minutes a day, with kids quietly surrounding and encouraging her. After the session, peers take it from her hands and lock it away in its case. By Valentine's Day Janice can play the famous riff from the song. By the end of the month, we have a sitar player.

Meanwhile, act 4 is ready. The blocking is done and the dance to "Crazy Little Thing Called Love" is in place. Rehearsals are whirlwinds, as the kids have so much of the show mapped out, there is more to rehearse. Thirty minutes of dance rehearsal, thirty minutes of blocking new scenes, and thirty minutes of rehearsing scenes from the previous months, and then it's time to go home.

February is a blur, but what a ride. And March means the finishing of the play. The kids are soaring.

March

Each month of rehearsal is more exciting than the previous one. In March the students finish blocking the hilarious act 5. This includes the mechanicals' presentation of *Pyramus and Thisbe*. With Stephen (Thisbe) wearing a dress, Jooho (Bottom) hamming up the longest death scene in history, and Ellen (Quince) correcting Bottom's mistake that the lion *devoured* and did not *deflower,* his love, the rehearsals are filled with peals of laughter bouncing off the classroom walls.

It's also shirt month. An important part of the production is that the students do not wear costumes. The players perform wearing Hobart Shakespearean T-shirts and jeans. This makes the language the star. The actors are here to tell a story, and without the help of fancy costumes, their ability to communicate the tale through language becomes the centerpiece of the show.

We use different color shirts to help tell the story. Kings usually wear purple, and jealous husbands green. For *Midsummer,* the mechanicals wear tan, with Bottom wearing dark brown to stand out from them. The fairies wear pink with phosphorescent paint that will glow under Craig's magical lighting scheme. The two sets of lovers are paired in red and gold, helping the audience remember who is linked with whom. It's fun for the kids to contribute ideas for the colors we will use. We are here to tell a story, and the kids are the architects of how that story will be told.

Many members of the audience who have watched a lot of Shakespeare remark every year that they have never heard

Shakespeare spoken so clearly. Some school productions spend enormous amounts of time worrying about sets and costumes. As our shows are done on a bare stage with practically no costumes or props, the kids have more time to work on understanding the language and speaking it beautifully. Returning to the mission, students with a command of language are going to have doors opened for them in the future. And that's why we all spend thousands of hours working. When all is said and done, the play's not really the thing. The students are.

As practically every student plays several roles, this requires them to change shirts quietly and efficiently while the play is going on. Janice, for example, will wear red as Titania but turquoise when she plays in the band. With forty kids moving constantly around the tiny room, we spend three days in March practicing what happens offstage. Each student knows when his shirt will be changed and another one left neatly to be used for a later scene. Audience members have told me that they like seeing the show twice: once to see the play, and once to watch what goes on behind the scenes. The choreography of the movement of the kids around (and sometimes under) the audience sitting in the risers is as diffi-cult to learn as the dialogue. And it's just as much fun.

April

The blocking of the show is completed. The rehearsals are no lon-ger divided into work on various pieces of the play. Instead, the children practice one of the five acts each day. Each act takes about thirty minutes to perform.

April is the month when tickets become available for the show. Our Web site announces the schedule. *A Midsummer Night's Dream* will be performed twelve times in June. There will be eve-ning shows Wednesdays, Thursdays, and Fridays. Saturday mati-nees make it possible for working parents and people who come from other states and countries to see the show on a weekend. Tickets are free but reservations are necessary. The tickets are gone quickly.

The students are now off book. Some of the lines are still shaky, but between fellow actors onstage and others offstage, anyone who stumbles is caught by a dozen different safety nets. The students have internalized that mistakes are fine. If a line is forgotten, no one gets upset. Instead, every mistake provides an opportunity for others to find creative ways to fix things. Without the fear of "messing up" the students rarely do.

The children laugh because April is the month of the dreaded "notes." The fifth graders who participated last year simultaneously laugh and groan when they see me take out a huge stack of yellow legal pads. The rest of the cast is puzzled until an explanation is provided. During April rehearsals, as the kids run an act, I sit in the back of the room scribbling furiously. In just thirty minutes I will make a note of at least fifty things I feel need improvement. Quince needs to be louder. Helena entered late. The band needs to look at one another when they play. The kids doing the sign language are not in perfect sync.

After a thirty-minute practice, the kids gather round and I go over the notes with them. They know my expectations so well, they can practically recite the notes before I read them. Once this session ends, we have enough time to do the act again with the criticisms fresh in the performers' minds. The second run-through is far better than the first.

The kids get better and better, but every rehearsal ends with the same question and answer. "When are we done?" I ask the children.

"Never," they respond in unison. And they are not unhappy with this reality. They are not the least bit concerned about the show, now less than sixty days away. Their journey is everything.

May

The kids are ready. They know all their lines and own their characters. Every rehearsal shows improvement. They are truly happy, and about to get happier.

Matt Scarpino comes to build the risers for the audience seating and additional platforms on the tiny stage. This allows the performers to speak to the audience from three different levels, which helps them tell the story from various angles to make the flow of the play smoother. When Matt is done, it feels like the first day of kindergarten, as the students have to rework their movement around platforms and seating that has not been with them for their ten months of rehearsals. Yes, we've put tape on the floor to mark where these areas would be, but that's not the same as negotiating dance moves on an eighteen-inch platform where a misstep could mean a spill. It's challenging and fun for the kids to get acclimated.

Yet the real fireworks haven't even started. Craig sets them off when he designs the lighting for the show. The kids are mesmerized and astonished as they discover how lights can help tell a story. A cloth dropped behind the students is used for spectacular projections, while thousands of colors from every possible angle create images never to be forgotten. After the month's work, the actors learn how to work with the lights, understanding that standing three inches to one side can make or break the effectiveness of a scene. It takes focus and disciplined practice to make such technology work, but the students have worked on these skills for the entire year. By Memorial Day they are ready to perform.

A nice tradition concerns the way the students take a bow. At the Oregon Shakespeare Festival, the company hangs shields outside their Elizabethan Theater announcing the titles of all the plays performed there in the past and the years they were performed. Our class does the same thing. At the beginning of the play, the students hang the shields on a wall to pay homage to the kids from the past who made the same voyage they are about to complete. During the final bow, when all the students are onstage listening to thunderous applause, fifth grade students leave first. The fourth graders, who will be back for another year, take out a shield hidden behind a picture of Shakespeare. This shield reveals next year's play, and the fourth graders wave to the audience and yell, "See you next year!" For the fourth graders performing *Midsummer,* they get to announce that *Measure for Measure* will be the next show.

The final work to be done involves the students who will be helping before the play, during intermission, and after the show. The hosts, as they are called, have specialized roles that they take very seriously. It is their job to greet every member of the audience in the parking lot before the show. Guests are guided to the room, and their hosts make sure they are comfortable. These kids help to plan intermission. The break after part 1 of the show is a lot of work. All sorts of delicious snacks are provided, along with hot and cold drinks, in an adjoining room. These children also help decorate the intermission room with fresh flowers and photographs of past shows. The hosts serve the guests treats and show appreciation for their taking the time to come. They guide people to the bathroom, and make sure to offer their arms to elderly guests who might have difficulty with stairs. After the show, they make sure all the guests get to the parking lot safely for a smooth trip home. Almost all of the cast does some of this work, and they believe hosting is as important as performing the play. They're right.

June

The shows are indescribably fun. The students are usually nervous the first night, but that tension lasts for about five minutes. They realize they are part of a marvelous production and spend the month laughing and celebrating. Between shows, they continue to improve and try new things. During the day, the class hosts third and fourth graders to watch selected scenes. Students not yet involved in the program learn how they can join next year's production.

During part 1 each evening, former students come to make sure all goes smoothly. They stay in the intermission room and put out fresh pastries or cold drinks just before hungry guests enter. They also tune instruments during the break, and put out any fires that might have started. Whether a guitar string broke or a lighting cable was disconnected, these problems are handled by the alumni faster than you can say "Shakespeare." Even during the show, the current students are surrounded by alumni who have a generosity of spirit that will hopefully be adopted by some of these young admirers.

I beg the kids to make sure they get enough sleep and stay in bed later than usual. With state testing finished and books completed, there is no reason to come to school early. They do not listen. Every morning practically the whole group shows up by 6:30 to clean up from the night before and begin setting up for another show. It's a community fueled by a camaraderie that none of them has ever been a part of before. As the final week approaches, some express sadness that one Saturday afternoon it will be over.

When the students take their final bows, they break down and cry. I remind them that the show might be over but the lessons they have learned will be with them for the rest of their lives. I also encourage them with the wisdom of Dr. Seuss, reminding them "Don't cry that it's over; smile that it happened."

In this age of standardized testing and people demanding data, how can the value of a production like this be measured? In the long term, the fact that these children consistently beat the odds and attend outstanding universities is a good start. Many of these kids return for the shows and express to me that the lessons they learned have carried them through good and bad times.

Yet in the short term, a detailed assessment of the value of the show comes from Clayton Stromberger, a fantastic teacher who lives in Austin, Texas. Clayton teaches Shakespeare to children and also works for the University of Texas. He is involved with Winedale, an outstanding Shakespeare camp where kids learn the same skills that the kids do at Hobart. After bringing two of his children to watch the show twice, Clayton offered the following observations. Teachers who want to include drama in their programs would do well to follow Clayton's wise reflections regarding what being in a play can mean for children and the audiences who watch them.

Rafe—

If it's not too late, please pass along my heartiest congratulations to all the Hobart Shakespeareans. The play was, to use one of my old Shakespeare professors' favorite words—but one he saved only for the best—splendid in every way.

I'm sure tonight will be another special moment, perhaps the most special.

I was thinking this morning that for me there are five main criteria for a great Shakespearean performance by ANYONE, be they fourth graders or RSC actors. (I tried to keep it to three, but I couldn't choose any to leave out!)

1. Did I learn something new about the play?
2. Did I wish I was IN the play, up there on stage with the players?
3. Is it clear that every single member of the ensemble, through a deep respect for the words of the text and for the mystery of the play—which, as Nick the Weaver puts it, "hath no bottom"—gave so fully of himself or herself

that the group became for those two hours greater than the sum of its parts? (In other words, do they undergo a creative experience parallel to that of Shakespeare and his players?)

4. Did I leave the performance feeling better about the world than when I arrived?

5. Did I both laugh and cry at some point?

The answer to all five of these was a resounding YES, especially #2 (oh, man, I wanted to sing, and swing my arms and dance and pound the drums and . . . darn it!) . . . . which in my experience is a very rare thing. I'm sure Sir Ian would agree with me on that one.

So congratulations to all of you, and thank you so much for your hard work.

We return to Texas energized, inspired, and feeling again the spirit of Bottom, who is ready and eager to play any role with courage and joy and enthusiasm. I won't soon forget Grace's sweet smiling lion, Anthony's put-upon Starveling (thankyouverymuch), Eugene's jolly Puck, Cindy's heartfelt Helena, Jooho's warm and playful Nick Bottom . . . the wonderful mystery of Evan's Theseus and Oberon . . . Cynthia's tough Hippolyta . . . Oscar's hilariously grouchy yet lyrical Egeus . . . Julie's sharp Hermia . . . the dueling Demetrius and Lysander of Brandon and Justin . . . Carlos's no-nonsense Philostrate . . . oh, and Stephen's amazing Thisbe, that face floating in all that white wig and dress . . . Rudy's tough Wall . . . Janice's down-to-earth-yet-otherworldly Titania (how did she do that?) . . . all the fairies and all of the dancers and singers . . . and of course everyone who played an instrument (which would mean repeating most of this list, or all of it?, over again) . . .

Did I leave anyone out? I hope not . . . but if I did, I will remember them later today as I replay the play in my mind . . . because seeing it twice was just the beginning of starting to notice all the little details that added up to something wonderful, i.e., full of wonder.

Sitting in the front row I saw what I didn't quite get the first night, the "citizens" whispering to each other during the opening scene. I also marveled again at the long moments of Evan and Cindy sitting on that center riser, just . . . being. Thinking. Feeling. With no big rush to "show" anything. Allowing us, the audience, the time to wonder, to ask our own questions. Which is such a clear example of what is lacking in most professional productions I see, sadly, which seem to carry on the ideas of bad high school theater, where it's all about showing off, being THE STAR, having a big party afterwards, having people give you compliments . . . and basically showing how much more clever you are than boring old Mr. Shakespeare.

I know there are professionals out there who go beyond that . . . but they are hard to find. You will discover this as you get older too. Where is that Hobart feeling? (For me, it's the "Winedale" feeling . . .) Why don't these actors have the same joy?

Well, they didn't have Rafe for a teacher . . . ! Or my teacher, Doc Ayres. You have been invited into a most rare vision. Keep those eyes open. (I guess I am speaking to the kids now . . . even if they can't hear me!)

I love the way the Hobart Shakespeareans clearly love and respect the words, the story, the play, and the guy who scratched it all out on paper with a quill pen 400-something years ago. That's the respect my teacher awakened in me almost 30 years ago at UT in my Shakespeare playing experience, and I've been shocked to realize, over the decades, just how rare that approach is.

You guys and gals all get it. That's why Sir Ian sits there and listens. YOU listen—to each other, to the words, to the music behind the words. You respect what Hamlet calls "the heart of my mystery"—the understanding that we can never say we are "done" with a play, we can never stop exploring and trying to make it better. And that this process continues after the house lights come back on and we walk or drive or bicycle home.

So yes, the mysterious thing is—if you understand this about Shakespeare, you somehow begin to understand it about life, too. How did Will do it? We will never know, I suppose. But somehow, to dive deep into his plays is to dive deep into life itself. You all did that, and it is something that will be with you for the rest of your life. And ours too. A gift you've given us, hand-made.

Thanks for your hard work and hospitality and generosity, and YES, we will see you next year for *Measure for Measure* . . . !

All the best, Clayton S.
(and of course Augie and Emma)

ACKNOWLEDGMENTS

With a Little Help from My Friends

A long, long time ago, in 1985, I used to sit at a lonely bus stop at 4:00 A.M. five days a week. It was my first year at Hobart and my third year of teaching. I lived in a small place over thirty miles from school, and did not have a car. I had spent all my money on the classroom.

There was no grand plan. I was just struggling to do my best with very little skill and even less knowledge. At the time, I didn't feel that getting up at 3:15 A.M. to go to work after working a second job until 11:00 P.M. seemed crazy. It was.

Then I met Barbara, who I would be lucky enough to marry. She brought the cool water when the fever ran high. She and my family removed the crazy and made everything make sense.

I was all alone once, but I am not alone any more. There are many who chose to sit by me on that bus bench and encouraged me to take their help.

This book, my fourth, has been written because Bonnie Solow was the first to recognize that the story of Room 56 could help others. My agent and friend, Bonnie saw the promise and the possibilities I could share with others. I am forever grateful to her.

Bonnie introduced me to a new group of friends at Penguin. In Clare Ferraro, I met an extraordinary person who genuinely cared about my students and what they represent. The legendary Wendy Wolf never compromised on the message; her incomparable integrity makes her the most brilliant and helpful editor a person could wish to know. When writing a book, the author must be able to trust the people who help him. How could I not trust Kevin Doughten? He not only helped craft my paragraphs but traded stories with me about Ray Davies and The Kinks. Kevin is indeed a well-respected man.

Real Talk for Real Teachers exists because of these friends, but there is no book without a story, and Room 56 is crowded with lovely human beings who have made it all possible.

Sir Ian McKellen was a Wizard for the Hobart Shakespeareans long before he brought Gandalf to life. And Hal Holbrook has always been with the children on their journey down the Mississippi River.

Thanks to Mary Alden, Bill Anderson, Helen Bing, Joann Burton, Judy Campbell, Bruce and Marty Coffey, Paul Cummins, Craig and Lili Foster, Bill Graham, Richard and Heidi Landers, Peter and Marsue MacNicol, Buzz McCoy, Jan Miller, Stephen and Kay Onderdonk, Larry Smead, Bill and Michelle Tessier, Kay Tornborg, Ann Wang, and the dozens of foundations that open up so many doors for the children.

Lois Sarkisian and Lee Cohen are the most wonderful of friends. Thanks for a million laughs, memorable evenings, Stove Top Stuffing, and fighting about important issues such as if The Moody Blues deserve to be called a rock 'n' roll band.

Outstanding teachers from around the world visit daily, and there are simply too many of you to list. Thank you for sharing so many laughs and tears. We remind each other that there is no reason to sit alone at 4:00 A.M. waiting for a bus.

There are so many parents who have given me their love and

trust. Thank you Doug and Cindy, and thank you to the Lees for my yearly birthday cake, even fifteen years after your daughters left my classroom.

Finally, of course, and most important of all, are some incredible Hobart Shakespeareans.

Thank you, Joann. If you were the only student I had ever taught, it would have been enough. You are the student who taught me more than I could ever teach you.

Thank you to Matt, Jefferson, Angela, In Yong, Hwi Yong, Joanna, Elizabeth, Oscar, Jiyeon, Rudy, Albert, Tracy, Linda, Abdiel, Damian, and Elsa. Your love and support means more than you will ever know.

Thank you everyone for putting so much back into the tree. A long, long time ago I was alone on a bench. Thanks to you, I am no longer alone, and the good times only get better.

I've gotten by with a little help from my friends.

AVAILABLE FROM PENGUIN

Lighting Their Fires
How Parents and Teachers Can Raise
Extraordinary Kids in a Mixed-up,
Muddled-up, Shook-up World

Bestselling author and educator Rafe Esquith
shows that children aren't born extraordinary;
they become that way as a result of good
parents and teachers. Esquith uses proven
methods to explain and demonstrate how
parents can equip their kids with the tools they
need to be thoughtful and honorable people—
as well as successful students—and to have fun
in the process.

ISBN 978-0-14-311766-7

Teach Like Your Hair's on Fire
The Methods and Madness
Inside Room 56

Perhaps the most famous fifth-grade teacher
in America, Rafe Esquith has won numerous
awards for his exceptional teaching methods.
This bestseller gives any teacher or parent all
the techniques, exercises, and innovations that
have made its author an educational icon, from
personal codes of behavior to tips on tackling
literature and algebra.

ISBN 978-0-14-311286-0

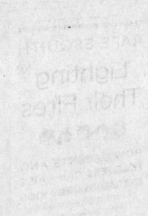